Media use as social action

A European approach to audience studies

ɔoks are to be returned on or before
last date below.

Media use as social action

A European approach to audience studies

Edited by
Karsten Renckstorf
Denis McQuail
and
Nicholas Jankowski

John Libbey

LONDON · PARIS · ROME

British Library Cataloguing in Publication Data

Media Use as Social Action: European
Approach to Audience Studies

    I. Renckstorf, Karsten
    302.23
    ISBN: 0 86196 485 3
    ISSN: 0956–9057

Series Editor: Manuel Alvarado

Published by

John Libbey & Company Ltd, 13 Smiths Yard, Summerley Street,
London SW18 4HR, England
Telephone: +44 (0)181-947 2777; Fax: +44 (0)181-947 2664
John Libbey Eurotext Ltd, 127 avenue de la République, 92120 Montrouge, France.
John Libbey - C.I.C. s.r.l., via Lazzaro Spallanzani 11, 00161 Rome, Italy

CONTENTS

Preface

We feel the time has come to intensify and focus discussions within the international community of communication researchers. Not only are media landscapes rapidly changing around the world, resulting in similar problems, but communication strategies are also emerging and being implemented on a global scale. In both cases the underlying logic is similar. The issue of 'media performance' as one of us formulated it elsewhere (McQuail, 1992) covers many of the still-unsolved problems of communication research such as measurement of quality and determination of responsibility.

Quite obviously, the perspectives chosen and the approaches employed by communication researchers differ from time to time, from society to society, and perhaps from community to community. Intensifying academic discourse within the discipline of communication research, then, is at the very least a sensible, perhaps even an urgently needed, task.

We have, of course, our academic journals for launching and engaging in discussion, but this avenue is not always sufficient. Mark Levy and Michael Gurevitch made a remark in this direction not long ago in their editorial note to the 'Future of the Field' theme issue of *Journal of Communication* when they wrote that 'some, but not enough (contributions), come from ... research traditions outside the United States.' Many discussions within communication research accordingly follow a pattern of one-way communication.

It is against this background that the idea developed to publish *Media Use as Social Action: A European Approach to Audience Studies*. Here, we present a recently developed research perspective which conceives of 'media use' as 'social action' – what we term the MASA approach – in a more comprehensive manner than possible in individual journal articles. This book represents a collection of recent theoretical and empirical labour, and ranks as one of the prominent contemporary European traditions of communication research.

This tradition merits a European label for several reasons. First of all, it represents the cooperative undertaking of Dutch and German colleagues who have initiated and conducted an extensive series of empirical studies at the Institute of Mass Communication at the University of Nijmegen in The Netherlands. Moreover, this approach to communication research is European in the sense that some of the central ideas and concepts of leading scholars of the social sciences who originally came from Europe – Paul F. Lazarsfeld, Kurt Lewin and Alfred Schütz to name a few – have been 're-imported' and their ideas have served as inspiration for our work.

There are many more ideas and viewpoints which have left their impact on the development of the MASA approach, particularly those from the uses and gratification tradition. Further, the contributions from many British, Swedish, Dutch and German scholars can be sensed in the pages of this volume. It should be stressed that MASA is just one of a number of emerging European approaches to the study of communication. In this book, though, we will be primarily concentrating on MASA; other approaches are only discussed in order to 'set the stage' for media use as social action.

We hope this collection of studies, published for the first time in English, contributes not only to a stimulating and critical discussion of the MASA approach, but helps reopen and renew debate throughout the community of scholars concerned with how audiences make use of media.

Many people contributed to completion of this volume. The authors, first of all, generously attended to our frequent requests for information and refinement of their manuscripts. One person in particular – Paul Hendriks Vettehen – 'came to our rescue' often, promptly delivering information we sought. Reinier Etienne, finally, assisted with processing the bibliography and proof-reading the manuscript. To all of our colleagues involved in this project, named and unnamed, we express our sincere appreciation.

Nijmegen/Amsterdam
Spring 1995

Karsten Renckstorf
Denis McQuail
Nicholas Jankowski

1 Social action perspectives in mass communication research: an introduction

Karsten Renckstorf and Denis McQuail

On reviewing the last 40 years of mass communication research it becomes evident that the notion 'active audience' is one of the central and comparably stable elements of communication theory and research. Nevertheless, there are good reasons to be critical of the way in which the notion has been conceptualized since Elihu Katz and Paul Lazarsfeld (1955) first identified the role of 'personal influence' in mass communication and stressed the 'part played by people' in the processes of mass communication. This introduction provides a critical sketch of this development and suggests the contours of an alternate conceptualization.

The audience has been central in mass communication research since the field has been an object of scientific study. Initially, the audience was perceived as an undifferentiated mass, as a passive target for persuasion and information, waiting – as it were – for media messages to come along so the audience members could respond to them in a quite uniform, foreseeable manner. Students of mass media effects soon came to recognize, however, that audiences were made up of real people, surrounded by and embedded in social groups, which can be characterized as networks of interpersonal relationships through which media effects are mediated. That is, essentially, why audiences can resist the influence often intended by media campaigners. People have their own varied reasons for using the mass media, and it is they who choose to attend to media messages – or not. 'The initial mistake,' according to a recent assessment, 'was to suppose that media choose their audiences. They aim to do so, but their selections are less decisive than the choices which audience members make of media channels and contents' (McQuail & Windahl, 1993:132).

Audience, audience activity and mass media use

Evidence of selective exposure, selective perception and selective retention soon accumulated, showing that audiences tend to match their media use – i.e. their choice of media channels and media content – to their own tastes, ideas and informational needs. Thus, the chance of change-oriented effects from the media diminished and the chance of reinforcement increased (cf. Klapper, 1960). It was about the time of that insight when Katz (1959:2) suggested mass communication researchers should pay less attention to 'what media do to people' and more to 'what people do with the media.' This is perhaps the most general formulation of the underlying premise of all approaches of communication research assuming an active audience. Since then, it is more or less considered common sense within important parts of the scientific community of communication researchers that mass media use must be conceptualized in terms of social action and, consequently, processes of mass communication must be studied from a social action perspective.

Accordingly, many efforts have been made to set up such a social action perspective for mass communication research (cf. Anderson & Meyer, 1988; McQuail & Gurevitch, 1974; Dervin, 1981; 1983; Renckstorf, 1977a; 1989; 1994; Renckstorf & Wester, 1992; Hunziker, 1988; Vorderer, 1992; Charlton & Neumann, 1985; Altheide, 1985; Lull, 1980b; 1988) that go beyond the classical formulation of these principles within the tradition of uses and gratifications research. The underlying logic of uses and gratifications studies has been summed up as follows:

They are concerned with (1) the social and psychological origins of (2) needs, which generate (3) expectations of (4) the mass media or other sources, which lead to (5) differential patterns of media exposure (or engagement in other activities), resulting in (6) need gratifications and (7) other consequences, perhaps mostly unintended ones (Katz *et al.*, 1974).

Clearly, a social action basis is at least implicit in the formulation of the uses and gratifications model for mass communication research:

> (1) The *audience* is conceived of as *active*, that is, an important part of mass media use is assumed to be *goal directed....*
> (2) In the mass communication process much initiative in linking *need gratification* and *media choice* lies within the audience member....
> (3) The media compete with other *sources of need satisfaction*. The needs served by mass communication constitute but a segment of the wider range of *human needs....*
> (4) Methodologically speaking, many of the goals of *mass media use* can be derived from data supplied by individual audience members themselves – that is, *people are sufficiently self-aware* to be able to report their *interests* and *motives* in particular cases....
> (5) Value judgements about the cultural significance of mass communication should be suspended while *audience orientations* are explored in their own terms.... (Katz *et al.*, 1974:21-22; italics added)

What is formulated here – twenty years ago – is the concept of a self-aware, goal-directed audience member, who is able to make sensible media choices in order to serve his/her interests (needs) and motives by means of media use. Thus, according to uses and gratifications research, media use normally does not happen by chance or at random, nor can it be imposed by the media themselves. Instead, media use is seen, albeit implicitly, as a form of social action. The term is even used in the Weberian sense,[1] for media use is described here as an activity that is planned, shaped and carried out by self-conscious actors who are interacting with the surrounding social context and, thus, taking a whole set of subjectively perceived functional alternatives into account.

However, within the tradition of uses and gratifications, emphasis has not been placed on the (further) development of a theory of social action (cf. McQuail & Gurevitch, 1974; McQuail, 1985) suitable for facing the central task of communication research, i.e. 'the task of assessing the nature and influence of mass communication...' (DeFleur/Ball-Ro-keach, 1982:12/13). Or, as Katz and Lazarsfeld (1955:18) put it:

> ...fundamentally, all of communications research aims at the study of effect. From the earliest theorizing on this subject to the most contemporary empirical research, there is, essentially only one underlying problem – though it may not always be explicit....

In the following sections we elaborate on some of the main theoretical perspectives in communication research as well as on recent approaches in mass communication research. This discussion allows us to illustrate the actual and/or potential relevance of social action perspectives for mass communication research – including some notes on a close cousin, i.e. audience reception theory and research. Finally, we will comment on the 'media use as social action' approach that has recently been developed as one of the European contributions to audience-centred mass communication research.

Epistemological and ontological premises

In their discussion of contemporary perspectives in communication research Max Kaase and Winfried Schulz (1989:10) state that 'the contours of mass communication research are unclear and fluid.' Karl Erik Rosengren recently raised the question whether there really is a 'field' of communication research, or, as he calls it, just many 'frog ponds' (Rosengren, 1993:6). Even more skeptical was John Durham Peters (1986:528) who commented some years ago on the 'state of the art' of communication research: 'Each department, school or university creates the field anew in its own image. Theory fails as a principle of definition, as does the attempt to define communication as a distinct subject

---

1   According to Max Weber, *action* is defined as '... any human attitude or activity (no matter whether involving external or internal acts, failure to act or passive acquiescence) if and in so far as the actor or actors associate a subjective meaning with it.' And *social action* according to Weber is '.. such action as, according to its subjective meaning to the actor or actors, involves the attitudes and actions of others and is oriented to them in its course.' (Weber, 1907/1956:3; translation by Parsons, 1937/1968:641).

matter.' One of the perhaps most critical comments on the recent state of the art stems from Klaus Krippendorff (1993:20-21):

> ... I dare say, no one really understands what makes the mass media into what they are. It is my contention that the failure to understand the mass media is not so much due to a lack of interest in the subject matter or caused by the absence of appropriate research funds, but a consequence of pursuing theory construction with *inadequate epistemologies* and from *disciplinary perspectives* that have their own separate agendas. (italics added)

Krippendorff thus questions whether communication theory is based on adequate epistemologies and communication research on disciplinary perspectives relevant to the field of communication. He considers, in other words, that discussion of the epistemological and ontological premises of the theoretical perspectives in communication research is strongly needed.

Stephen W. Littlejohn (1983) some years ago presented a meta-theoretical scheme that, at least for heuristic purposes, is useful for providing some order to the theoretical perspectives underlying the multitude of theories, models and approaches in communication research (cf. McQuail & Windahl, 1993; DeFleur & Ball-Rokeach, 1982; Fauconnier, 1986; Maletzke, 1988; McQuail, 1994; Wright, 1986). The first dimension of Littlejohn's (1983:19 ff) two-dimensional scheme (see Figure 1) concerns the *epistemological* premises of research, the second the *ontological* assumptions. In communication research, according to Littlejohn, usually one of the following two epistemological positions is held.

The first epistemological position is characterized by the assumption that human beings are surrounded by a physical, more or less completely knowable world; Littlejohn labels this (positivistic) position 'World View I' and sums it up as follows:

> This tradition is based on empiricist and rationalist ideas. It treats reality as distinct from the human being, something that people discover outside themselves. It assumes a physical, knowable reality that is self-evident to the trained observer. Discovery is important in this position; the world is waiting for the scientist to find it. Since knowledge is viewed as something acquired from outside oneself. (Littlejohn, 1983:20–21)

The second epistemological position is characterized by serious doubts in the human capability for acquiring such (positivistic) knowledge of an 'objective' world. Here, knowing is seen as interpreting, an activity everybody is assumed to be engaged in. This (hermeneutic) position is termed 'World View II':[2]

---

2   It is evident, that these fundamental epistemological positions underlying communication research, which Littlejohn calls World View I and World View II have been described elsewhere with somewhat more familiar labels: materialistic *vs* idealistic (cf. Klaus, 1970:316–326), positivistic *vs* hermeneutic (e.g. Adorno, 1970; Popper, 1970; Seiffert, 1972; 1973) and, more specifically, as a contrast between science and scientists, on the one hand, and humanities and scholars on the other (cf. Berger & Luckmann, 1967; Maletzke, 1967).

> This tradition takes a different turn by relying heavily on constructivism, viewing the world in process. In this view people take an active role in creating knowledge. A world of things exists outside the person, but the individual can conceptualize these things in a variety of useful ways. Knowledge therefore arises not out of our discovery but from interaction between knower and known. For this reason perceptual and interpretive processes of the individuals are important objects for study. (Littlejohn, 1983:21)

The second dimension of Littlejohn's scheme, that of ontology, deals with the nature of phenomena communication researchers seek to know. Essentially, there are two ontological positions to be found in communication research. Littlejohn (1983) labels them: (1) the 'non-actional' position and (2) the 'actional' position. Both positions are characterized by typical assumptions concerning the concept of man, the concept of human action as well as the concept of human interaction.

Non-actional theory, according to Littlejohn (1983:22), 'assumes that behaviour is determined by and responsive to past pressures. Covering laws are usually viewed as appropriate in this tradition; active interpretation by the individual is downplayed.' Peter Hunziker (1988:72) continues this argument as follows:

The *non-actional approach* normally reduces the material under investigation to empirically (objectively) observable events that can be identified and tested intersubjectively. Scientific efforts are made to relate empirically observed phenomena in order to formulate hypotheses. In the case of human action, directly observable are overt *behavioural responses*; as factors playing on overt behaviour (observed) external influences, i.e. *behavioural stimuli*, are taken.

Actional theory, instead (Littlejohn, 1983:22), assumes '... that individuals create meanings, they have intentions, they make real choices. The actional view rests on a teleological base, which says that people make decisions that are designed to achieve goals. Theorists of the actional tradition are reluctant to seek covering laws ... instead, they assume that people behave differently in different situations because rules change form one situation to another.' Hunziker (1988:73) sums this position up succinctly:

The *action-theoretical approach* postulates that human social action is based on *subjective meanings* ('subjektive Sinngebung'). Research efforts are made to understand these subjective meanings as well as the underlying motives and the social nexus within which social action takes place. The problem of *verstehen* is due to the fact that neither motives, nor orientations or perspectives of the actors can be investigated directly.

The combination of both dimensions, i.e. the epistemiological and the ontological of communication research, thus, allows the discrimination of four theoretical perspectives[3] underlying contemporary communication research: (a) the *behaviouristic*, (b) the *trans-*

---

3   A theoretical persepective can be described as 'a point of view, a way of conceptualizing an area of study' (Littlejohn, 1983:22), or, in other words, a way of organizing research on the basis of specified epistemological as well as ontological premises.

missional, (c) the *interactional* and (d) the *transactional perspective.* It is obvious that alternative classifications are possible, but at least for heuristic purposes Littlejohn's scheme seems quite fruitful; see Fig. 1.

Behaviouristic perspective

The *behaviouristic perspective* of communication research, often considered the oldest of the four perspectives, has been developed within behavioural psychology. This perspective is based on the stimulus-response (S-R) model: human behaviour is understood in terms of 'release,' i.e. a response to external stimuli. Communication research within this tradition aims – via field studies or experiments – at the discovery of invariant, mechanistic relations between 'causes,' i.e. media messages, and 'effects,' i.e. subsequent audience behaviour (cf. Hovland, 1959). Communication research based on the behaviouristic perspective (cf. Hunziker, 1988; Littlejohn, 1983) characteristically takes the epistemological position of Littlejohn's World View I and seeks to explain human action in terms of behaviour.

Transmissional perspective

The *transmissional perspective* of communication research conceptualizes communication as a transfer of information from source to destination; this perspective, according to Schulz, implies not only the assumption of linearity, but also the assumptions that communication processes are *asymmetrical, individual, intended* and *episodical* (Schulz, 1982:52). Communication research based on the transmissional perspective, postulating a transmission or a transfer model of communication, is often used in advertising research; it has been described by Katz (1959; quoted by Chaney, 1972:11) as the 'book-keeping tradition' of communication research. The transmissional perspective of communication research, too, is characterized by the epistemological positions of World View I and, again, seeks to explain human action in terms of behaviour.

Interactional perspective

Communication research based on an *interactional perspective* usually takes Littlejohn's World View II as a starting point; reality is conceived as socially constructed. Audiences are looked upon as (actively) 'meaning making' subjects of communication processes; thus, media messages are not conceptualized here as stimuli, but as objects that need to be interpreted. Communication is no longer thought to be linear, but conceptualized as an on-going social process with many feedbacks. While early functional versions of communication research based on an interactional perspective (cf. Blumler & Katz, 1974; Rosengren *et al.,* 1985) – often implicitly – used non-actional (behavioural) assumptions, the more recent variants explicitly use actional concepts in order to explain audience activities (cf. Renckstorf, 1977a; 1989; Renckstorf & Wester, 1992; Anderson & Meyer, 1988; Charlton & Neumann, 1985; Altheide, 1985).

6

Transactional perspective

Finally, the *transactional perspective* of communication research, much in line with Raymond A. Bauer (1964; 1973) and W. Phillips Davison (1960), conceptualizes communication processes as 'transaction;' it is stressed, that in communication both partners – communicators as well as their audiences – are participating ('bargaining') actively (cf. Barnlund, 1970; Sereno & Mortensen, 1970). Communication is seen here as a mutual and dynamic process in which all participants are actively engaged. The epistemological position of this transactional perspective is that of Littlejohn's World View II and, here, usually actional assumptions are made.

These four theoretical perspectives, of course, do not entirely cover the whole range of communication research, but we can be rather certain they have at least covered the 'major divisions of the field' (Littlejohn, 1983:23). With the aid of this scheme (see Fig. 1) we can easily place the four theoretical perspectives and characterize them in terms of their epistemology and ontology. It is evident, that each of these perspectives carries its own set of assumptions; against this background of different epistemological and ontological premises it becomes quite plausible, why – as Krippendorff and many others before him (cf. Hovland, 1959; Peters, 1986; Rosengren, 1993) have pointed out – communication research has been producing such a confusing variety of questions and answers, such a multitude of contradictory findings concerning its central problem, the problem of media impact. In any event, as has been shown, social action perspectives obviously play an important role in contemporary communication research. Not only can the development of theoretical perspectives be adequately described by using social action concepts, but – as will be illustrated in the following section – also recent approaches of communication research can thus be characterized.

Frames of reference, concepts of action and the problem of media impact

As has been argued above, the problem of media impact can be regarded as the crucial problem of mass communication research as such, and the problematic effects of mass communication form the *raison d'être* of communication science as an academic discipline – from the very beginning on.[4] It seems that Lazarsfeld and Merton in 1948 described the impetus of society, as well as the impetus of communication researchers, in the early days of communication research very well by quoting the credo: '...the power of radio can be compared only with the power of the atomic bomb...' (Lazarsfeld & Merton, 1948/1960:492-493).

Today, still, questions about the *impact* of televised violence, sex and crime, brutality or horror scenes on television, video or in the movies, questions about the *effects* of contemporary media mixture of informational and entertainment content ('infotainment') as well as questions about the *influence* of, for example, television news or (political)

---

4 Cf. for example, Gerhard Maletzke (1963:187): 'Die Frage nach den Wirkungen der Massenkommunikation ... stellt das zentrale Problem der Lehre von der Massenkommunikation dar.'

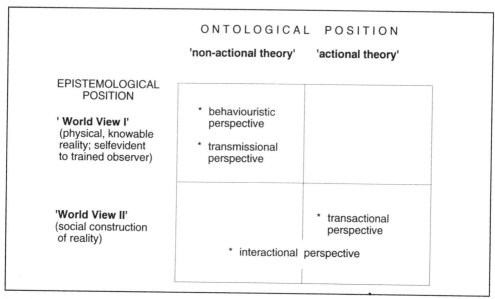

Fig. 1. Classification of theoretical perspectives in communication research.

commercials on children, on adults or specific subgroups such as ethnic minorities dominate the research agenda of contemporary mass communication research. Questions about the *effectiveness* of certain media campaigns (cf. AIDS-prevention, cancer prevention or family planning) the social *consequences* of extensive media use (heavy viewing) or questions about the responsibility of the media (media performance, social responsibility of television) are further examples. During the last 40 years students of communication research have also been busy with different concerns but the central aim of communication research has remained essentially unchanged: 'The task of assessing the nature and influence of mass communication' (DeFleur & Ball-Rokeach, 1982:12/13). Or, as Hsia (1988:3) formulates the issue:

> ...we are exposed to thousands of television and radio commercials, programmes, news, articles, advertisements, books, and films. Each has some influence on our lives. This is the reason communication must be studied and researched.

Hence, Winfried Schulz (1993) recently posed the question whether the concept of media effects has been conceptualized properly in the past. Schulz reminds us of the fact that Paul F. Lazarsfeld and Robert K. Merton (1948/1960:495) as early as 1948 already pointed out, that '...to search out "the effects" of mass media upon society is to set upon an ill-defined problem.'

Schulz argues that contemporary conceptualizations of media effects, i.e. what he calls 'diffuser Wirkungsbegriff' (Schulz, 1993:5; cf. Katz, 1980), in most cases not only proved to be rather useless but the concept of media effect has been discredited by the abuse for political goals. According to Schulz, the concept of media effects should be handled with caution: it should be seriously reconceptualized[5] – or given up altogether. According to McQuail (1987:251), '...the entire study of mass communication is based on the premise that there are effects from the media, yet it seems to be the issue on which there is least certainty and least agreement.'

And indeed, one cannot deny the fact that there is a long and impressive history of – almost chronic – contradictory research findings concerning media effects; and this holds true especially between the several traditions of empirical communication research (cf. Hovland, 1959; Renckstorf, 1995) Basically, there are at least three traditions of communication research that involved a specific understanding of mass communication and developed different basic models of mass communication processes. As a matter of fact, there are at least three basic models underlying empirical mass communication research: i.e. the *media-centred* model, the *audience-centred* model and the *culture-centred* model of communication research (cf. Chaffee & Izcaray, 1975; Renckstorf, 1994; 1995; McQuail & Windahl, 1993; McQuail, 1994; Davis & Puckett, 1992). And each of these three traditions developed and used a concept of media impact of its own:[6]

- The *media-centred model* of communication research (cf. Chaffee & Izcaray, 1975; McQuail & Windahl, 1993) essentially is based on the assumptions of the behaviouristic and/or the transmissional perspective developed by Littlejohn. Here, according to Lasswell's (1948) 'effect analysis,' the question of media impact usually is posed in terms of effects.

- The *audience-centred model* of communication research (cf. Chaffee & Izcaray, 1975; McQuail & Windahl, 1993) on the other side, is based on assumptions of the transactional and/or the interactional perspective. The question of media impact here, typically, is treated in terms of consequences.

- The *culture-centred model* of communication research (cf. Adoni & Mane, 1984; Davis & Puckett, 1992; McQuail, 1994), finally, represents a third tradition that is

---

5 According to Lazarsfeld and Merton's proposal (1948/1960:495), three research questions should be answered by communication research (1) 'the effects of the existence of the(se) mass media in our society,'; (2) 'the effects of the particular structure of ownership and operation of mass media,' and (3) the effects of particular contents disseminated through the mass media'. Much in line with Lazarsfeld and Merton, and Schulz (1993) as well, Melvin L. DeFleur and Sandra Ball-Rokeach (1982:13) argued some years ago; they presented the following three research questions: (1) *'What is the impact of a society on its mass media?* That is, what have been the political, economic, and cultural conditions that have led the mass media in their present form?; (2) *How does mass communication take place?* In other words, does it differ in principle or only in detail form more direct interpersonal communication? (3). *What does exposure to mass communication do to people?* That is, how does it influence them psychologically, socially and culturally?'. And, as DeFleur and Ball-Rokeach (1982:13, cf. Lowery & DeFleur, 1988) add, '... it is to the third question that the majority of mass communication research has ... been addressed.'

6 Corresponding to this, Denis McQuail recently distinguished three traditions of research into audiences, i.e. the structural, the behaviourist and the social–cultural tradition (McQuail, 1994:294–298) of audience research.

9

characterized by a variety of underlying assumption not easily fitting into one of Littlejohn's perspectives. The social-cultural tradition of communication research as McQuail (1994:297) termed it, characteristically poses the question of media impact in terms of results of mass communication for the social-cultural environment, or the symbolic milieu (cf. Gerbner, 1964; 1969; Gerbner & Gross, 1976a).

In order to classify recent approaches of mass communication research (cf. McQuail, 1987, 1994; McQuail & Windahl, 1993; Schulz, 1982; 1993; Schenk, 1978; 1987; Stappers *et al.*, 1990) we may use two central aspects underlying recent research approaches. First, we can discriminate different *frames of reference*[7] handled within different approaches and, second, we can differentiate several traditions of communication research by investigating the respectively assumed *concepts of action* (cf. Wilson, 1970; Krappmann, 1969).[8] Thus, we come to a classification of recent approaches of mass communication research for the study of mass media impact, i.e. effects, consequences or results of processes of mass communication (cf. Renckstorf, 1994:31). See Fig. 2.

The more traditional forms of research on media impact, such as Lasswell's (1948) 'effect-analysis,' taking Schulz's (1982) 'transfer-model' as a point of departure, usually conceive *media impact in terms of effects*, i.e. as media induced and intended changes in audience behaviour. Characteristically, this tradition of research takes the communicator intentions as a frame of reference and conceptualizes social action according to the normative/dispositional understanding; this tradition is therefore subsumed under the *media-centred model*. As has been argued elsewhere (cf. Renckstorf, 1994; 1995), there are at least two recent approaches of communication research that use the *media-centred model* as a starting point, i.e. the 'agenda setting approach' (AS) as well as Noelle-Neumann's (1973; 1991) 'spiral of silence' approach (SP).

Many of the more recent, alternative approaches in communication research thematize the way people handle the media and make use of mediated messages and, thus, try to measure, describe and explain audience activity. This tradition usually conceptualizes *media impact in terms of consequences*; this tradition, that takes audience interests as points of reference and normally conceptualizes social action in accordance with an interpretive under-

---

7   Obviously, the conceptualization as well as the measurement of media impact requires a certain 'frame of reference', i.e. in order to measure, analyse and interpret certain '(non-)changes' we have to define and use references. In recent communication at least three of such references have been used to determine media impact: (1) communicator intentions; (2) audience interests; and (3) social–cultural goals (cf. Renckstorf, 1994).

8   According to the *normative/dispositional paradigm* of social action existing prescriptions and rules of behaviour or human dispositions, respectively, stand central and pregiven rules, or basic dispositions, respectively, are assumed to determine human action. According to the *interpretive paradigm* of social action, the meaning making capability of (inter)acting human individuals stands central. Here, meanings and actions are conceived as social products, emerging from ongoing processes of defining and redefining within social interactions (cf. Wilson, 1970; Krappmann, 1969; 1972; Renckstorf, 1994; 1995).

standing, in Figure 2 is termed the *audience-centred model.*[9] Here, again, at least five recent approaches of mass communication research can be identified that are based on an *audience-centred model,* i.e. the 'uses and gratifications approach' (U&G), the 'dynamisch-transaktionaler Ansatz' (DTA), the 'information seeking approach' (ISA), the sense-making research (SMR), and the 'media use as social action' (MASA) approach.

Last but not least, in Figure 2 some research approaches are included, which are based on the *culture-centred model* of communication research. Here, the problem of *media impact* usually has been defined in *terms of social–cultural results* of mass communication processes, i.e. the process of social construction of reality – and the role mass media play herein – is under investigation (cf. Adoni & Mane, 1984) or, more specifically, the role the mass media play in forming social–cultural milieus, such as the symbolic environment (cf. Gerbner, 1969), is studied. Here, at least four approaches of communication research and/or media studies can be identified, which are based on a culture-centred model, i.e. the 'cultivation analysis' (CA), the 'cultural studies' (CS), the 'knowledge gap' approach (KG), and the tradition of so-called 'critical communication research' which especially has been inspired by the Frankfurt school.

As was the case in the discussion of theoretical perspectives of communication research, we can state that social action perspectives again play an important role in the development of recent approaches of communication research.

Audience reception theory and research

We are here primarily concerned with a theoretical development (that of social action theory) which grew out of sociology, in an attempt to understand audience behaviour and to contribute to an understanding of potential media impact. The social-cultural tradition of audience study, mentioned above (especially under the cultural studies label), has different origins and objectives, despite certain similarities of approach with social action theory. Since this has been and is still an influential school in European media research, we need to briefly assess these similarities and differences. The link between cultural studies and reception research is discussed by Jensen and Rosengren (1990:222):

Drawing on methods of analysis-cum-interpretation from the literary tradition and the conception of communication and cultural processes as socially situated discourses from cultural studies, *reception analysis* can be said to perform a comparative reading of media discourses and audience discourses in order to understand the process of reception.

The origins of the reception approach are mixed, drawing about equally on critical theory, textual and literary analysis and work on popular culture. A key founding text was Hall's

9   It has been pointed out by many critics that the central terms in U&G studies are not always conceptualized in an appropriate manner (cf. Swanson, 1977; Elliott, 1974); this holds especially true in the case of the concept of social action. As has been argued elsewhere (cf. Renckstorf, 1977:11) some of the U&G studies are based on 'normative' (or: 'dispositional') concepts of social action whereas some newer studies within the U&G tradition clearly hold a more 'interpretive' view; in Fig. 2 this is indicated by U&G(N).

(1973/1980) seminal article 'Encoding and decoding in the television discourse,' which offered a model emphasizing the fact that the meaning of media messages was reconstituted by their 'readers' according to their own life experiences and knowledge, which often sharply diverge from the perspectives of those who produce and transmit messages. The emphasis was thus placed on 'differential decoding' and initial work, e.g. Morley (1980), concentrated on political and social class differences as determinants of such decoding.

Subsequently, this emphasis changed and during the 1980s and 1990s, reception research has moved away from an openly political framework of understanding, under the influence of the cultural studies school. Questions of genre and gender, of youth and street culture, of minority experience and the realm of 'everyday life' for ordinary people in homes and families came to the fore. This shift can be seen reflected in the later work of Morley (1986; 1992), of Fiske (1987), of Silverstone (1994) and many others (see, e.g. Seiter *et al.*, 1989). Empirical reception research has focused especially on the most popular narrative genres (e.g. soap operas) and on the detailed social practices which surround and shape media use. The following are the main defining characteristics of reception research:

- an emphasis on the multiplicity of meanings (polysemy) of all media content, which cannot be arrived at by conventional content analysis and which are ultimately dependent on the sense-making 'work' of audiences;

- a strong preference for small-scale, in-depth, ethnographic, holistic and interpretative forms of enquiry, although more traditional, social-psychological methodologies can be represented, as in the work of Liebes and Katz (1990) or Livingstone (1990);

- a concentration on popular forms of narrative and entertainment, although news can be studied according to the same paradigm and principles, e.g. Jensen (1990);

- giving an equal place to the meaning of media use practices as is given to the meaning of message content.

Some of the similarities between reception and social action theory will be obvious. Both share an emphasis on the importance of social context and on the influence of the immediate environment on media use activity. Both emphasize the need for interpretive and qualitative methods. They hold in common a rather similar notion of audience 'activity,' although in the cultural studies/reception research school, the behaviouristic and rational-individualistic connotations are rather frowned upon. Some of the similarities result from largely unacknowledged borrowing by cultural studies from certain sociological traditions, especially symbolic interactionism and phenomenology. The theoretical eclecticism of reception research is both a strength and a weakness.

The differences are also not so hard to identify. One such difference is the continued attention by many reception researchers, in the cultural studies tradition to the *text*, either as symbolically encoded in the vehicle of expression, or as selectively reconstructed by 'readers' or as a discourse performed by readers around the use of the text. This centrality of text and discourse reflects a particular intellectual choice or bias. Social action theory

CONCEPT OF ACTION

FRAME OF REFERENCE	'normative'/ 'dispositional' paradigm	'interpretative' paradigm	CONCEPT OF MEDIA IMPACT
communicator intentions 'media-centred model'	1 * AS * SP	2 * AS (N)	**effects**
audience interests 'audience-centred model'	3 * U&G	4 * DTA * U&G (N) * ISA * SMR * MASA	**consequences**
social-cultural goals 'culture-centred model'	5 * CA * KG * Critical Communication Research	6 * CA (N) * CS * KG (N)	**results**

Fig. 2. Classification of recent approaches in mass communication research.

works at a somewhat higher level of generality and maintains a commitment to the possibility of scientific generalization about patterns of audience behaviour (or practices, or activity) in choosing and responding to media content and applying the experience in the rest of life. It remains true, that is to say, to a notion of media effect (or consequence) which is of little interest or relevance to many practitioners of reception research, whose goal is only a deeper and more nuanced understanding of the meaning of media in relation to other (often more significant) features of personal, social and cultural life. The notion of cause and effect connections of the traditional kind is not welcome. One should not, however, underestimate the potential and flexibility of the reception research approach for shedding light on possible effects (e.g. in the case of popular understanding of news texts), should the aim of investigating effects be chosen.

It looks as if reception research and social action theory are running along tracks which sometimes coincide and lead in the same direction and sometimes diverge quite sharply. The existence of these alternatives at the same time is not accidental. Both reflect a theoretical enrichment which has accrued through research and experience and both, in their own way, can be shown to 'work.' Even so, because of different intellectual origins and assumptions, sometimes of ideology and principle, we cannot expect these two traditions to merge or be fully reconciled. Morley and Silverstone (1991) stress the moral/political dimension of audience ethnography, although it is not entirely clear that this is intrinsic to the method. Both approaches discussed here seem to have their own committed followers and it will be interesting to look back in a decade or two to see which has seemed to work best and with what kind of yield.

In a concluding section, we go a little further and comment on one social action perspective underlying a part of recent European communication research. We will do so by sketching some traits of this developing tradition, called 'media use as social action.'

Media use as social action

As will be worked out in the following chapters of this book more extensively, the social action perspective conceives media use[10] as social action and characteristically places the audience as central and dominant in the mass communication process (cf. Renckstorf, 1989, 1994; Renckstorf & Wester, 1992; Bosman *et al.*, 1989; Frissen, 1992; Nelissen, 1991; Renckstorf *et al.*, 1993; Hendriks Vettehen, 1993). As is the case with other approaches within the audience-centred tradition of communication research (cf. Anderson & Meyer, 1988; Charlton & Neumann, 1986; Altheide, 1985; Vorderer, 1992), the focus is on human beings engaged in a multitude of interactional relations. People, as is postulated here, engage in activities on the basis of their own objectives, intentions and interests; they are linked via a diversity of interactions with each other, and are capable of reflecting on their own actions and interactions with others. They are aware of existing social-cultural goals and at least sufficiently self-aware of subjective aims and personal interests; thus, they are not only capable of reflecting on (own) roles and (other's) expectations, they are also able to interact in a sense-making, meaningful way within social contexts. During the course of everyday life the individual comes in contact with a large number of material and immaterial events, persons, objects, considerations and questions. Individuals are able to *act* upon all of these objects in the environment, to which the mass media and their messages also belong.

Such action, however, must be given form by the individuals themselves. According to the *normative paradigm* of social action (cf. Wilson, 1970; Krappmann, 1969; 1972) existing prescriptions for action and rules of behaviour stand central and pregiven rules are assumed to guide action. In *interpretive approaches* of social action, such as in symbolic interactionism (Mead, 1934; Blumer, 1969; Manis & Meltzer, 1972), but also in the action theory of Schütz (1932, 1964; Schütz & Luckmann, 1979; 1984; Berger & Luckmann, 1967), the meaning-making activity of individuals stands central. In contrast to the animal world where behaviour, to a relatively large degree, is determined or instinctively regulated (e.g. Claessens, 1968), man does not live in a type-specific environment in which the instincts of the organism provide acceptable reactions (Berger & Luckmann, 1967:47). Human beings must create their lifeworld (Schütz, 1932), which

---

10 What is meant by 'media use' can here best be described in terms of selecting, referring to, dealing with, making (differentiated) use of mass media and mediated messages; for a more complete discussion see Renckstorf (1989) and Chapter 2.

is shared with others. In everyday life the individual is regularly confronted with repetitive situations in which solutions are developed and methods of response are tried out, to which others in turn react. In this manner the individual develops 'recipe knowledge' (Berger & Luckmann, 1967:42) with respect to potential situations and routines which can be employed therein. And, society can be considered as the sedimented form of such shared meanings and actions.

The social action perspective for mass communication research, labelled 'media use as social action' in this volume, is explicitly based on an interpretive understanding of social action. Essentially, three central assumptions underlay this perspective:

- The mass media, by distributing messages, can only *offer* information about things, actions and/or events to their audiences: information that may be accepted by individuals as objects of their environment that need to be perceived and thematized – or not. Thus, mediated messages are not viewed here as stimuli causing responses. Instead, mediated messages are conceived as environmental objects, requiring interpretation, just as any other object in the environment of an actor. Such objects need to be interpreted against the background of a (subjective) system of relevancies (cf. Schütz & Luckmann, 1979:229-270).
- It is assumed here (cf. Hunziker, 1988) that media and mediated messages form but a part of the sense-making symbolic environment of modern post-industrial man, and that the relative importance of media and mediated messages is determined by social situations and circumstances as well as the individual characteristics and personality of men.
- Consequently, it is assumed that the role of viewers, listeners and readers is misunderstood if they are conceptualized as pure recipients of mediated messages; rather, viewers, listeners and readers are seen here as the factual creators of messages (cf. Renckstorf, 1989:331), i.e. during the subjective processes of meaning-making, the really and in fact action-relevant messages are produced by the people, the (active) audiences, themselves.

The research perspective offered by the 'media use as social action' approach has thus far been transformed into two formalized models. First, a more general social action model for communication research, a so-called reference model, has been developed in order to direct and stimulate communication research (cf. Renckstorf, 1989; Renckstorf & Wester, 1992; Chapter 2) and, second, a reduced research model has been set up in order to guide empirical communication research in a more detailed way – and to integrate research findings (cf. Renckstorf *et al.*, 1993; Chapter 3). These models serve as guidelines for empirical studies and are used in the context of quantitative projects as well as for qualitative (*verstehende*) studies. Up to now, empirical research has in most cases been carried out in the Netherlands (cf. Renckstorf *et al.*, 1993); these studies, to name just a few, thus far have been directed to problems such as heavy viewing (cf. Frissen, 1992; Chapter 5), non-viewing (cf. Renckstorf & Hendriks-Vettehen, 1994; Chapter 6), use of television news (Chapters 10, 11 and 12), watching foreign television channels (Chapter 8), and television use in the family context (Chapter 7).

Presently, data from the second wave of a national survey carried out in the Netherlands (n =971, called MASSAT '94), are being analyzed. These data shall be used in the context of about twenty quantitative studies, accompanied by a series of qualitative studies as well; more generally, it is precisely this combination of quantitative *and* qualitative studies that is presumed here to be the most adequate methodological strategy (see Chapter 3). Similar research efforts are being made by other recent traditions of contemporary mass communication research as well; although it seems to be a challenging task, we could not discuss them here in an appropriate manner. Nevertheless, it seems obvious by now, that social action perspectives, by filling in the notions of 'active audience,' 'personal influence' and the 'part played by people' in the flow of mass communication, have gained a central role in recent mass communication theory and research.

Concluding remarks

It is clear from this overview of research into the audience that there have been persistent tensions within the field from the very beginning. More pragmatic researchers may see this simply as a reflection of different disciplines and methodologies applied to similar problems of media choice, use and interpretation. The more theoretically committed, especially among critical researchers, do not generally accept the possibility of compromise. However, the core of the dispute has been defined in more than one way and it would be a pity if theoretical dispute were to stand in the way of inquiry of the many inter-relations which exist between media use practices, social life and media 'texts.'

At an earlier point, when audience research was largely a preserve of 'media sociology,' the main dispute was between functionalists and critical theorists, who emphasized structural factors. It was argued by one of the present authors (in McQuail & Gurevitch, 1974) that an 'action-motivational' approach based on the phenomenological sociology of Alfred Schütz might offer a viable alternative. Such an approach would aim to '... explore the source of *meanings* present in media use situation' and it would also allow investigations to go beyond the study of individual circumstances to find patterns and regularities. It was also argued that 'patterns might show themselves because individuals sharing a set of situational circumstances are likely to choose, and give meaning to their choices, in similar ways – not because common circumstances *cause* common behaviour but because meanings given to acts of choice *take account of*, and are consistent with, what is involved in those circumstances' (McQuail & Gurevitch, 1974:296).

This theoretical model was not at that time explicitly represented in audience research but it is very close in essentials to what has been described in this chapter as the Media Use as Social Action (MASA) approach. And it is this which provides the theoretical basis for the studies reported in this book. The locus of dispute and its contours have changed somewhat in the past twenty years. The main opposition is now between an alleged 'dominant paradigm' (not so different from earlier functionalism) which is behaviouristic and quantitative in its research demands and a cultural-critical alternative which is interpretative and qualitative in approach and devoted to exploring the minutiae of media meanings and experience.

We are inclined to suggest that the social action approach can still serve as a viable alternative to these opposed camps for those who want to combine qualitative theory and empirical-quantitative methods in the study of the audience. The MASA approach offers a conceptual bridge between opposed schools of research, since it is emphatically inter-pretive and sensitive to social-cultural contexts, yet at the same time capable of uncovering regularities and suggesting general explanations of audience phenomena. Nor is it not just a fudged compromise, since it derives from a distinctive and coherent sociological tradition.

The studies in this book represent the application of such an approach to a range of questions about the media audience, although more in conception, mode of analysis and interpretation of findings than in the choice of data-collection method. Survey research, as used in several of these studies, for practical reasons, does not fully or adequately meet the preferred requirements of the theory, as noted above. Nevertheless, the reader has the opportunity to assess the potential of the theoretical model and also the validity of its claim to provide a bridge between current oppositions.

2 Media use as social action: a theoretical perspective

Karsten Renckstorf

Current audience-centred approaches in mass communication research –
such as uses and gratifications, 'dynamisch-transaktionaler Ansatz,' sense-
making research, and information seeking – focus on the measurement,
description and explanation of audience activity. As has been pointed out
elsewhere, these research approaches essentially fail in conceptualizing the
notion of an active audience in a theoretically satisfying manner. In this
chapter, an action-based theoretical perspective on mass communication is
outlined that conceives of media use as social action, and a reference model
for mass communication research is presented grounded in an interpretive
view of human action.

A major concern in communication research has always been to study media impact, i.e. to measure, describe and explain the influence of television, radio, newspapers and more recent media such as telematics, on individuals, groups and society as a whole. As many scholars have pointed out (Lazarsfeld *et al.*, 1948; Lazarsfeld & Merton, 1960; Katz & Lazarsfeld, 1955; DeFleur & Ball-Rokeach, 1982; Katz, 1987; McQuail, 1994), the problematic *effects of mass communication processes* constitute the central task of communication research.

During the past twenty years, however, the focus of attention in communication research has gradually shifted away from processes on the message production side (i.e. research on media and/or communicators) to processes and conditions related to the message consumption side (i.e. research on audience and reception; see Katz, 1980; Schulz, 1982; Stappers *et al.*, 1990; Renckstorf, 1989; 1994). This change in attention is paralleled by a change in conceptual models of communication research. The latter development, from a so-called *media-centred* model to an *audience-centred* model or a *culture-centred* model respectively, of course, involves more than a change in the focus of attention (cf. Chaffee & Izcaray, 1975; McQuail & Windahl, 1993; McQuail, 1994; Davis, & Pucket, 1992; Renckstorf & Wester, 1992). In fact, the theoretical perspective for mass communication itself has come under discussion. In media-centred models, for example, it is assumed that

CONCEPT OF ACTION

FRAME OF REFERENCE	'normative'/ 'dispositional' paradigm	'interpretative' paradigm	CONCEPT OF MEDIA IMPACT
communicator intentions 'media-centred model'	1	2	effects
audience interests 'audience-centred model'	3	4	consequences
social-cultural goals 'culture-centred model'	5	6	results

Fig. 1. Approaches to mass communication research and mass media impact. Source: Renckstorf (1994).

mass communication processes are dominated by the media and the intentions of (purposive) communicators; the role of the audience is down played because human actors are primarily seen as determined by predispositions (according to the normative paradigm of action) or attitudes (according to the dispositional paradigm; see Wilson, 1970; Krappmann, 1972). In audience-centred models, in contrast, it is postulated that the audience takes on a central and dominant place and, consequently, social action, including use of the media, has to be conceptualized according to the so-called interpretive paradigm (see Wilson, 1970) as the core element in the theoretical conceptualization of mass communication processes.

With the aid of the notion 'frame of reference,'[1] i.e. focus of attention, and the concept of 'action,' i.e. the theoretical perspective on human action, it is possible to classify recent approaches in mass communication research into six major types; see Fig. 1.

Traditional mass communication research, conceptualized within the tradition of media-centred models, and particularly in the tradition of 'effect analysis' (Lasswell, 1948), can be placed in the first cell. The above mentioned developments in the field, however, suggests serious reorientations – sometimes even called paradigm change (Kepplinger,

---

1   What is meant by 'frame of reference' is – very briefly – the theoretical framework, including fixed aspects, i.e. 'references', used by communication researchers to decide whether 'media impact' has been measured. In the case of the media-centred model, for example, intentions of (purposive) communicators serve as such points of reference; that is, in order to determine effects, researchers within this tradition have to examine (or evaluate) whether the intended behaviour (intended by communicators) has been carried out by (parts of) the audience.

1979) – toward cells four and six in the figure, a reorientation of recent mass communication research employing an interpretative action theory perspective within an audience and/or culture-centred model (cf. Jensen & Rosengren, 1990).

On the basis of previously conducted examinations of recent approaches in mass communication research,[2] the principles of a new perspective for mass communication research are presented. Further, a reference model is outlined based on an interpretive theory of social action which indicates consequences for further empirical research (see Renckstorf & Nelissen, 1989; Bosman *et al.*, 1989).

Three basic frameworks in mass communication research

The above mentioned development of three basic frameworks in communication research, termed media-centred, audience-centred and culture-centred models, will be examined shortly. Second, media use as social action will be elaborated upon. Afterwards, a reference model for mass communication research based on the interpretative paradigm of social action is presented. Finally, the methodological implications and some of the more practical consequences of the model are noted. These implications and consequences are best understood in the context of a broader discussion of the qualitative or interpretive research tradition, as well as the quantitative or inferential tradition of social science research. A more extensive elaboration of this task is reserved for the following chapter.

Media-centred model

The media-centred model, often formulated in terms of Lasswell's (1948) well-known formula 'who says what to whom in which channel with what effect,' is essentially based on four underlying assumptions:

> (1) purposeful mass media are successful in reaching almost every single member of a given society;
> (2) these individual members are capable and willing to pay attention to the messages proliferated by the media;
> (3) the messages represent direct, i.e. necessary and sufficient, impulses for subsequent audience behaviour, thus,
> (4) the recipients will act in accordance with these mediated massages and therefore in accordance with the intentions of mass media communicators.
> (Renckstorf, 1977:99)

The central task for communication research, the study of media impact, in media-centred models is thus usually formulated in terms of effects: What can (purposive) media and/ or communicators do to people? Communication research within this tradition typically has to search out the 'know how' and the 'know why' of processes in influencing (target) audiences.

2　This presentation must, inevitably, be restricted to the main principles of the perspective, called 'Social action model of media use' (see McQuail & Windahl, 1993). For more detailed discussion, see Renckstorf (1989; 1994:143–144), Renckstorf & Wester (1992) and Renckstorf *et al.* (1993).

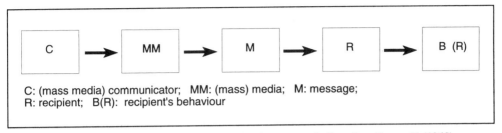

C: (mass media) communicator;   MM: (mass) media;   M: message;
R: recipient;   B(R): recipient's behaviour

Fig. 2. Media-centred model for mass communication research. Based on Lasswell (1948).

Given the omnipresence, actuality and attraction of mass media, the assumptions of the media-centred model seem to be self-evident. The linearity and one-sidedness of this model, however, which conceptualizes media communicators as creative and initiating actors and, at the same time, defines the audience as passive recipients merely waiting for messages from the media, should be apparent. See Fig. 2.

Activity, here, is almost exclusively thematized with respect to communicators, who were thought to hold a monopoly on taking initiatives and have a talent for manipulation (cf. Naschold, 1973; Renckstorf, 1977; 1984). According to Schulz (1982:52) the central assumptions of the so-called 'transfer model' imply that communication and the processes of mass communication are seen as *asymmetrical, individual, intended* and *episodic*. These assumptions in the meantime proved untenable, as demonstrated in various empirical research projects. With publication of the now classic studies *The People's Choice* (Lazarsfeld *et al.*, 1948) and *Personal Influence* (Katz & Lazarsfeld, 1955), it came to be clear that the traditional model of the 'all powerful media' was no longer defensible. Since the early 1960s, signs appeared of a basic reorientation in communication research regarding media effects – a transformation sometimes referred to as a paradigm change (Kepplinger, 1979).

Audience-centred model

Nearly forty years ago Katz (1959) had already indicated such a transformation of the central research concern when he suggested that the question was not 'What do the media do to people?' but instead 'What do people do with the media?' This version of the central issue marked the starting point for a turn in communication research and theoretical development. In fact, this reformulation of the old research question points to and demands an alternative framework. That is why the audience-centred model for communication research approaches the central problem of media impact not in terms of effects but in terms of consequences, i.e. consequences of mass communication processes for the audiences.

Audience-centred models focus on the audience of mass communication and – at least implicitly applying a social action perspective – thematize how people relate to mass media, choose and use mass media and mediated messages in the context of their daily lives. The activities of audience members, media directed or not, are not looked at as specific forms of (media) behaviour, but are considered in terms of everyday forms of meaningful social action, are seen as *'Normalfall' sozialen Handelns* (Renckstorf, 1977).

Within the tradition of the uses and gratifications approach (see Blumler & Katz, 1974), the most prominent approach based on the audience-centred model, the principles of this view are formulated as follows:

> (1) The *audience* is conceived of as *active*, that is, an important part of mass media use is assumed to be *goal oriented* (McQuail *et al.*, 1972)...(2) In the mass communication process much of the initiative in linking *need gratification* and *media choice* lies within the audience member. This places a strong limitation on theorizing about any form of straight-line effect of media content on attitudes and behaviour. As Schramm *et al.* (1961) wrote: 'In a sense the term "effect" is misleading because it suggests that television "does something" to children ... Nothing can be further from the fact. It is they who use television rather than television which uses them' ... (3) The media compete with other *sources of need satisfaction*. The needs served by mass communication constitute but a segment of the wider range of *human needs* ... a proper view of the role of the media in need satisfaction should take into account other functional alternatives ... (Katz *et al.*, 1974:21-22)

In addition to the uses and gratifications approach, further recent approaches in mass communications research in which the audience-centred model is fundamental should be noted. For example, Renckstorf and Nelissen (1989) and Renckstorf (1989) refer to the *dynamisch-transaktionale Ansatz*, the information seeking approach, the *Nutzenansatz*, and projects conducted in the tradition of sense-making research. Although there are clear differences between these approaches, it is nevertheless possible to identify common themes regarding fundamental principles. At the core of audience-centred models is the concept of human behaviour seen in terms of social action; human action taking place within the context of a given *society* (including mass media and other social, political and economical institutions) undergoing interaction with certain *individual and social characteristics* of the human actor (including plans, goals and values). Against this – more or less tension free – background, situations and problems have to be identified; the combination of (perceived) *problems* and (perceived) *solutions* constitutes differential *motives* for further *(external) action*, for example media use, which later is to be *evaluated* in terms of goal attainment. These central aspects of the audience-centred model, inspired by Rosengren's model (1974:271), are graphically presented in Fig. 3.

Culture-centred model

In the context of culture-centered models of communication research the media impact problem is usually formulated in terms of what has been called 'results' – here called media-caused or media-induced changes of the social-cultural symbolic environment (see also Gerbner, 1964; 1969). Some examples of communication studies within this tradition are: examinations of the relation between mass media and political culture (Kraus & Davis, 1976), mass media and ideology (Hall, 1982), and mass media and the distribution of

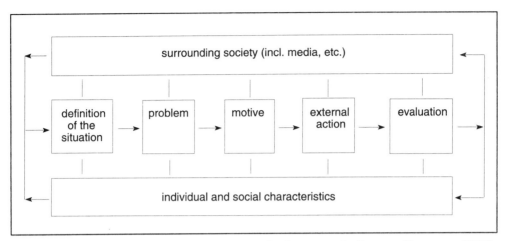

Fig. 3. Audience-centred model for mass communication research. Sources: Rosengren (1974); Renckstorf (1989).

knowledge in whole societies (Saxer, 1985) or in special segments within societies (knowledge gap; see Tichenor *et al.*, 1970). Mass media are here characteristically looked at as institutions of the culture industry (Horkheimer & Adorno, 1969; Adorno, 1963a; 1963b). More generally, this tradition focuses on processes of the social construction of reality by means of mediated communication, or as Adoni and Mane formulated it: 'The role of the mass media in the process of the social construction of reality holds a central place in communication research.' (Adoni & Mane, 1984:323)

Thus, media impact is described here neither in terms of effects of purposive communicators on their audience(s), nor in terms of consequences the use of mediated messages may have for the users. Rather, it is seen as the role of mass media in defining, shaping and constructing societal beliefs, the norms and values of a culture of a given society. Typically, most of the projects carried out within this long and rich tradition of communication studies, are based on literary criticism, semiology and discourse analysis (McQuail & Windahl, 1993:145) and therefore often lack an empirical orientation[3] as usually expected in the social sciences:

> Their works investigate the interaction among the social system, the media (their structure, occupational practices, and products), and individual perceptions and acceptance of the social reality in which they live....Their conclusion regarding the impact of the media at the macro-level are based on historical and ideological reasoning, while their conclusions regarding the impact of the media on the individual's subjective reality are highly speculative. (Adoni & Mane, 1984:333)

---

3   It should be noted here, that some of the recent approaches within this tradition – 'reception analysis' (Jensen, 1990; Jensen & Rosengren, 1990) and Morley's version of 'cultural studies' (Morley, 1989; Lull, 1980; 1988) – are taking steps toward applying social science research methodology.

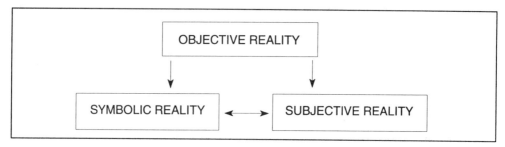

Fig. 4. Culture-centred model for mass communication research. Slightly modified from Adoni & Mane, 1984; see also Renckstorf, 1995.

Within this culture-centered tradition of communication studies, and especially in the case of holistic approaches (see Horkheimer & Adorno, 1969), the process of the social construction of reality is conceived as a dialectical process in which human beings play an important role both as subjects, creators, and as objects and products of their social world. The media come into the picture insofar as the different types of 'world' or 'reality' involved are influenced by their performance. For heuristic purposes, three types of reality can be discriminated:

> (1) the *objective social reality*, i.e. the reality that is experienced as the objective world existing outside the individual, in other words, this is the world of 'facts' that is apprehended as 'reality par excellence,'
> (2) the *symbolic social reality*, i.e. the (multiple) reality that consists of any form of symbolic expression of an objective reality, such as art, literature, or media contents,
> (3) the *subjective social reality*, i.e. the reality that individuals create or construct on their own where both the objective and the symbolic realities serve as inputs. (cf. Adoni & Mane, 1984:325-326)

The mass media, then, are assumed to play an important role in constructing these realities; the more holistic approaches simultaneously examine the interactions among the three types of reality, whereas other studies focus on the interaction between the symbolic and one of the other realities. In order to design a culture-centered model for communication research that would be more or less accepted within this tradition of communication studies, the model developed by Adoni and Mane (1984)[4] serves as a valuable starting point. See Fig. 4.

Conceptualizing media use as social action: towards a theoretical model

The audience-centered model is the only one which has a concept of man as an action oriented being at its core. Here, people engage in activity on the basis of their own objectives, intentions and interests; they are linked via a diversity of interactions with each

---

4   Adoni & Mane included, for their purposes, two underlying dimensions: '.. the dialectical process of the social construction of reality can be defined as a system consisting of two dimensions – *type of reality* (objective, symbolic, subjective) and *distance of social elements from direct experience.*' (Adoni & Mane, 1984:327; italics added)

other, and are capable of reflecting on their own actions and interactions with others. During the course of everyday life the individual comes in contact with a large number of material and immaterial events, persons, objects, considerations and questions. Individuals are able to act upon all of these 'objects' in the environment, to which the mass media and messages also belong. Such action, however, must be given form by the individuals themselves.

In contrast to the animal world, where behaviour to a relatively large degree is determined or instinctively regulated (e.g. Claessens, 1968), man does not live in an environment in which instinct capabilities of the organism provide acceptable reactions (Berger & Luckmann, 1967:47). Human beings must, therefore, create their life-world (Schütz, 1932) which is shared with others. In everyday life the individual is regularly confronted with repetitive situations in which solutions are developed and methods of response are tried out, to which others in turn react. In this manner the individual develops 'recipe knowledge' (Berger & Luckmann, 1967:42) with respect to potential situations and routines which can be employed therein. Society can be considered as the sedimented form of such shared meanings and actions.

As social beings – that is to say, as more or less successfully socialized beings – people generally know how to behave, how to act relative to a particular role or position in relation to happenings, persons, objects or questions (Helle, 1968; Zijderveld, 1974a). In the normative view of social action (Wilson, 1970; Krappmann, 1969; 1972) such prescriptions for action and rules of behaviour stand central: the pre-given rules guide action.

However, the concrete situation in which action takes place is seldom completely identical to the situation in which 'correct' action was previously exercised. Moreover, the role of the individual consists, in fact, of an entire set of sometimes conflicting roles. In addition – and this point can be equally problematic – it is also the case that the 'object' for which the personal actions must be designed is generally understood, but one can never be completely sure of this because the context is continually changing. So the individual's actual action proceeds much less problem free than one would expect on the basis of normative or dispositional assumptions of a theory of social action (Wilson, 1970).

In interpretive approaches to social action, such as in symbolic interactionism (Mead, 1934; Blumer, 1969; Manis & Meltzer, 1972), but also in the action theory of Schütz (1932; 1972; see also Schütz & Luckmann, 1979; 1984; Berger & Luckmann, 1967), which constitutes the foundation of the more recent variants of the sociology of knowledge (Zijderveld, 1974a), the meaning-making activity of the acting person stands central. The exceptional nature of human action is marked by the fact that the acting individual must interpret all components of such action – the *situation*, the *objects*, the *action of the other*, and the *action of the individual* – in order to provide them with meaning and in so doing to give form to the action. This does not mean that each interactional situation again is necessarily problematic. Schütz remarks that the majority of everyday experiences are *routinely stored* in the everyday 'stock of knowledge' – that is, in accordance with former experiences – and are thus given an appropriate meaning without difficulty. A subjective

25

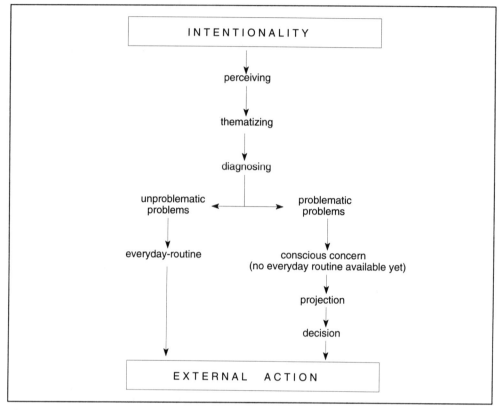

Fig. 5. Steps in the process of defining the situation. Source: Bosman *et al.*, (1989); Renckstorf (1989; 1994)

problem with which an individual must consciously be concerned only arises: '...if an actual experience does not readily 'fit' into a type at hand in the stock of knowledge...' (Schütz & Luckmann, 1984:202).

The normal procedure regarding the performance of an action in everyday reality is that the everyday situation as a problem is characterized *as unproblematic*. Such problems are naturally, and in a certain sense *pre-reflexively* (Zijderveld, 1974a:70) provided with meaning whereby action is made possible. See Fig. 5.

In an interpretive, action-based theoretical perspective, human action in general, and human social action especially, is not to be considered a reaction to an objective action or even more generally an object, but as carefully planned activity in the light of the person's own hierarchy of relevances. Or, as Blumer expressed it:

> The human being is seen as 'social' in a...profound sense – in the sense of an organism that engages in *social interaction with itself* by making indications to itself and responding to such indications....Instead of being merely an organism that responds to the play of factors on or through it, the human being is seen as an

organism that has to deal with what it notes. It meets what it so notes by engaging in a process of self-indication in which it makes an object of what it notes, gives it meaning, and uses the meaning as basis for directing its action. Its behaviour with regard to what it notes....is an *action* that arises out of the interpretation made through the process of self-indication. (Blumer (1969), italics added)

Naturally, in defining the situation and in interpreting action and objects (Thomas, 1932) a certain degree of help is provided by the social stock of knowledge (Schütz & Luckmann, 1979) that is created in each culture and is transferred through learning processes. But given that these patterns are applicable only within a particular cultural range and are relatively situation specific, they are, taken on their own, necessarily too general to really guide actions in the sense of making action problem free for the actor.

Frequently, definitions of situations are created through negotiations with others, and thus frameworks for meaning and interpretation are formulated anew. The meaning attached cannot thereby be considered permanent, but is rather, in principle, subject to continuous reinterpretation and redefinition (see Wilson, 1970; Blumer, 1969).

The above represents the general principles of the interpretive perspective of social action and social reality. Of course, these principles can also be applied to themes in communication research. The result of such application is evident: mass media and their messages are merely objects in the social environment, which provide the individual actions and events. These actions and events are also objects for (acting) individuals, which they first observe and perceive and then, depending on the situation, thematize and diagnose. From this perspective the messages of mass media are not to be considered stimuli on their own, but rather events which, from the background of a (subjective) system of relevance (Schütz & Luckmann, 1979:229-270; see also Haferkamp, 1972), are perceived, thematized and diagnosed and thereby considered objects which require interpretation. For the mass media and their messages this means that the media form but a part of the meaning-producing symbolic environment of human actors (see further Hunziker, 1988).

In this perspective viewers, listeners and readers are shortchanged if they are only conceptualized as recipients of mass media messages. In the framework of this perspective, media users are active individuals who interpret media messages on the basis of their own objectives, values and plans, and then carefully construct their (external) actions.

It is important to realize that the process of interpretation cannot be entirely explained on the basis of individual characteristics; the individual comes to an interpretation by himself, but this is not primarily an individually-oriented activity (Lüscher, 1975:99). Meanings are social products, they emerge from procedures for defining within social interactions, and they constitute part of the identity of the individual as participant in the society (Blumer, 1969:5). Interpretation occurs on the basis of the image the individual has of himself; it is a form of self-interaction in which experiences are confronted with the (subjective) knowledge system as well as with the structure of relevances (Kleefmann, 1985). Interpretation, in short, manifests itself within the framework of the individual's

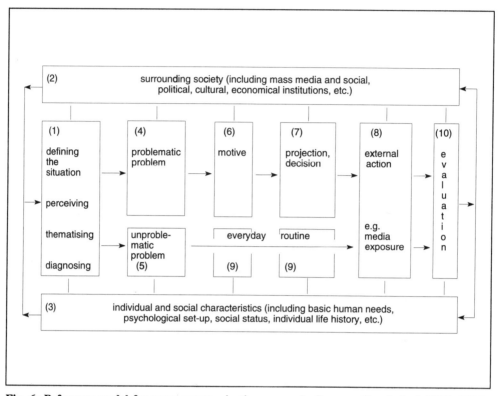

Fig. 6: Reference model for mass communication research. Sources: Renckstorf (1989, 1994); Bosman *et al.* (1989).

actual and potential patterns of social action and interaction (see Schütz & Luckmann, 1979; 1984).

On the basis of these considerations it is now possible to design a reference model for mass communication research that structures processes of mass communication according to an interpretive action-based theoretical perspective; see Fig. 6.

As McQuail and Windahl (1993:144) note, the model shows similarity with Rosengren's (1974) model; that is, mass communication is assumed here, too, to be an interactive and recurrent process. Nevertheless, as they indicate, the starting point of the reference model is different and alternative options are presented:

> At the outset (1) we see the individual adopting or having a definition of the situation, in which experience from everyday life and interaction are perceived, thematized and interpreted. The factors of individual make-up, social position and experience (2 and 3) enter into the defining and interpreting processes. The route followed is then either conceived as 'problematic' (4) or 'unproblematic' (5). If the former, action on the problem is contemplated, motives (6) are formulated and decisions about action taken (7). These can include media selection and use as

one type of external action (8). The alternative, unproblematic route can also lead, by way of everyday routines (9), to similar actions, also including media use. Whether motivated or not, media use is subject to evaluation (10) by the individual and is followed by a new sequence of definition and interpretation. (McQuail & Windahl, 1993:144)

In Figure 6 *media use,* not to be confounded with *media exposure,* is not situated in a single, fixed place in the reference model. Obviously, that fact itself does not signify improvement, but with the aid of the model it is possible to identify, to separate, and to integrate various relevant aspects of media use. For example, *instrumental* as well as *ritualized* forms of media use (Rubin, 1984), which often have been described as antagonistic concepts in communication research, are integrated within one model here. And, with regard to the process of defining the situation – in the internal phases of perceiving, thematizing and diagnosing – it is reasonable to conceptualize media use as *referring to information* formerly distributed via mass media, or, as 'making use of clusters' of information related to complex images of reality which compare with what Lippmann (1922) called the 'pictures in our heads.' Furthermore, in the internal phase of the (ideal type of) action process – the phase which relates to the internal solution of a problem – media use could be, again, conceptualized as the preferred internal reference to information distributed via the media. In the phase of external action, i.e. what is often meant by overt behaviour (Mead, 1934; Hulett, 1966) – the phase which relates to the external solution of problems – in addition to *media exposure* in general and the exposure to specified types of mediated information in particular, media use can also be conceived of as the adoption of models for action, as these have been found in mass media programmes.

Some consequences for mass communication research

The most important function of the proposed action-based reference model, of course, is to initiate and direct empirical mass communication research. Accordingly, most of the studies published in this volume are more or less explicitly based on this model. In the proposed framework, dealing with mass media and using their messages is conceived as a form of social action which is not only concerned with *external action,* but also with *internal action* or self-interaction during interpretation processes. This means that there is a need felt – and formulated – for a change in perspective in comparison with conventional research in the field of mass communication and the study of media impact, what is usually regarded as the study of effects of mediated messages. The consequences of such a change for the research design and the methods employed will be considered in the following chapter. Here, though, a number of consequences for communication research are sketched in general terms.

In relation to research projects focusing on the consequences of communication processes, the proposed framework implies, regarding the research approach, a choice for a methodology which does justice to the perspective of the actor. This means, in general, that a more *verstehende* or interpretive methodology is employed in which explicit attention is paid to the reconstruction of the world of those involved, both communicators and recipients. Such proposals for research, of course, have already been formulated (cf. Frissen & Wester, 1990; Jankowski & Wester, 1991): for example, in the case of research on the problem of 'heavy viewing' (see Frissen *et al.*, 1989; Frissen, 1992; Chapter 5 in this volume), or, the use of television news by women (see Hermans & Van Snippenburg, 1993; Chapter 10 in this volume).

In line with such a research approach, the *case study* should be used more often as a research design (e.g. Charlton & Neumann, 1985; Lull, 1988). This involves a clear reorientation towards the investigation of a relatively small number of cases chosen on an analytical basis rather than large scale surveys (see Barton, 1968; Strauss, 1987; Wester, 1991).

Clearly, this is not to say that (large scale) survey research in particular, or quantitative research methods in general, could not be useful in approaching research problems within the field of mass communication; on the contrary, provided that the problem statement is clear and the researcher is conducting the investigation from well defined concepts related to explicit hypotheses, pure quantitative research may prove extremely useful. Sometimes survey research is, in fact, essential, but in relation to the framework presented here survey research cannot be the only or, without further specification, the preferred method of mass communication research.

The shift in accent from external observable action to internal action processes – perceiving, thematizing, diagnosing and, further, projection and decision of action – and the related need for more insight into these processes places certain demands on the research strategy. Evidently, internal action processes cannot be measured in the same way as external action (overt behaviour). The former involves a more qualitative research strategy to determine whether and how internal action processes can be made visible. Qualitative research can provide the analytical framework as well as the research instruments to do that (see Wester, 1991; Peters & Wester, 1989). In this regard, biographical research, such as life history research, of (types of) recipients may be undertaken. The insights gained may later be used to develop large scale descriptive or hypothesis testing quantitative research.

The above mentioned consequences lead to the need for an integrated planning of various types of research – exploratory, theory building, hypothesis testing and evaluation research – around questions formulated on the basis of the presented theoretical framework. In such a programme for mass communication research, applied and fundamental research projects should be closely related. The status quo in mass communication research nowadays is such that large scale continuous and quantifying research projects are solely characterized as relevant in a policy context. Often not recognized, however, is that many small scale qualitative research projects can contribute substantially and often fit better in a policy context (Patton, 1980). Thus, the recommendation here is an integration of both qualitative and quantifying research. Through planning and co-ordination, it should be possible that these types of research can cross pollinate. One may also consider the formula whereby research of the one type is in principle related to research questions of the other type. The reference model presented in this chapter may function as a source of guidance both for large scale quantitative and small scale qualitative research – as well as for their integration.

3 Media use as social action: methodological issues

Paul Hendriks Vettehen, Karsten Renckstorf and Fred Wester

As stated in Chapter 2, the most important function of the social action perspective and reference model presented there is to initiate, stimulate and guide empirical studies of mass communication research. How an audience deals with the mass media and its messages is considered a form of social action, not only conceptualized as external action, but also as external action with accompanying internal or self-interaction during the process of interpretation. This change in perspective implies a shift of accent in mass communication research. A number of the considerations for and consequences of this shift for research design and methods are presented in this chapter.

As elaborated in Chapter 2, social action theory regards intentionality, interpretation and reflection as central aspects of human social action. Media use, i.e. the use of mass media and its messages, is therefore conceptualized as a form of social action which not only needs to be described and explained in terms of external action (overt behaviour), but also as internal action (covert behaviour), as a process of interpretation. In the reference model presented in Chapter 2, the whole process of defining and interpreting the situation is presented as a number of successive steps, thereby stressing the importance of the process.

In investigating the subjective aspect of this perspective problems arise regarding observation and analysis inasmuch as the perspective focuses on those processes which take place in the minds of the actors. These are mental processes which can hardly be observed and measured directly. The various analytically distinguished phases in these processes are also difficult to operationalize. However, the research which has been undertaken does not aim at describing these internal processes as such, but in relation to patterns of media use. For this reason, as an initial form of empirical study, a less elaborate version of the model is employed, taking into account only the major concepts and their interconnections. Figure 1 provides a schematic representation of this more limited version of the model.

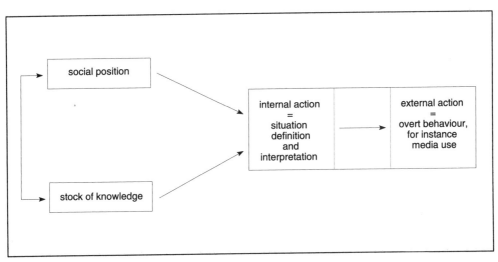

Fig. 1. Limited version of reference model.

The model is composed of four components: (1) social position, (2) background knowledge, (3) internal process of defining and interpreting a situation, and (4) external action based on the other components. Actors continuously define situations internally and subsequently react to these situations externally through, for example, using particular media against the background of their actual social position and their individual stock of knowledge. As a result of some action their actual situation[1] and stock of knowledge[2] changes, which in turn may be the starting point for a new process of defining and interpreting the situation. Clearly, most central to the model is the intermediate concept of situation definition and interpretation, as described more elaborately in Chapter 2.

However, even when beginning from this simplified version of the model, problems arise regarding the operationalization of the main concept, the internal process of situation definition and interpretation. The main concern, then, in conducting research along this social action perspective is how to obtain an idea of the interpretational processes related to media use.

In general, a social action perspective of communication processes implies a methodological stance which does justice to the perspective of the actor (Renckstorf & Wester, 1992; see also Chapter 2). This means that a *verstehende* or interpretive methodology should be employed where explicit attention is paid to the reconstruction of the world of those involved, both communicators and recipients. Qualitative methods, such as participant observation, in-depth interviews and group discussions are the widely accepted techniques for exploring this personal world. The empirical material thus obtained, can

---

1 This can also be changed through actions of others in the 'surrounding society;' see discussion of the social action model in Chapter 2.

2 The whole definition and interpretation process which leads to the action and the awareness that this action has been completed, forms a new addition to the stock of knowledge.

sometimes help to reconstruct an image of the processes involved in the use of certain forms of media. However, in Chapter 2 it was suggested that (large scale) survey research in particular and quantitative research methods in general could also be useful in approaching these research problems. The main feature of this approach is inference of definition and interpretation processes from relations found between background characteristics of various groups of users (particularly characteristics of social position and stock of knowledge) and the media use of those groups. This can be done both in an explorative or hypothetico-deductive manner.

In the following section, both of these approaches to interpretive communication research are discussed in more detail. Then, a combination of qualitative and quantitative methods is considered as a fruitful approach for reconstructing internal action processes.

Qualitative methods

Qualitative studies of media use are generally designed on the basis of principles for interpretive research. The interpretive approach has developed in both content and scope in recent years. There is, however, not one, but several interpretative traditions which employ the same methodological basis (cf. Jensen & Jankowski, 1991; Denzin & Lincoln, 1994).

Perhaps the most significant approach for the development of qualitative research is symbolic interactionism which has become widely known through the work of Herbert Blumer (1969), Howard Becker (1973; Becker *et al.*, 1961), Anselm Strauss (1969), Everett Hughes (1958), and Erving Goffman (1959). This form of research focuses on the natural social world of people involved in interaction.

The second important research tradition is phenomenologically inspired and based on theoretical notions developed by Alfred Schütz (1967/1932), and Peter Berger and Thomas Luckmann (1967). This approach is directed toward structures of meaning establishment and the process of social interaction. Related to this approach is ethnomethodological research (Garfinkel, 1967) which focusses on the rules constituting everyday life. An exceptional form of this approach is conversation analysis where everyday conversations are the object of research activity.

The third important tradition is ethnography which is related to anthropological research. This approach is concerned with the reconstruction of (sub)cultures (Spradley, 1980) and with investigation of everyday life. Although coming from a different background, that of humanistic scholarship, cultural studies shares with the ethnographic tradition an accent on cultural analysis.

Feminist research also has affinity with the interpretive approach (see Rubin, 1979) and should be mentioned in such an overview. Of particular relevance in this regard is the central importance attached to everyday experiences of the research subjects (an approach sometimes referred to as biographical research). Finally, the case study approach in organization research (Patton, 1980) deserves mention. This involves in-depth investigation of a single or limited number of cases, mostly related to complex organizations.

All of these forms of interpretive research share a number of principles, four of which are briefly described here. First, the basis of *verstehen* and symbolic interactionism is the meaning people ascribe to their everyday environment. People act on the basis of the meanings they attach to objects, which together constitute their world; Schütz (1967:21) refers to this as 'life-world.' The object of research is, then, a pre-interpreted reality.

Second, in order to study the behaviour of people as meaningful conduct, an interpretative oriented researcher has to view the objects as they are perceived by actors in their everyday life situation. The researcher has the task, in fact, of reconstructing that reality (Schwartz & Jacobs, 1979:1-15). A central notion in qualitative methodology is thus called the method of *verstehen*. In the terminology of Mead (1934/1970:76-79), this means 'role taking' – the ability to place oneself in the position of an individual or group in order to determine the meaning of situations according to the actor's definition of that situation.

Third, there are methodological implications regarding the research design. Blumer's (1969:47) phrase 'direct examination of the empirical social world' refers to the world of group life and conduct. The procedure is not to first formulate concepts, operationalize and then measure them, but to respect the nature of the empirical world of everyday experience and to become acquainted with the sphere of social life under study. Theories and concepts are to be elaborated through exploration and inspection of that world. The research procedure is to be as open as possible and is to be directed toward direct contact with the reality studied. This is the reason for a preference for participant observation and case studies. Filstead (1970:2) in this regard considered qualitative methodology as 'firsthand involvement in the social world'. Different data collection techniques are employed in order to achieve an as detailed as possible description of events.

Fourth, the researcher should not only be content with a description in terms of the actor's perspective; the meaningful reality must be objectified in concepts. This principle constitutes the core of qualitative analysis. Schütz (1964:17-19) and Bruyn (1966) mention in this regard the 'ideal type' as an aid; Blumer (1969:40-44) speaks in terms of 'sensitizing concepts.'

Against this background, it is sensible to give an alternative definition to qualitative research inasmuch as 'qualitative' refers to different aspects of research: the nature of the data, the relationship between data and concepts, and the research design. Regarding the nature of the data, the inner world of the participants stands central in the social action model. One objective of this type of research is to provide a description of the world from the perspective of the people under study. The data, then, are meant to reflect these meanings; qualitative here means that kind of research material in which the meanings of the people under study are expressed – the 'actor's point of view' and 'member's knowledge' are two expressions commonly used to convey this aspect.

Since the data sought are not known *ex ante*, this view has consequences for the relation between data and concepts. The relation is open and must be demonstrated during the investigation itself. Qualitative here means an open and developing perspective on reality, which is to be related to theoretical perspectives in the final analysis. This is not to say that cumulation of theoretical insights does not take place; the developed concepts may always be applied in further research. Nevertheless, the empirical examples that fit the concepts developed must be found in each research project anew; the world of those investigated is not known beforehand.

With regard to the research design, it follows from the previous points that the researcher should have extensive contact with the reality under study. The research design should include procedures which facilitate gaining a clear picture of the social reality under study (Blumer, 1969:27), and may involve open observation techniques and participation within that social reality. Qualitative means in this case an open research design allowing the researcher to test the developed insights in direct contact with and through different approaches to that social reality.

The object of the interpretive approach is thus closely associated with the life world of those involved, the meanings they attach to their situations and their construction of everyday reality. This is the reason for an alternative approach to conducting research: beginning with a description of the life world under study and on the basis of that developing theory. Although there is not an unambiguous qualitative methodology developed for all forms of interpretive research (Jankowski & Wester, 1991), there is nevertheless a common methodological ground. In this shared perspective on interpretive research, the methodological and theoretical views of symbolic interactionism play a central part (cf. Denzin & Lincoln, 1994:5).

The most important principle of symbolic interactionism is that the researcher:

> ...needs to discover the actor's 'definition of the situation' – that is, his perception and interpretation of reality and how these relate to his behaviour. Further, the actor's perception of reality turns on this ongoing interpretation of social interactions that he and others participate in, which, in turn, pivots on his use of symbols in general and language in particular. Finally, in order for the researcher to come to such an understanding he must be able (albeit imperfectly) to put himself in the other person's shoes. (Schwartz & Jacobs, 1979:7-8)

The aspects mentioned above by Schwartz and Jacobs refer to a central mechanism in symbolic interaction theory that plays a crucial role in its methodology: role taking. It points to the person's ability to take the position of an individual or group. In order to allow this role taking to function the researcher should participate as much as possible in the social world under study.

The continual contact which the researcher has with the research object makes it possible to develop concepts which relate to the situation under investigation. These concepts are not used as precisely defined concepts, but are more like guidelines for analysing the situation. The social reality, however, is obdurate: the concepts are as open as possible and their meaning becomes clearer during the process of analysis. Blumer (1969:40-44) refers in this sense to 'sensitizing concepts,' concepts which provide direction and indication of the area of concern to the researcher. Such sensitizing concepts are not a reflection of the directly perceived experience, but of the problematic character of these experiences; they are not prescriptions of what must be seen, but suggestions as to which aspects are relevant. They are important because the researcher (like any other human being) does not operate with a blank mind, but has ideas and preconceptions. Sensitizing concepts gain empirical substance through the continual contact which the researcher has with the topic and actors under study.

Once the investigator has obtained a clear image of the research object in the above manner, he/she proceeds with the phase in which the research object is analyzed or inspected from a theoretically directed perspective. The investigations are now directed toward the empirical content of the tentative concepts which were developed during the exploration phase, and toward the relations between these concepts.

The prototype of inspection is represented by our handling of a strange physical object: we may pick it up, look at it closely, turn it over as we view it, look at it from this or that angle, raise questions as to what it might be, go back and handle it again in the light of our questions, try it out, and test it in one way or another (Blumer, 1969:44).

Also in the inspection phase of research is Blumer's (1969:46) phrase 'direct examination of the empirical world' relevant. In addition, emphasis is placed on the principle that the research does not follow rigid predetermined procedures, but is flexible; the researcher is free, in other words, to consider new directions. In this manner sensitizing concepts become definitive as well as generic; that is to say, the concepts become formed by empirical content and can be used as elements for theory development.

Although theory development is the most important objective of interpretive research, not all qualitative studies aim to define and elaborate new theory. Some studies pretend no more than a first but thorough exploration of the specific field under study, others present a description of the field on the basis of substantive field-related concepts. In regard to the diversity in research objectives and related specifications of the research design, three main forms of qualitative research may be distinguished: the ethnographic study, the case study and the qualitative survey.

The ethnographic – sometimes termed naturalistic – study is based on participant observation in the life world of a specific culture or group. An ethnography has an anthropological accent and is aimed at a description of the cultural elements that are central in the life world of the group under study. Data collection is based on broad participation by the researcher in group activities, including unstructured observation, conversational interviews and document analysis. Ethnographic analysis is directed at the description of cultural domains and its components, and the cultural themes that structure several domains (cf. Spradley, 1980). Other participatory studies (Guba, 1981) are directed to describe the ongoing processes in the field under study. The studies presented by Lull (1988) are examples of research into media use with a participant observation design. Although Lull labels these studies ethnographic, they lack specific emphasis on cultural elements. The participant observation methods are mainly used here to describe patterns of television usage in families from different parts of the world, taking 'what is said' by the family members as the main categories of description.

The case study is aimed at the diagnosis of a (problematic) situation in a specific case or some specific cases through exploration and analytic description. The case, often an organization or institution, is studied in all its complexity by integrating data collected through interviewing, document analysis, observations during meetings and similar techniques. The objective is to perform a diagnosis of the situation in theoretical terms and sometimes to formulate possible solutions to specific problems. The analysis is based on comparisons between cases directed by a well developed theoretical perspective (cf. Yin, 1984; Miles & Huberman, 1984:28-33). Radway's study (1984) of readers of romantic fiction is based on such a case study design. Through individual and group interviews she tried to reconstruct the reading practice of her respondents. The main categories of description and interpretation come from the researcher's perspectives. The same is true for the case studies described by Charlton and Neumann (1986:8). They focus their observations on the media use of a specific child in the family and analyse the data in view of their *strukturanalytische Rezeptionsforschung* framework.

The qualitative survey is aimed at theory development through comparison of a relatively large number of diverse cases. Although all kinds of observational methods may be applied, in most studies data collection is based mainly on a single method, particularly interviewing. These studies often follow the grounded theory method. Starting with some sensitizing concepts as a provisional analytic framework, the theory is elaborated in four phases. The initial, exploratory phase is intended to extract preliminary, field-related concepts from the collected material. In the second or defining phase, the researcher tries to construct variables based on the field-related substantive concepts. In the third phase or reduction phase, the aim is to formulate the core of the theory. In the final phase, termed integration, the concepts are related to one another and the relations tested on the data.

The cycle of reflection, observation, and analysis is repeated throughout the research process in each of the four phases, until the theoretical formulations have exhausted available data. Although the agent of analysis at each step of theory formulation is the researcher, the computer is an important administrative aid in all kinds of manipulations on the data (Peters & Wester, 1994). Morley's (1986) study of television use in the family is an example of a qualitative survey based on interviews with members of families from different social classes. Although this study does not accentuate theory development, it nevertheless demonstrates specific patterns of television usage for men and women.

The study presented in Chapter 11 of this volume is an illustration of a qualitative survey conducted from the perspective of the social action model for media use elaborated in Chapter 2. Another example is Brehm's (1994) investigation of patterns of television viewing in the context of everyday activities through interviews with persons living together. She elaborated a typology of viewing patterns and found that, although every household had a dominant pattern for watching together, there were different watching patterns for the partners watching alone.

Quantitative methods and the social action model

Many of the research questions concerning media use are based on feelings of surprise among researchers about the regularities people have in their media use. For example: why do certain people generally read the newspapers in great detail whereas others seldom or never read newspapers at all? Why do certain people continuously change television channels whereas others stick to one channel? Why do certain people watch television each day for at least four hours whereas others watch no more than half an hour, if at all? Communication research tries to explain, among other things, why certain actions occur relatively frequent – or relatively seldom – within a given period of time.

Quantitative methods can help much in discovering regularities in the processes of a situation definition and interpretation that bring about such patterns in media use. Therefore, regularities in a whole series of actions are measured and not just during one or two isolated actions. The same goes for characteristics of the actor's social situation and stock of knowledge: it is the structural aspects which are first measured. Next, the regularities in actions are related to the regularities in social situation and stock of knowledge characteristics. Finally, regularities in the intermediating processes are inferred from these relations.

The following example may help illustrate this aspect. Suppose the research question is: to what extent is interest in sports a factor of importance in the choice process leading to watching sports programmes? To answer this question, data are collected by means of a survey on the frequency of viewing sports programmes and interest in sports. If the analysis of these data reveals that there is a statistical relation between a relatively strong interest in sports and the relatively high frequency of viewing sports programmes, then this may indicate that interest (in sports) is indeed a factor in the choice process that leads to watching (sports) programmes. Furthermore, one may raise the question to what extent the possibly deviant interests of housemates play a role in the choice process (see Chapter 7). The more people there are in a household, the greater the chance that there will be housemates who have different interests and programme preferences. If these possibly deviant preferences of housemates are factors in the choice of programmes, then this will mean that people in larger households will quite often not be able to watch programmes they would normally choose on the basis of their own interests. Single people, on the other hand, are practically always able to watch a programme they would choose on the basis of their interests. If the survey includes data on the number of housemates, then one can also test the probability of this possible influence. This can be done by checking whether the statistical relation between interests and programme preferences is stronger in single person households than in larger households.

Likewise one may check to what extent other individual or combined factors are related to a relatively high frequency of watching sports programmes. In the same way one can try to describe other forms of media use. Thus, one obtains a large number of data allowing inferences concerning regularities in interpretation processes that form the basis for media use.

Of course, the application of quantitative methods as we have sketched here presents a rather rosy picture. In practice, caution is required, especially in case of a causal interpretation of the research model. As already described, in applying quantitative methods one measures characteristics of social position, aspects of the stock of knowledge and external action (media use included) within a certain period of time, mostly by means of a cross-sectional study based on a standardized questionnaire.

A significant feature, particularly of cross-sectional studies, is that the causal sequence of the concepts measured within the period of time is often not known. In such studies, caution is required in making inferences concerning the causal effects of definition processes from observed relationships between the various concepts. For instance, in our example of watching sports programmes an influence of interest in sports on watching sport programmes is presupposed. However, it is also imaginable that a certain interest in sports is developed by regularly watching sports programmes. Both causal processes would lead to a correlation between these two concepts. If we want to explain the correlation in one of these two ways, then we will need strong arguments to exclude the other. It may be clear that a valid (i.e. plausible) argument supporting a particular inference concerning definition processes is much easier to find for relations between media use and influence of stable background characteristics such as sex, age and education than for relations between media use and less stable characteristics such as characteristics of the stock of knowledge.

A more fundamental problem connected with survey research concerns the reliance on preconstructed questionnaire items, whether applied in a cross-sectional study, a panel study or an experimental study. The use of these items is based on the assumption that the item has the same meaning for each respondent (Anderson, 1987:70). From the standpoint of a social action perspective, stressing the dependency of meaning attachment on individual and situational circumstances is at least problematic. The most extreme position one may take on this issue is to abandon the use of questionnaires. A more moderate position may be to include only items in a questionnaire the meaning of which seems to be shared. And once more, it is obvious that the meanings of direct observable background characteristics such as sex, age and education and the also observable external action are much more shared than the meanings of beliefs, needs and the like.

A common solution to these three problems is that only the most obvious aspects of social position, external action and (sometimes) stock of knowledge are measured. However, as a result the reconstruction of the intermediary processes of situation definition and interpretation is often rather poor (Anderson & Meyer, 1988; Blumer, 1969). A better solution may be the use of extensive pilot studies to formulate items that fit the perspective to be measured.

40

Combining qualitative and quantitative research

As we have seen, the shift in accent from external observable action to internal action processes (perceiving, thematizing, diagnosing and projection and decision of action) and the related need for more insight into these processes poses some significant problems for empirical research because internal action processes cannot be 'measured' in the same way as external action (overt behaviour). In general, the former involves a more qualitative research strategy to determine whether and how internal action processes can be made visible. Qualitative research can provide the analytic framework as well as the research instruments to do that (see Wester, 1991:25-29; Peters & Wester, 1989). In this regard, biographical research, such as life histories of (types of) recipients may be undertaken. However, as we have also shown, quantitative methods may also help to provide some insight into the processes leading essentially to media use. We would now like to address the question whether a combined application of both approaches of research may be fruitful as a general research strategy for reconstructing internal action processes.

Various authors have argued for a combined application of different research methods. For instance, Denzin (1978) considers methods as interaction strategies which the researcher may employ to get acquainted with the social reality under study. Some methods provide for a good registration of the perspectives of the participants, some are more focused on the social and situational context; some methods are apt to analyse stable behaviour patterns, other methods are sensitive for the process aspects of human behaviour. Some methods are more suitable for studying interaction patterns and others for considering symbols and meaning structures. Inasmuch as every method is able to contribute to understanding specific aspects of a phenomenon, it is recommended that researchers employ multiple methods in investigating social reality. Denzin (1978:291) refers in this regard to methodological triangulation. As a second example we mention the work of Glaser (1978), Glaser & Strauss (1967) and Strauss (1987), who criticize the one-sidedness of the hypothetico-deductive research model. This model is restricted to quantitative methods and is only appropriate for testing hypotheses. This leads, they contend, to the formulation of all kinds of speculative ideas about reality, which only increases the gap between theory and the empirical social world. They propose, in contrast, the development of 'grounded theory,' which is developed step by step on the basis of acquaintance with the social reality under investigation. Clearly, qualitative methods play a crucial role in the grounding of theories. However, Glaser and Strauss also point out that quantitative methods may contribute substantially to the grounding of theories provided they are used in an explorative and flexible manner.

A combined application of different research methods is also sometimes supported in the work of more positivist oriented authors, such as in the methodological treatise of De Groot (1969:27) and his 'cycle of empirical-scientific research.' De Groot's empirical research cycle starts with a dual phase in which the researcher formulates inductively some general hypotheses on the basis of a literature study and an (empirical) exploration. In this phase, the researcher has considerable freedom in choosing a research design and methods. It is only in the following deductive phase that hypotheses are tested. Quantitative methods are best suited for this phase of testing hypotheses. However, the deductive phase may give rise to new research questions, which need (inductive) exploration.

In line with these ideas, we see no reason for a policy of restrictiveness concerning choice of research methods, even from a social action perspective. On the contrary, we think qualitative and quantitative methods may in some instances be complementary, which we hope to illustrate elsewhere in this volume.

Qualitative methods are especially suitable as a method of exploration because of their flexibility (Wester 1991:55-58). With the use of methods such as participant observation, in-depth interviews and group discussions it is possible to acquire very detailed, empirical material. These enable us to reconstruct intermediary definition and interpretation processes more accurately and to develop theories on a more abstract level about the way in which these processes work. The contribution by Hermans and Van Snippenburg in this volume (Chapter 11) illustrates the way in which qualitative methods may contribute in generating insights on some topic. The authors investigate the place watching the news has in the everyday activities of women living in a family context. In this qualitative survey several women from different social backgrounds were interviewed. The authors explore the ways the women watch television news in relation to use of other news sources, the reasons for watching and in which news topics the women are specifically interested.

Quantitative methods, on the other hand, have attractive aspects such as the relatively easy processing of data and the possibility of generalizing research results statistically for larger populations than those that were studied. This is why these methods are best suited for hypothetico-deductive research. Van Snippenburg's study (Chapter 9) is an example of such a traditional application of hypothetico-deductive investigations. Based on notions from social stratification theory and the uses and gratifications approach, he develops a conceptual model for explaining exposure to information-oriented media content. The model is tested using survey data and regression analysis.

However, as we have seen, quantitative methods also may serve as a method of exploration, providing used in a flexible manner. The study reported by Renckstorf and Hendriks Vettehen on non-viewers (Chapter 6) is one example of the way in which quantitative methods may be used to generate insight about a specific phenomenon. Simple and straight-forward comparisons between non-viewers, light viewers, moderate viewers and heavy viewers on the basis of survey data enable the authors to gain insight into possible motivations for non-viewing.

To summarize, both qualitative and quantitative research methods may contribute to research developed from a social action perspective. Each approach has its own merits. A combined application of both may, indeed, be the ideal solution. However, due to the usual constraints of time and resources, it will remain difficult to realize such an idealized design within single research projects. It may only, in fact, be possible within research programmes which combine and prioritize individual projects.

4 Information needs: problems, interests and consumption

Jan Bosman and Karsten Renckstorf

The need for information as a predictor of information consumption has been criticized from various sides in recent years, particularly because it was often used in communication studies as an autonomous explanatory factor. This chapter tries to establish the determinants of information needs. A distinction is made between intrinsic and extrinsic motivation for information consumption and an examination is made into the relative importance of subjectively experienced problems as an extrinsic motivation in explaining information needs and consumption.

The concept of 'information needs,' which is quite important in recent communication studies, has been under attack from all sides during the past few years. Problems concerning social desirability and the instability of the information needs measured have caused researchers such as Van Cuilenburg (1983) to conclude that 'information needs research in its present form produces results which are not very reliable, valid or accurate, and therefore useless for policy making.' More substantial criticism came from Bosman *et al.*, (1989:24-25) who assert that the concept of information needs has no sound theoretical basis. By using information needs as a point of departure for analysis, it is given the status of an autonomous explanatory factor, although it is in fact an *ad hoc* notion created for practical purposes in order to predict information-seeking behaviour and information consumption. It is rather obvious that people who consume much information on a certain subject will also state that they have a certain need for this information. From this point of view, one may expect an empirical relation between both notions. Notwithstanding the methodical objections posed by Van Cuilenburg, such a relation is indeed found in most cases.

However, if one wants to explain why some people do and others do not consume certain information, the information needs concept is as elucidating as, for instance, explaining criminal behaviour on the basis of hypothetical 'criminality needs.'[1]

---

1 Concepts such as the need for cognition (NC; see Petty & Cacioppo, 1986) seem to suggest

Information needs, motivation and information consumption

The information needs concept plays, therefore, at the most an intermediary role between more deeply seated factors and information-seeking behaviour or information consumption. After examining the available literature, Van Cuilenburg states that such factors include, among other things, problems, insecurity, cognitive dissonance, interests, and the need to form opinions. He also states that, at a higher abstraction level, these factors can be described in terms of utility,[2] and that the literature distinguishes between instrumental and social utility.[3]

The difference between instrumental and social utility is that instrumental utility refers to the utility of information as such (e.g. knowing how to solve a problem), whereas social utility refers to the utility of knowledge as a part of social action (e.g. showing off with your knowledge about the solution of a problem). In both cases, the information is instrumental in order to achieve a certain goal. Van Cuilenburg's distinction between instrumental and social utility incorrectly suggests that social utility is not instrumental.

Atkin (1973) uses a somewhat different distinction. He differentiates between instrumental utility and non-instrumental considerations as the determinants of information-seeking behaviour and information consumption. In this concept – although Atkin does not state this explicitly – instrumental utility includes social utility, whereas amongst the non-instrumental considerations one finds personal interest (a notion which Van Cuilenburg lists under the heading of 'instrumental utility'), as well as the entertainment value of information. Apparently, there is still no agreement on how the various factors underlying the information needs concept should be categorized.

From Atkin's point of view, non-instrumental considerations refer to information which is not instrumental for the realization of a certain utility. However, this does not mean that these non-instrumental considerations do not have any utility value. If someone, for example, is interested in certain information, then the consumption of that information will in general give satisfaction, fulfilment or pleasure[4] (not taking into consideration other possible benefits he/she may gain from this information and presuming that he/she does not expect these other benefits). Such a utility, however, is not instrumental for the achievement of other goals, but a goal in itself.

Atkin (1973:205, italics added) defines instrumental utility value as: 'A message has instrumental utility for the receiver when it provides him with a helpful input for

---

(contd) differently, however. Even if we suppose that different people reliably differ in their NC, then such an NC still cannot explain why people want information from certain domains while rejecting information from other domains.

2 See further the notion *Nutzenansatz* as discussed by Renckstorf (1977: 12–34).

3 Van Cuilenburg (1983: 62) also states that the factors concerned are so obvious that they do not need any further scientific foundation, while on the other hand they are 'so general and empty that they can hardly be used for concrete information policies.'

4 See further notion of gratification as developed by Katz *et al.* (1974).

responding to everyday stimuli for defending personal predispositions. He may need information to keep him abreast of governmental actions, to guide his consumer decision making, or to reinforce his political preferences. These types of informational needs generate *extrinsic* motivation to seek messages from mass media sources.'

Thus, Atkin actually makes a distinction between extrinsic motivation to consume information and intrinsic motivation. Both can be described in terms of utility value. In the case of intrinsic motivation, the utility value is intrinsically related to the consumption of the information itself. With extrinsic motivation the utility is not found in the consumption of the information itself but in the fact that the information can be used (i.e. it is instrumental) to realize another utility.

Note that the introduction of the notion of intrinsic utility is in fact a reintroduction of the notion of information needs: seeking antecedents of information needs is the same as seeking other needs to which the information concerned is instrumental. The assumption of intrinsic utility or non-instrumental considerations indicates that the value of the information concerned can be found in the information itself (or in the processing of the information) and not in the fact that it serves other needs.

The expectancy value theory of Fischbein and Ajzen (1975) can be used in order to place some of this in a broader theoretical framework. Recently, this theory has also been incorporated in a number of variants of the uses and gratifications approach (cf. Palmgreen & Rayburn, 1982: Rayburn & Palmgreen, 1984). The expectancy value theory states that the attitude towards an object (or a certain behaviour) depends on the characteristics of that object (or the consequences of the behaviour) and the evaluation of those characteristics (or consequences). Mathematically, the theory is expressed as follows:

$$A_g = \sum_{i=1}^{n} (b_i * e_i)$$

The attitude towards a certain behaviour (A_g) is the product of the expectation (b_i: belief) that behaviour has consequence 'i' and the evaluation of that consequence (e_i: evaluation), summed for the relevant consequences. In the theory of Fischbein and Ajzen, the attitude, together with the subjective norm, determines the behavioural intention. The subjective norm consists of two factors: the expectation that important other people think that one should or should not engage in such behaviour (normative belief) and the motivation to comply with these other people (motivation to comply). Although the subjective norm is presented as a separate component in the theory of Fischbein and Ajzen, it may be stated that the way in which others judge one's behaviour is just one of the consequences of that behaviour, and that the motivation to comply with that opinion is the evaluation of that consequence. Hence, the subjective norm is nothing but the attitude towards the social consequences of a certain behaviour, and it is therefore only a variant of the more general formula for attitude.

Van Cuilenburg's distinction between instrumental and social utility can therefore also be found in the notions of attitude and subjective norm in the expectancy value theory of

Fischbein and Ajzen. Both can be criticized for the same reason: social utility is a part of instrumental utility and the social norm is a part of the notion of attitude.

In order to be able to incorporate Atkin's distinction between instrumental utility and non-instrumental considerations (here named extrinsic and intrinsic motivation) in the expectancy value theory, Fischbein and Ajzen's basic formula – $A_g = \sum(b_i * e_i)$ – needs further examination. This formula states that our evaluation (or attitude or some other concept expressing evaluation) towards a certain object (or a person, a behaviour; anything one can evaluate) depends on the evaluation (attitude) of the distinguishable aspects of the object. Of course this raises the question what the evaluation of these aspects subsequently depends upon.

The simple answer that the expectancy value theory can also be used for these aspects is not sufficient because it leads to a *regressum ad infinitum*: nothing is valued for what it is, but only because of its aspects (or consequences), and those aspects are in turn only valued according to their sub-aspects. It is clear, for example, that sex can be valued for what it is and not for its consequences.

So, the problematic distinction between extrinsic and intrinsic motivation can also be found in the expectancy value theory of Fischbein and Ajzen, be it somewhat camouflaged. Was the (implicit) introduction of the notion of intrinsic motivation in Atkin's work actually a reintroduction of the notion of information needs, the same can be said of the attitude towards an aspect (e_i: evaluation) in the expectancy value theory, which is in fact a reintroduction of the notion of attitude which the theory tries to explain. In other words: our attitude towards a sack of potatoes is the sum total of our attitudes towards each of the potatoes separately.

This is, of course, not wholly unjustified. Some things have no value of their own, but are only useful insofar as they are the key to other things or events. But eventually, if we do not want to end up in a *regressum ad infinitum*, these other things or events should always lead to something with intrinsic value.[5] The question then becomes to what extent our attitude towards a certain object or behaviour is determined by either extrinsic or intrinsic factors. The formula of the expectancy value theory wrongly suggests that the determinants of the attitude towards an object or a behaviour should always be sought at a deeper level.

As far as information needs or attitudes towards the consumption of information are concerned, the literature (for instance, the items often used in the uses and gratifications approach) roughly suggests three categories of determinants of those attitudes or needs in agreement with the above mentioned categories: social utility (e.g. in order to have topics

---

5   Actually the formula of Fischbein and Ajzen gives a recursive definition of the notion of attitude. Recursive definitions are characterized by the fact that the notion to be defined recurs in the definition. Such procedures are often criticized, but do not necessarily produce nonsense. The faculty of n, for example, is defined mathematically as: $n! = n*(n-1)!$. Such a regressive formula does of course need a stop rule. In this case: stop if $n-1 = 0$. In Fischbein and Ajzen's formula this would be: stop if it concerns an intrinsic value.

of conversation), instrumental utility (e.g. in order to decide whether to buy something) and intrinsic utility (e.g. the entertainment value of the information offered). Alternatively, one may use the terms intrinsic utility and extrinsic (social and instrumental) utility.

One problem is the fact that these categories have no clear boundaries and may overlap each other. A programme which has entertainment value may also be suitable as a topic of conversation. A more fundamental problem is the fact that the subjective value of information is probably (also) the product of a long personal history of social and instrumental (i.e. extrinsic) utility of (similar) information. From a cognitive viewpoint such a history leads to the general and abstract expectation that similar information will again be useful in the future (extrinsic utility; the uses and gratifications approach employs the term surveillance information in this respect). Along the lines of conditioning theories, however, such a history leads to the observation that the information has been rewarded time and time again in the history of the individual, and thus that the information has obtained intrinsic value through principles of conditioning.

Information interests, problems experienced and information consumption

Hence, the different categories cannot always be distinguished clearly. Nonetheless, it does seem important in communication studies to know to what extent people use mass media for extrinsic reasons and therefore seek certain information that (subjectively) fits the personal circumstances and the problems of the receiver. Or, to what extent people evaluate the media on less pragmatic grounds and are guided in their choice by intrinsic factors like entertainment value.

The clearest form of extrinsic motivation is the case in which information is used in order to cope with other situations, as Atkin (1973:205) puts it. In other words: when information is used to improve the decision-making process in those other situations, or to solve problems. Problems as underlying determinants of information needs are also mentioned by Bosman et al., (1989:40-41) and Van Cuilenburg (1983:62). Apart from other factors (e.g. involvement and interests), problems as major predictors of information-seeking behaviour are also mentioned by Dervin (1983:172).

Bosman et al. (1989:40-41) describe subjectively experienced problems as the central factor in the creation of a demand for information, and therefore in the pursuit of knowledge. From this point of view, problems are the driving force behind the process of acquiring knowledge. This chapter tries to take the first steps towards an explanation of the relative importance of extrinsic motivation, in the form of problems, in the explanation of information needs and information consumption. The data are taken from a survey (MASSAT, '89) conducted in 1989 by the Department of Communication at the University of Nijmegen in the Netherlands. This survey was conducted with a random sample (n=956) of the Dutch population (for more details, see Arts et al., 1990b).

For this particular study, the most important variables were the problems people experience in certain domains (i.e. the extrinsic motivation for information consumption), the

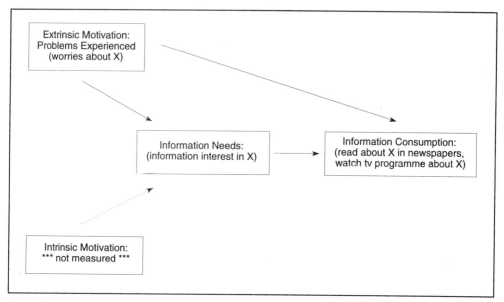

Fig. 1. Relation between problems experienced, information needs and information consumption.

information needs and the actual information consumption with respect to these domains. The problems experienced were operationalized by means of items where the respondents had to indicate to what extent they were worried about certain topics (for example: 'I am worried about the political future of our country'). Information needs were not measured directly. Information interest (earlier described as one of the underlying intrinsic factors of information needs) is regarded as an indicator of information needs as we assumed that respondents would not perceive questions with respect to information interest as matters concerning intrinsic interest as defined here. Such questions concerning information interest function rather as a repository for all kinds of factors that constitute information needs. For the respondents, the extrinsic value of information (e.g. functionality with respect to solving a certain problem) will also fall under the heading 'interest'. Finally, information consumption was operationalized as the frequency with which respondents actually read about these topics in the newspapers or watched television programmes on these topics. In total, six domains could be distinguished for which data on problems with respect to these domains as well as on information needs and information consumption were available. The topics concerned were politics, crime, scientific developments, health, finance and natural disasters. In a number of cases there were more items to measure a certain variable. In these cases, the scores on these items were averaged.

As already mentioned, we consider problems to be one of the major underlying determinants of information needs. We shall determine to what extent information needs predict information consumption, to what extent information needs are predicted by problems and to what extent problems predict information consumption. Furthermore, we shall determine whether problems have a direct or indirect influence (i.e. via information needs) on information consumption.

Results

Table 1 shows the correlations between problems experienced, information needs and information consumption for the topics investigated.

Table 1. Problems, information needs and information consumption

	Problems correlated with needs	Needs correlated with consumption	Problems correlated with consumption
Domains			
Criminality	0.26	0.42	0.10
Science	0.28	0.53	0.22
Disasters	0.24	0.43	0.15
Politics	0.46	0.65	0.32
Health	0.24	0.33	0.10
Finances	0.04*	0.61	0.06
Total[†]	0.28	0.51	0.18

* not significant at $P = 0.05$; [†]mean correlations over the six domains according to the formula: $r = \sqrt{\sum (r^2) / n}$

The correlations between information needs and information consumption are generally rather strong. The mean correlation is 0.51. Somewhat lower correlations are found between problems and information needs ($r = 0.28$) and between problems and information consumption ($r = 0.18$). With one exception, all correlations form a regular pattern per domain, in which the relation between information needs and information consumption is the highest and the relation between problems and information consumption the lowest. The one exception concerns the domain of finances, in which the relation between problems and information needs is the lowest and problems hardly have any relation with information needs and information consumption. Apparently, financial worries cannot be alleviated by information in the eyes of the respondents.

This pattern (in which the highest correlations are between information needs and information consumption and the lowest between problems and information consumption) is in agreement with the hypothesis that influences of problems upon information consumption are mediated by the information needs concept, and that problems as extrinsic motivators for information consumption constitute one of the determinants of information needs.

In order to test this hypothesis more carefully, the partial correlations between problems and consumption were determined with the influence of the information needs upon information consumption was partialled out. If the influence of problems upon information consumption is indeed exerted via information needs, then these partial correlations should be negligibly small.[6] Table 2 shows the partial correlations for the different domains, together with the original correlations between problems and information consumption.

Table 2. Problems and information consumption (Rpc), and problems and consumption (PRpc.n) partialled out for information needs

	Correlations Rpc	Partial correlations PRpc.n
Domains		
Criminality	0.10	0.00*
Science	0.22	0.11
Disasters	0.15	0.06
Politics	0.32	0.04*
Health	0.10	0.02*
Finances	0.06	0.05*
Total[†]	0.18	0.06

* not significant at $P = 0.05$;
[†]mean correlations over the six domains according to the formula $r = \sqrt{\sum (r^2)/n}$

One can see that, by partialling out the information needs, the correlations between the problems experienced and information consumption have generally fallen to a non-significant level. On average the correlation for all domains together has dropped from 0.18 to 0.06. In terms of explained variance this means that 89 per cent of the covariance between problems and information consumption is accounted for by information needs.

Conclusions

These data are in accord with the hypothesis that external motivation in the form of problems experienced is one of the determinants of information needs and the influence of those problems on information consumption occurs via information needs.

Generally speaking, however, the correlations that were found between problems and needs on the one hand and between problems and information consumption on the other are low[7] ($r^2 = 0.08$ and $r^2 = 0.03$ respectively). A rather obvious interpretation thereof may be that problems are a relatively unimportant factor in information seeking behaviour and consumption.

---

6   This does not mean that the reverse is also true, i.e. that if partial correlations are indeed negligibly small, the hypothesis is confirmed. It is just not falsified and it is possible that the supposed causal order (from problems through needs to consumption) is incorrect, and that, for example, consumption of information leads to problems.

7   Even these low correlations may be somewhat inflated. For example, part of the correlation between problems and information consumption may be due to the influence of information consumption on the problems experienced by the respondents (see also previous footnote), and external variables, such as age and education, can be partly responsible for, for example, the correlation between information needs and information consumption.

There may, however, be other causes for these low correlations. First of all, information consumption behaviour is not only determined by the personal wishes and needs of the respondents (especially with respect to television viewing), but also for a large part by the needs and preferences of members of the household (Mutsaers, 1993; see also Chapter 7). Such an influence by members of the household will especially have to manifest itself in the relations between the antecedents of information consumption, and information consumption and will have little or no influence on the relation between problems and information needs. Table 3 shows the correlations between problems, information needs and information consumption for the whole group of respondents, together with the correlations for the respondents who live in a single household.

Table 3. Problems, information needs and information consumption for respondents living in single households

	Problems & Needs		Needs & Consumption		Problems & Consumption	
Domain						
Criminality	(0.26)	0.33	(0.42)	0.51	(0.10)	0.17*
Science	(0.28)	0.30	(0.53)	0.61	(0.22)	0.35
Disasters	(0.24)	0.15*	(0.43)	0.59	(0.15)	0.04*
Politics	(0.46)	0.45	(0.65)	0.69	(0.32)	0.35
Health	(0.24)	0.25	(0.33)	0.25	(0.10)	0.00*
Finances	(0.04)	0.11*	(0.61)	0.73	(0.06)	0.22
Total[†]	(0.28)	0.29	(0.51)	0.58	(0.18)	0.23

Note: the correlations for the entire sample are in brackets. *not significant at $P = 0.05$; [†]mean correlations over the six domains according to the formula: $r = \sqrt{\sum(r^2)/n}$

One can see that the correlations between needs and consumption and between problems and consumption are indeed higher for respondents living alone, and that the correlation between problems and needs is not influenced by leaving out multiple households. The variance of information consumption which is accounted for by information needs, increases from 26 per cent to 34 per cent ($P = 0.01$)[8] and the variance accounted for by problems increases from 3 per cent to 5 per cent (n.s.).

A second cause for the low correlations between problems and information consumption might be found in our basic assumptions. We have assumed that information is (or can be) instrumental in solving problems. However, people differ in the way they believe that they can influence their environment (internal versus external control) and, likewise, they differ in the way they perceive information as being instrumental in solving their problems. As an indicator for such differences we used the fatalism scale (Arts et al., 1990b:285) and performed separate analyses for the half of the respondents who scored highest and for

---

8   The calculations of the explained variances are based on the mean correlations; the calculation of the significance of the difference is based on the smallest N.

the half who scored lowest. Those analyses did not show any differences between the respondents who had more and those who had less fatalistic tendencies.

Finally, non-optimal operationalizations may also be the cause of the relatively low correlations. This study is based on an analysis of secondary data and that implies that the available variables were not entirely tailored to our questions. On the one hand this meant that the number of domains which we could analyse were limited. With respect to environmental problems, for example, there were questions available concerning problems and needs, but not concerning information consumption. On the other hand, the use of secondary data meant that all variables did not always correspond well with each other, even in the domains for which the variables were available. Having problems in the domain of criminality, for example, was operationalized by asking the respondents whether they ever worried about 'criminality, violence, public safety,' whereas information consumption was operationalized as reading (in the newspapers) about 'crimes and court cases.' Such imperfections – common when working with secondary data – surely do not improve the relations that were found. Additional research using better operationalizations is therefore necessary to assess the role of problems in explaining information consumption. However, even though such additional research might yield more promising results for the concept problems, it should also be noted that in the present design problems have a monopoly position in explaining information needs and information consumption. Additional research should therefore include alternative motivational variables such as intrinsic motivation and social utility to compete with problems in explaining information need and consumption. The authors are currently working on such a design.

5   Heavy viewing as social action

Valerie Frissen

In spite of the considerable social and scientific interest for heavy viewers, research has been driven by a rather one-sided and stereotypical image of this group. A theoretical perspective on heaving viewing has been absent which has impeded interpretation of research findings. In this chapter a theoretical perspective is developed by which heavy viewing is considered a form of social action. This perspective constitutes an integration of concepts from the uses and gratifications approach and interpretative approaches based on social action.

The television audience has been a focal point of public and academic discourses, virtually since the widespread introduction of that medium after World War II. However, as Ang (1991) argues, despite the existence of such discourses, there is still no great theoretical and empirical understanding of the social world of audiences. In Ang's terms the television audience exists only as an abstract discursive construct, 'onto which large scale economic and cultural aspirations and expectations, policies and planning schemes are projected' (Ang, 1991:3).

> The audience is treated as a conceptually non-problematic category, consisting of a definite, unknown but knowable set of people...an aggregate of individuals whose characteristics can then presumably be operationalized, examined, categorized and accumulated into an even more complete picture. (Ang, 1991:11)

This has led to a neglection of what Ang calls 'the social world of actual audiences.'

Heavy viewers can be seen as such an 'actual audience,' which during the past years has been a subject of considerable social and academic concern and interest. As I have argued elsewhere (Frissen, 1992), since the introduction of television there has been an ongoing debate about heavy viewers as a social problem. This social concern has generated much academic research. However, the result of these studies is a rather restricted and biased image of heavy viewers because this research concentrates generally on only a few recurrent themes. The fact that social and cultural discourses on the television audience have dominated academic research so strongly implies a predominant ad hoc character of the questions asked and a lack of theoretical reflection in the research undertaken.

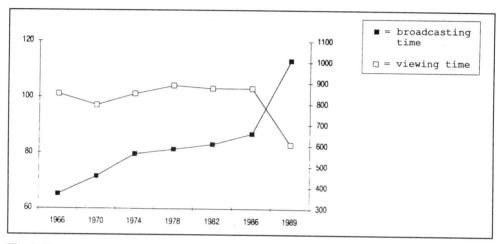

Fig. 1. Viewing and broadcasting of Dutch channels. Note: Average amount of viewing time and broadcasting time of the Dutch channels in minutes between 1965 and 1989 after 6.30 pm. Source: NOS, 1990.

In this chapter I shall argue that, in order to describe and explain the social world of an actual audience such as heavy viewers adequately, a theoretical perspective on the social character of media use is required. The aim of this chapter is to describe such a theoretical perspective and to present empirical data illustrating the usefulness of the perspective. But first I shall briefly review and criticize research on heavy viewing conducted in the field of mass communication.

Academic research on heavy viewing[1]

Television landscape

The first regular and large scale television broadcasts in the United States and Europe began shortly after the end of World War 2. The technology developed very quickly into the basis for a mass medium. In the early 1950s, particularly in the United States, the supply of programmes was already quite extensive. Consequently, Americans could spend virtually all of their leisure time watching television. This led to many more or less speculative debates on the implications of heavy viewing for the individual (particularly the child), the family and society in general (see, for example, Schramm *et al.*, 1961:2-5). It is not surprising that these discourses of social concern influenced research on the television audience in general and heavy viewers in particular. And, of course, in the United States there was some reason for this concern because television seemed to change daily life and leisure patterns quite dramatically. According to Schramm *et al.* (1961) in their classic study of children's use of television, children tended to spend as much time watching television as they did attending school. Therefore, it is not surprising that most

---

1   For more extensive reviews, see Frissen (1992) and Huth (1982).

research literature on heavy viewers during the early decades of television originates from the United States where heavy viewing was considered to be a serious social problem.

In the late 1970s and early 1980s increasing academic interest in the problem of heavy viewing arose in Europe, particularly in West Germany, but also in the Netherlands. This should be seen against the background of the introduction of cable and satellite television in several European countries. The resulting expansion of the supply of programmes was expected to lead to an increase in the number of heavy viewers and in the average viewing time. Research into the implications of these developments was considered desirable (e.g. Sturm, 1981a; 1981b; Schulz, 1986b; Kiefer, 1987). However, the actual facts concerning development of television viewing behaviour in the Netherlands, show clearly that there is no real support for the thesis that an increase in the supply of programmes automatically leads to an increase of the average amount of television viewing. Figure 1 indicates that, in the Netherlands at least, the recent development may be even opposite to the one expected.

This figure clearly illustrates that the average broadcasting time has increased dramatically, while the average viewing time has not changed substantially changed over the years. Even when daytime viewing is taken into account, there is no fundamental change in the general trend as presented in this figure. The most crucial recent development in the Netherlands was the introduction of the commercial channel RTL-4 in 1989. This channel soon was very successful and in a few years became the leading Dutch television channel in terms of audience appeal. This resulted in 1991 in a slight increase in the average viewing time of Dutch viewers. However, compared to the explosive growth of broadcasting time since the 1980s, the average amount of viewing by the Dutch audience has not changed fundamentally.

Such facts, of course, do not imply that heavy viewing is an unimportant issue, but they do make clear that the matter of heavy viewing is not very well defined. Heavy viewing is not a natural and logical effect of certain developments in the field of mass communication, an effect that applies to everyone who owns a television set. The important issue, in fact, is why some people watch a lot of television and others do not. Which factors contribute to the importance of television in the everyday social world of the individual? To describe and explain heavy viewing, two questions in particular need to be addressed:

- How can heavy viewing be defined and/or conceptualized adequately, and what distinguishes heavy viewing from other patterns of television use?
- How can the fact be explained that some people spend many hours per day watching television while others very few?

In the following discussion of some of the central themes in the research on heavy viewing I shall argue that these questions have not yet been adequately answered.

Definitions of heavy viewing

An important consideration is how heavy viewing is defined in the academic literature. The concept of heavy viewing has become so familiar in popular and academic discourses that it seems to be more or less clear what it means. A closer look at the literature, however, shows that there is no consensus as to how heavy viewing is defined. Mostly the problem of definition – put more precisely, the operationalization of a concept not theoretically defined – is solved pragmatically and arbitrarily. Heavy viewing can be defined in terms of the number of hours television is watched, which can range from two hours per day or more, but also three or four or even six hours per day (Gerbner, *et al.*, 1979, Jackson-Beeck & Sobal, 1980; Buß, 1985), depending on, for instance, the average amount of viewing in a particular population. Another pragmatic solution is defining heavy viewers as the 25 per cent to 30 per cent of a population which spends the most time watching television (e.g. Himmelweit *et al.*, 1958; Schulz, 1986b).

In academic research on heavy viewing the considerations for choosing a particular definition are almost never of a theoretical nature.[2] It must, as a consequence, be concluded that heavy viewing has not yet been adequately conceptualized given the absence of a theoretical basis. It is difficult, then, to answer the question as to what distinguishes heavy viewing, on a definition level, from other patterns of viewing behaviour. The only conclusion which can be drawn from research that is based on such pragmatic operational definitions is that in a certain population those people who spend the most time watching television are, relatively speaking, older, poorer and unemployed. However, this does not lead to a clear conceptual distinction of heavy viewing from other patterns of viewing behaviour because, evidently, not all older or unemployed people are heavy viewers.

Statistical correlates between patterns of viewing behaviour on the one hand and, for example, certain socio-demographic characteristics or certain conceptions of social reality (Gerbner & Gross, 1976a; Gerbner *et al.*, 1979) on the other hand, tend to lead to more or less static and reified typifications of viewer categories, such as heavy viewers. The result of such research is merely the construction of an 'ideal type' of heavy viewers, or as Ang (1991) argues, an artefact, an abstract discursive construct. The construction of this stereotype image of heavy viewers is illustrated in greater detail in the following section.

Explanations of heavy viewing

In an earlier review of academic and popular literature on heavy viewing (Frissen, 1988) I have argued that, although heavy viewing has been of considerable interest to communication researchers in the past decades, they have not yet reached the point where they describe and explain this phenomenon from an explicit theoretical point of view. Research is often based on ad hoc questions derived from public debates, particularly on the harmful effects of watching (too much) television. The central concepts in the research on heavy

---

2   An exception to this is a definition used by Smith (1986). Smith stresses that although television 'addicts' may not watch television heavily in terms of number of hours, they may still report spending all or most of their free time watching television. In order to define television addiction adequately, Smith considers it important not only to measure the absolute amount of time watching television, but also the proportion of free time spent viewing. A definition that relates heavy viewing to the total amount of leisure time available is one step towards a more theoretical understanding of heavy television use as a pattern as social behaviour.

viewing have often been taken directly from public discourses without consideration of their validity. Consequently, academic attempts towards the explanation of heavy viewing are rather restricted and biased, and dominated by only a few themes.

First of all, in the cultural indicators approach (e.g. Gerbner & Cross, 1976a; 1976b; Gerbner *et al.*, 1979) the relationship between heavy viewing and certain 'conceptions of social reality' – such as anxiety, anomy, alienation, mistrust – has been explored. This relationship is interpreted as an effect of heavy viewing, an interpretation which has caused a great deal of criticism in communication research (see Hirsch, 1980; 1981; Hughes, 1980; Schulz, 1987). Gerbner *et al.* claim that people who spend a lot of time in 'the world of television' tend to perceive social reality in terms of the reality presented on television. Because of the violence-laden nature of American television drama, heavy viewers are more fearful, anxious, alienated and mistrusting than light viewers. According to Gerbner *et al.*, heavy viewing is part of a complex syndrome, which includes lower education, lower mobility, lower aspirations, higher anxieties and other class and sex related characteristics (see also Gerbner & Gross, 1976a:191).

This notion of a 'heavy viewer syndrome' as a term for a complexity of psycho-social characteristics has greatly influenced the debate on heavy viewing. There have been many replications of cultural indicators research in and outside the United States.[3] Furthermore, in recent studies of heavy viewing in Europe the concept, or elements of it are referred to quite often (e.g. Sturm, 1981a; 1981b; Groebel, 1981; Burdach, 1981; Peters, 1989; Schulz, 1986b; 1987; Vierkant, 1987). Schulz (1986b), for instance, explores the relationship between heavy viewing and a number of psychological dispositions, divided into two dimensions: depressivity and fatalism. In the Netherlands Peters (1989) and Vierkant (1987) found that heavy viewing was strongly correlated with anomy.

The results of descriptive studies of heavy viewers (Buß, 1985; Kiefer, 1987; Jackson-Beeck & Sobal, 1980; Vierkant, 1987) indicate that heavy viewers are often less educated, elderly, unemployed, from the lower classes and often live alone. If this socio-demographic profile is linked to the idea that these people are suffering from a heavy viewer syndrome, the result is a rather negative and bleak image of a group of viewers who are psychologically and socially deprived, alienated and who have very few alternatives and resources.

There has been, understandably, considerable discussion as to how to interpret this negative and disturbing image of heavy viewers. Does watching television make people feel depressed and anxious (the cultivation hypothesis), or do anxious and depressed people find relief in watching television (the escape hypothesis)? The latter explanation, the use of television for escapist reasons, to retreat from tensions and problems experienced in real life, is another recurrent theme in academic literature on heavy viewing, especially during the early decades of the television era (e.g. Maccoby, 1954; Pearlin,

---

3   See, for example, Bonfadelli (1983), Bouwman (1987), Doob and MacDonald (1979), Hawkins and Pingree (1980), Hirsch (1981; 1981), Hughes (1980), Schulz (1986a) and Wober (1978).

1959; Himmelweit *et al.*, 1958; Schramm *et al.*, 1961; Riley & Riley, 1951). The use of the escape concept in the 1950s as an overall explanation for quite diverse aspects of media use has been roundly criticized:

> The label 'escapist' has been used to characterize the psychological drives that motivate exposure, the extent of exposure itself, the contexts in which exposure takes place, the content of the media, the psychological processes involved in attending, and the consequences of all these things. (Katz & Foulkes, 1962:386-387)

Katz and Foulkes argue that escapist content may be put to uses that are not at all implied by that label (Katz & Foulkes, 1962:383). Furthermore, high exposure cannot automatically be equated with escape, as is often done in escape studies. Most authors, according to Katz and Foulkes, are ultimately, and most of them implicitly, concerned with the consequences of high exposure, particularly the 'narcotizing dysfunctions.'

Some of the criticisms put forward by Katz and Foulkes have been taken seriously by scholars within the uses and gratifications approach. Studies such as those by McQuail *et al.* (1972) and Greenberg (1974) explore the possibility of differential gratifications of the television audience. These scholars demonstrate that different viewers can have different motives and gratifications for watching television that are equally as important as the use of television for escapist reasons. In these studies, typologies of viewer gratifications are developed showing a certain diversity and complexity of motives for viewing behaviour. 'Escape' appears to be only one of the possible orientations of the viewer towards television. However, in spite of this more sophisticated view of a range of possible motives for television exposure, it must be concluded that the central concept (gratifications) as used in the uses and gratifications approach still fails to explain heavy viewing adequately. In these studies it remains unclear from where these divergent viewer orientations originate: 'The psychological, cultural and social bases of any given class of function or gratification' (Greenberg, 1974:90) are left unattended.

Summarizing, heavy viewing has been described and explained for the most part as a rather problematic pattern of audience behaviour. Correlations have been found with various negative psychological and socio-demographic characteristics, adequately encapsuled in the concept 'heavy viewer syndrome.' Whether such a psycho-social syndrome should be interpreted as an effect or a cause of heavy viewing is an issue on which communication researchers do not agree. This concept has not been derived from an explicit and well defined theoretical framework. Consequently, it is primarily an ad hoc conceptualization generated mainly by discourses of social concern regarding the television audience.

However, attempts via the uses and gratifications approach to explain heavy viewing as a motivated pattern of audience behaviour – motivations which are assumed to be rather diverse and complex – can be seen as a first step towards development of a theoretically grounded perspective on heavy viewing. McQuail *et al.* have questioned the derogatory assumptions about the typical relationship between television and the viewer:

> The general bearing of this set of views is to see the experience of watching television as largely lacking in meaning, hardly deserving of serious interest or respect, a chance outcome of a set of market circumstances....So the evidence showing long hours of time spent watching television is not interpreted as pointing to the influence of powerful attraction or strong need, but as indicative instead of a vacancy of outlook, an emptiness of life and a uniformity of response. (McQuail *et al.*, 1972:140-41)

Heavy viewing, in the uses and gratifications perspective advocated by McQuail *et al.* (1972), should be conceptualized as active, motivated and goal-directed audience behaviour. Uses and gratifications research is concerned with the explanation of patterns of media use in terms of people's 'needs' and the social and psychological origins of these needs (Katz *et al.*, 1974:20). In this approach many useful typologies have been developed to describe the relationship between patterns of media use on the one hand and gratifications ('satisfied needs') on the other hand. To explain media use, these typologies are unfortunately inadequate, as has been argued by many critics of the approach. The reason for this inadequacy is that, until now, little theoretical work has been done concerning the social origins of these needs, giving these typologies an ad hoc character.

A theoretical framework

What is needed, then, is a theoretical framework of the social character of media use which enables heaving viewing to be conceptualized as a pattern of 'social action'.[4] In this section I shall argue that an integration of concepts from the uses and gratifications approach (central concept: 'audience activity') and interpretative approaches to human social action (central concept: 'definition of the situation') is useful for development of such a framework (see also Adoni & Mane, 1984; Altheide, 1985; Renckstorf, 1977; 1989).

The assumptions underlying this theoretical framework are:

- Heavy viewing is not an isolated, coincidental or extreme case of social action, but is one of the many possible social action alternatives available for a particular situation (Renckstorf, 1977).

- To explain heavy viewing, the starting point must be the audience, or in the terminology of uses and gratifications: the question is not what do media do to people, but what do people do with the media (Blumler & Katz, 1974; Schramm *et al.*, 1961).

---

4   The term 'social action' is used here as opposed to 'social behaviour'. The concept of *soziales Handeln*, as used by Weber (1956) was described by him as: 'Action is social insofar as, by virtue of the subjective meaning attached to it by the acting individual (or individuals), it takes account of the behaviour of others, and is thereby oriented in its course' (Weber, quoted in Schütz, 1972: 144.) Hunziker (1988:72–73) and Renckstorf (1977) make a distinction between theories of human social behaviour and theories of human social action. In the first type of theories social behaviour is described as directly observable behavioural reactions to objective stimuli, while the second approach describes social action as the result of processes of interpretation in which people are involved, of subjective definitions of the situation. The term social action thus stresses the active, constructive nature of social behaviour.

Heavy viewing should be conceptualized as an active and goal-directed pattern of media use.

- This 'audience activity' must be understood from an interpretative point of view; social action, and consequently heavy viewing should be conceptualized as a social construction (Lull, 1980) and not as a reaction to external stimuli such as an increase in broadcasting time. Heavy viewing results from subjective definitions of the situation. This interpretative paradigm implies that the concept of interpretation, or 'sense making' is crucial to explain human social action (see also Dervin, 1983).

The latter assumption takes us, in fact, back to the roots of the interpretative (*verstehende Soziologie*) tradition in social research and to one of the founding fathers of modern sociology, Max Weber. Weber basically laid the foundations onto which later research traditions such as symbolic interactionism, ethnomethodology and ethnography were built. In this chapter the theoretical relevance of these older interpretative approaches is stressed. Particularly the work of Schütz, Berger and Luckmann (Schütz, 1932; 1972; Schütz & Luckmann, 1979; 1984; Berger & Luckmann, 1970) is drawn attention to, all of whom have elaborated on work initiated by Weber. In the following paragraph I shall briefly describe some of the key elements of this approach.

An interpretative approach to human social action

In interpretative approaches to human social action, such as symbolic interactionism (Mead, 1934; Thomas, 1928) and the sociology of knowledge developed by Schütz (1932; 1972), Berger and Luckmann (1970), it is assumed that the individual is incessantly involved in a process of 'meaning creation.' Every object, every situation and every interaction with other people and with oneself is being given sense to, is constantly being interpreted. Put more radically, these objects and situations do not in fact become real, do not really exist, before they are actually given meaning by individuals. In this perspective social reality is not an objective reality, but a subjective construction, a result of meaning production, of *subjektiv gemeinter Sinn*. The following well-known quotation taken from Thomas expresses this view clearly: 'If men define situations as real, they are real in their consequences' (Thomas, 1932:572).

According to Schütz (1932), in these interpretative processes people are constantly leaning on the knowledge they have developed through the everyday social world in which they live. This knowledge gives them clues to understanding everyday life and how to act accordingly in a certain role, situation or interaction. Essential to the theory developed by Schütz, and later elaborated by Berger and Luckmann (1970) is that these interpretative processes are to a certain extent ritualized and have become routinized. In Schütz' view, we usually experience the social world we are living in as objective, as 'a world taken for granted.' This is a result of 'common sense' knowledge, which enables us to act most of the time in a relative unproblematic and habitual way. These routine actions ensure both our own existence and interactions with others (Adoni & Mane, 1984:326).

Another word for this common sense knowledge used by Schütz (1972) is the 'recipe knowledge' of the social world. In recipe knowledge, both individual experiences and the shared meanings of a culture or society are stored. In this respect knowledge is social, but the way this knowledge is structured is very individual (in specific structures or 'zones' of relevance). This individually constructed subjective reality provides the basis for the individual's social actions. Recipe knowledge implies that a great deal of everyday experience can be given sense in a seemingly automatic and semi-natural manner. However, the everyday common sense knowledge we are relying upon is not always sufficient to construct meaning, to define the situation. This forces us to reflect more consciously upon the situation and to rearrange or expand the knowledge we would otherwise apply in a ritualistic and relatively unproblematic way (cf. Adoni & Mane, 1984; Renckstorf, 1989; 1994). As a result, social actions have to be more instrumental to solve such a problem, which is a result of the inability to immediately define the situation.

Towards a conceptualization of heavy viewing as social action

The distinction thus made between an unproblematic, ritualized and 'taken-for-granted' way of experiencing the social world, and a more reflective and instrumental (problem solving) way can be useful for explaining patterns of media use such as heavy viewing (cf. Rubin, 1984). Renckstorf (1994; see also Chapter 1) has developed such a theoretical framework for explaining media use as social action.

In many cases, media use can be conceptualized as a ritualized and habitual pattern of social action, and this is particularly relevant when discussing heavy viewing. In most popular and academic discourses, heavy viewing is seen as an extremely passive, unse-

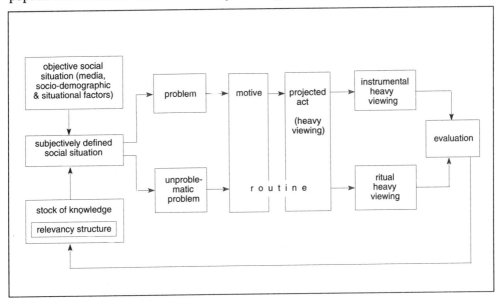

Fig. 2. Heavy viewing as social action.

lective and consequently senseless pattern of media use, therefore 'hardly deserving of serious interest or respect' (McQuail *et al*, 1972:141). If the aim is to explain heavy viewing by grounding it in a more fundamental perspective on human social action, like the one described above, it then may be valuable to describe and explain both ritualized (unselective) and instrumental patterns of heavy viewing, conceptualizing both of them as active, goal-directed patterns of social action, rooted in *subjektiv gemeinter Sinn*.

Schematically, this action perspective on heavy viewing can be expressed in the following conceptual model.

The key element in this model is the concept '*definition of the situation*'. Heavy viewing is conceptualized as a phenomenon which has an 'internal' and an 'external' component (cf. Mead's (1934) discussion of both 'overt' and 'covert' behaviour). This implies that concrete observable 'external' behaviour (viewing patterns) should be described, but in order to explain this behaviour it is necessary to take into account the 'internal,' interpretative actions in which the individual is involved.

Definitions of a situation are conceptualized here as interactions between aspects of an *objective social situation* (indicators such as socio-demographic factors, social structure and media structure variables) and elements of the specific *knowledge* an individual is relying upon to define everyday experiences, interactions and situations (indicators such as symbolic and subjective representations of the objective world, including values, interests, world views, images of oneself and other people). The combination of these elements leads to a certain experienced or *subjective social situation*. This provides the basis for individual social actions, in this case patterns of heavy viewing. The central question, then, is: What definitions of the situation do some people have who watch a lot of television; how are these definitions different from those of other people? How does the subjectively defined social situation of heavy viewers compare to that of light and moderate viewers?

Two basic patterns of heavy viewing are distinguished in the above model. Although these two patterns represent quite different forms of television use, both are rooted in definitions of the situation. As previously argued, the knowledge people have of their social world is, in most cases, sufficient to define a situation. This means that everyday experience has trained most people to act adequately in a certain situation. Considering heavy viewing, this pattern of television use may have been a suitable strategy in the past to solve certain problems (in this case 'problem' is defined as a lack of or discrepancy in the ability to give sense to everyday social life). Watching television may well be a solution to such a problem as, for instance, when an individual actively seeks 'sense' in the knowledge offered through the television screen, or when watching television offers the possibility of forgetting about the problem (through distraction or escape). All kinds of different *motives* (indicators include patterns of 'gratifications' or motives such as developed in the uses and gratifications research tradition) may be the result of a particular definition of the situation.

According to this model, a *ritual pattern of heavy viewing* results from a relatively unproblematic definition of the situation. Because the strategy of heavy viewing has in the past been suitable, it is stored as a useful 'solution' in individual knowledge and repeated in a rather unreflective and ritualized manner. The definition of the situation underlying this viewing pattern is thus in a way 'hidden,' which makes such habitualized behaviour look like unselective, passive behaviour with no purpose whatsoever. But again, in this model it is stressed that both ritual and instrumental patterns of heavy viewing do have a purpose, a purpose that is rooted in subjectively defined social situations which must be described if we want to adequately explain heavy viewing. An *instrumental pattern of heavy viewing* according to this perspective results from a definition of the situation as problematic, which means that knowledge is not sufficient to give sense to a certain situation. Heavy viewing, then, is a more consciously reflected upon and instrumental strategy for filling this gap (see Dervin, 1983).

One way to find clues to the more or less hidden definitions of the situation is to look at the kinds of television content selected by heavy viewers and the way this content is interpreted. This means that heavy viewing should not be treated as a mere quantitative concept, but also as a qualitative one. Not only the question why some people watch television a lot, but also what they are watching is important to gain insight into the way their actual behaviour is related to their objective and subjective situation. In this way, heavy viewing is treated as a thoroughly social action, and not as a coincidental effect of external circumstances, or a mere statistical correlation with certain socio-demographic variables.

Finally, the concept of *evaluation* in the model refers to the usefulness of the chosen strategy. If heavy viewing is experienced as an adequate action compared to the motives underlying this action,[5] this experience is stored in individual knowledge – the totality of experiences on which an individual relies in order to define a situation and act accordingly.

Empirical data

I have argued earlier that an adequate explanation of heavy viewing has failed to materialize mainly because a theoretical perspective which treats heavy viewing as a pattern of social action has not yet been developed. The primary aim of this contribution is to present such a theoretical framework, based on an integration of concepts from the uses and gratifications tradition and from interpretative perspectives on human social action. A subsequent step is to expand these theoretical considerations through operationalization of the central concepts and specification of the relationships between the concepts, and further to ground the model in empirical data. However, before presenting some empirical support, methodological considerations for the model are presented.

---

5   See further the distinction in the uses and gratifications approach between 'gratifications sought' and 'gratifications obtained' (Palmgreen *et al.*, 1985:27).

Methodological considerations

Inasmuch as heavy viewing is considered a social pattern of action, a rather complex research design is required to integrate the variables. This situation favours use of small samples and a qualitative design. Another reason for choosing a qualitative design is the key concept is the 'definition of the situation'. Qualitative methodologies have been developed to reconstruct such subjectively defined situations (Glaser & Strauss, 1967; Wester, 1987). A third reason for choosing a qualitative design is that qualitative methodologies are particularly suited to observe and analyse ritualized, 'taken-for-granted' patterns of social action (Zijderveld, 1974b).

In this study, however, we have tried to find empirical evidence for the usefulness of this perspective by conducting a secondary analysis of data from a large-scale survey, described in a number of the other chapters in this volume (see also Arts *et al.*, 1990b). The reason for using these data was that they provided a wealth of information which could be used to operationalize the concepts in the conceptual model. However, the consequence of using data from this survey is that the process by which the definition of the situation is formed cannot be reconstructed. With these data, only global indications of 'subjective social situations,' can be found, operationalized as relations between aspects of the 'objective social situation' and aspects of 'knowledge'.

In the dataset many variables are available for operationalizing these two concepts. Furthermore, this survey provides data which can be used to operationalize 'motives' and 'television use.' To summarize, these data make it possible to describe the relations between 'subjective social situations,' 'motives' and 'television use.' Using this dataset

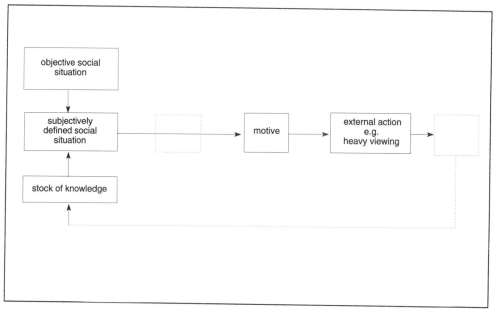

Fig. 3. Adapted conceptual model.

Table 1. Operationalization of central concepts

Concept	Variable	Label
Objective social situation	– work situation	– WORK
	– family size	– FAMSIZE
	– size of local network	– LOCNET
	– education (SES)	– EDUC
	– income (SES)	– INCOME
	– health	– HEALTH
	– leisure time	– LEISURE
	– mobility	– MOBIL
Aspects of knowledge	– family values	– FAMVAL
	– localism	– LOCAL
	– fatalism	– FATAL
	– fear of losing status	– STALOSS
Motives	– entertainment	– ENTERT
	– social use	– SOCUSE
	– escape	– ESCAPE
Action	– viewing time	– VIEWT

implies that the conceptual model, as presented in Fig. 2, has to be simplified as shown in Fig. 3.[6]

In Table 1 an overview of the variables used to operationalize these concepts is presented.

Results

The conceptual model shown in Fig. 3, then, when using variables from this dataset, can be transformed into the relationships shown in Fig. 4. This model serves as the starting point for analysing heavy viewing in four different age groups.

A social action perspective of heavy viewing implies that it is impossible to find one, all embracing, explanation. A crucial assumption of this perspective is that social action is grounded in different definitions of the situation, indicated by what has been termed 'subjective social situation.' The reason for analysing age groups is that we assume that in different stages of the life cycle individuals will define their social situation differently. This implies that in each age group different factors will probably be important for explaining heavy viewing.

Differences are anticipated in the objective situation of these age groups (e.g. work situation, family size, income, health), as well as in their 'knowledge' of the situation, as indicated by value orientations (such as family values, localism, fatalism). Furthermore, in different phases of the life cycle different motives related to television use are expected.

---

6   The dotted lines show the parts of the original conceptual model and that cannot be taken into account in the analysis presented.

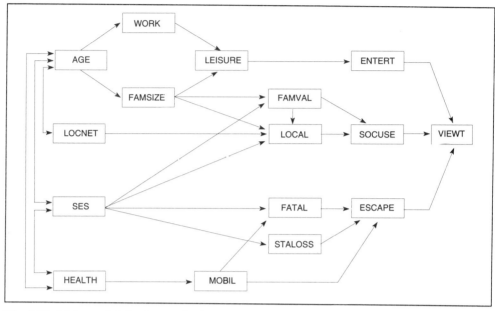

Fig. 4. Model for explaining heavy viewing.

By finding empirical clues for these differences it may be possible to demonstrate that heavy television use is rooted in different 'subjective social situations,' which lead to different motives for heavy television use.

Many other studies on heavy viewers have concluded that particularly older people are heavy viewers, a finding which tends to function as a pseudo explanation of heavy viewing. Heavy viewing, as formulated here, represents a pattern of social action which can be important in all phases of the life cycle. Therefore, in each age group it is assumed different factors will be important for explaining heavy viewing.

The results of the analysis of television viewing for different age groups are presented below. A more elaborate description of this analysis is provided elsewhere (Frissen, 1992). The factor analysis programme Lisrel was used to analysed the models developed for each age group. Some of the variables described in Fig. 4 had to be removed from these more specific models for statistical reasons (for example, the variable ENTERT, which did not explain much of the variation in viewing time). Other variables in the original model were not used in a particular analysis for theoretical reasons; for instance, the variable STA-LOSS is probably less important among young people and therefore need not be included in the model. On the basis of the Lisrel analysis, some of the expected relations were shown to be non-significant. In the results below, then, these non-significant relations have been removed.

Although the fit of this model, as indicated by the statistics X2 and AGFI, is not perfect, the total amount of variance explained by this model is 30 per cent. Three factors contribute

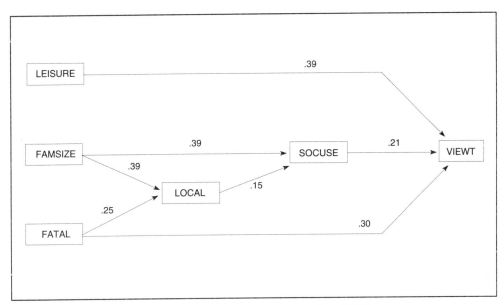

Fig. 5. Model for explaining heavy viewing among the young (age 16-25).

substantially to the explanation of heavy viewing among the young: the amount of leisure time, the social use motive and fatalism. Interestingly, the escape motive does not appear to be important. Social uses apparently are more crucial in this phase of the life cycle. This motive, in turn, can be explained largely by family size (apart from the value orientation localism): this finding might indicate that particularly for those young people who still live with their parents and/or other siblings, the social use motive is important.

The fit of this model is reasonable and the total amount of variance in viewing time explained by the model is 27 per cent. Again, there is a clear effect of the variables fatalism and leisure on viewing time; the effect of leisure, however, is not as strong. The social use motive is also important, but when factors that might explain this motive are examined, other aspects appear to be important. This motive is more strongly connected to value orientations such as localism and indirectly to family values. Family values, in turn, are strongly influenced by family size, a finding that indicates that people who have formed a family in this stage of life attach great importance to marriage, domestic life and having children.

The fit of this model is not ideal; the X2 value is reasonable, but the AGFI is rather low. This model explains 27 per cent of the variance of viewing time. The most remarkable finding, compared to the other two models is that both the social use and the escape motives contribute substantially to the explanation of heavy viewing.[7] Escape as a motive for heavy

---

7   The analysis of this model caused a problem: the variables, measuring the motives 'social use' and
     'escape' appear to correlate rather strongly (probably caused by inadequate measurement). The model

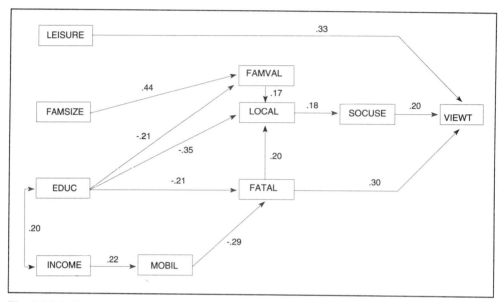

Fig. 6. Model for explaining heavy viewing among young adults (age 25-35).

television seems to be influenced by mobility: the lower the mobility in this phase of the life cycle, the stronger the escape motive. The results indicate that low mobility can be caused by low income or by a feeling of poor health. The social use motive appears to be important for those who are strongly oriented towards family life and the local environment.

Furthermore, these results suggest that the amount of leisure time is less important for these older viewers than in the younger age groups, a finding which could be expected inasmuch as in this phase of the life people seldom have much leisure time (due to family and work obligations). The results indicate that unemployed persons in this age group have a particularly large amount of leisure time. Finally, the effect of fatalism on viewing time is also weaker for this age group.

Although the fit of this model is not perfect, the total variance explained by this model is 31 per cent. The most striking result is that leisure time contributes the most variance (0.50) to the model, which can be explained by the fact that most older people no longer are employed. Apart from this, there is a considerable effect of fatalism on viewing time, which is strongest among those with a low socio-economic status.

---

is not able to explain this correlation through the paths that have been included in this model. This correlation has a strong negative effect on the fit of the total model. Because other variables cannot be included to increase the fit of the model, an artificial solution is used here which is to create a model in which the error terms of the two variables are correlated (indicated by a correlation between the thetas in the model).

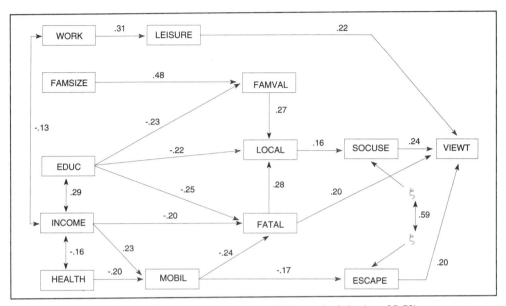

Fig. 7. Model for explaining heavy viewing among middle-aged adults (age 35-50).

It was expected that in this age group health and mobility problems in particular, would cause the escape motive to be more important for explaining heavy viewing. However, this motive seems to play no role whatsoever, and neither does the social use motive. Because of the importance of the variable leisure time, it might be concluded that for older people heavy viewing is a less problematic pattern of social action than is often assumed in public discourses about heavy viewers. Older people are often assumed to be lonely and strongly limited in their mobility, which causes them to escape into the 'world of television.' Few empirical clues have been found which support this assumption. For older people, heavy viewing seems to be simply a relatively unproblematic way of spending an abundance of free time.

Conclusions

In previous sections of this chapter it has been argued that research on heavy viewers in communication studies can be characterized by *ad hoc* research questions and a lack of theoretical reflection. Most studies seem to be inspired by not particularly subtle public debates about the negative social implications of heavy viewing. The result of this has been a rather biased and restricted image of heavy viewers, who are almost never seen as subjects acting intentionally and meaningfully. On the other hand, heavy viewing is mainly considered as a seemingly unchangeable, problematic form of behaviour, attributed to a category of viewers defined in very narrow terms.

It has been argued here that heavy viewing should be conceptualized as a multi-faceted phenomenon: a pattern of social action which can take on different forms and follow different definitions of the situation. In this chapter I have sketched a theoretical perspec-

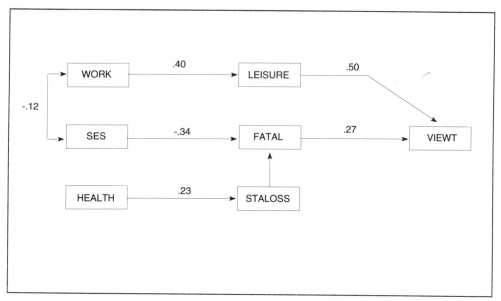

Fig. 8. Model for explaining heavy viewing among older people (age 50 and older).

tive of heavy viewing based on this argument. I have also presented some preliminary empirical findings to support this argument. Consequently, I have not aimed to find one, all-embracing explanation of heavy viewing, but have searched for empirical clues for different, situation-specific explanations of the phenomenon of heavy viewing in different stages of the life cycle.

The findings presented are valuable in that they enable us to refine the biased image of heavy viewing as a fixed and problematic pattern of behaviour by describing and explaining heavy viewing as a complex and meaningful pattern of social action. However, many elements of the theoretical perspective presented require further exploration. The data used for this empirical study did not allow full exploration of the rather crucial process of defining social situations. As a result, it was not possible to operationalize the two patterns of social action considered important in the theoretical model: ritual and instrumental patterns of heavy viewing.

The conceptualization of heavy viewing as a ritualized form of social action seems particularly promising, and needs empirical support. A qualitative design is much more suited for exploring these parts of the theoretical framework, especially given that a qualitative approach aims to reconstruct definitions of social reality often taken for granted in everyday life.

6 Non-viewers in the Netherlands

Karsten Renckstorf and Paul Hendriks Vettehen

This chapter examines the small portion of the Dutch population which never watches television. Descriptive analysis of data taken from a Dutch nationwide survey in 1989 suggests that there are two distinct types of non-viewers. First, there are the very religious Calvinist non-viewers who often belong to the lower socio-economic strata and second, the non-Calvinist non-viewers from the higher socio-economic strata. These two types of non-viewers have totally different values and attitudes. They also differ in their social activities and use of other media. The findings question the commonly held position that non-viewing is a sign of social disintegration.

Television use is widespread. Nevertheless, there are still people, also in the Netherlands, who never take advantage of the communicative possibilities available through the medium. In communication studies these structural non-viewers have ceased to play any role of importance.[1] In the last few decades they have hardly ever featured as subjects of research. As a result, non-viewers have become the inhabitants of a *terra incognita* in communication studies.

In the first generation of studies on the impact of mass media, the category of structural non-viewers still played an important role within the framework of research, namely a control group in so-called 'natural experiments'.[2] In the 1950s, for instance, two groups of children were regularly compared who were of the same age and grew up under similar conditions, but who differed in one respect: only one group grew up with television. This was done to determine the impact of television on children (e.g. Maccoby, 1964; Himmel-

---

1   Some studies published in Germany and the United States also have 'non-viewers' as topic for discussion. These non-viewers, however, are defined as people who either watch television less than 30 min per day (Jackson-Beeck, 1977; Tankerd & Harris, 1980) or do not watch during a given period of time in which viewing time is measured (Buß, 1985). For these categories the term 'incidental non-viewers' seems more appropriate in order to distinguish them from the category of structural non-viewers.

2   One of the last studies in this genre is that of Williams (1986) entitled 'The impact of television. A natural experiment in three communities'. This research was conducted in a Canadian municipality where, due to technical problems, television had not been introduced until 1973.

weit *et al.*, 1958; Schramm *et al.*, 1961). Furthermore, calculations of media reach in the longitudinal research on *Mediennutzung und -bewertung in der Bundesrepublik* (Kiefer, 1987a) were on the basis of the total population as well as on the basis of the members of the population living in a 'television household,' indicating the presence of significant numbers of non-viewers.[3] However, the fact that subsequent studies hardly ever pay attention to this illustrates how non-viewing as a phenomenon has been abandoned to the periphery of communication research.

This lack of interest in non-viewers is rather remarkable, inasmuch as they constitute a substantial group in society. In some Western European countries, such as the Netherlands (Felling *et al.*, 1987:44; NOS/KLO, 1990:59) and the former Federal Republic of Germany (Schulz, 1986a:161; Kiefer, 1987a:21), the amount of structural non-viewers are estimated to be between 3 and 4 per cent of the adult population. This means that the Netherlands has 400,000 structural non-viewers and the former Federal Republic of Germany 1,800,000. The size of these figures alone is reason to initiate further study around this special category of people.

Another reason for attending to non-viewers is the increased importance of participation in mass communication processes as a form of social participation. In a very short time the use of mass media, television in particular, has become a normal ingredient of everyday life for almost everyone. Already in the late 1960s McQuail (1969:3) asserted that 'It now makes sense to regard a moderate degree of exposure to mass media at least a mark and possibly even a requirement of membership of modern society.' It is precisely because the participation in mass communication processes has become the norm, that the phenomenon of non-participation in these processes gains importance. Not participating in a major form of social communication, i.e. television use, might then be an indication of social disintegration. McQuail (1969:3) states quite boldly: 'While it is common to find abnormally high levels of mass media use considered as deviant behaviour, the same could well be true of the avoidance of contact with mass communications.'

However, non-viewers can compensate for their lack of social participation through use of television by other forms of involvement with the surrounding society, including other forms of media use. This suggests that there does not necessarily have to be a direct relationship between non-viewing and social disintegration. Even when people consciously avoid the use of television or – more extremely – of all media, disintegration is only possible if the non-viewing is part of a broader life pattern which includes a conscious retreat from social life. Thus, knowledge of this broader life pattern concerning social participation is a necessary prerequisite for the formulation of meaningful statements about the relationship between non-viewing and disintegration. In this chapter we focus on particular aspects of the non-viewers' participation in social life.

---

3   Kiefer (1987a:28) defines *Fernsehhaushalte* as households in which at least one television set is available. Although not possessing a television set does not guarantee non-viewing, just as the possession of a television set does not necessarily lead to viewing, these people in *Nicht-Fernsehhaushalte* mostly fall in the same category as the people this study refers to as (structural) non-viewers.

Last but not least, there is yet another reason to pay more attention to non-viewers which lies more in the methodological-analytical sphere. Although non-viewers no longer feature frequently or explicitly in contemporary communication research, they do receive from time to time in the context of other discussions. For instance, Schulz (1986a:61) calls them *Fernsehverweigerer* and places them in the same class as the *Fernsehasketen*, the light viewers, in contrast to the *Extremseher* or heavy viewers.[4] His analyses of the data, however, is somewhat inconsistent. In some cases he includes the non-viewers in the category of light viewers, whereas in others he does not. This categorization, however, remains unwarranted. Moreover, *Fernsehverweigerer* and *Fernsehasketen*, the terms used by Schulz, suggest that these are two conceptually distinct categories. Put briefly, the question becomes: to what extent can non-viewing be regarded as an extreme form of light viewing and be grouped in the same category, e.g. in the comparisons between heavy and light viewers?

Key questions

As there is relatively little known about non-viewers, this study was directed at profiling the group. Despite lack of knowledge concerning non-viewers, descriptive research need not be done haphazardly, without formulation of suppositions. The special emphasis on the aspects of social participation has already been mentioned above. Further, current theories of mass communication provide guidelines for the description of non-viewers.

One such guideline is found in the theoretical notions of the American research team led by George Gerbner (see Gerbner & Gross, 1976). Gerbner presumes that television has a strong cultivating effect which results, especially among heavy viewers, in a distorted world view. Heavy viewers, more than light viewers, tend to see the world as evil and frightening. Other characteristics frequently mentioned in later research include fatalism, depression and feelings of uselessness (Gerbner & Gross, 1976) – sometimes referred to collectively as the 'Heavy Viewer Syndrome' (Schulz, 1986b:770). Furthermore, when compared to light viewers, heavy viewers are often found to be older, female, less educated and more often in the lower socio-economic strata (Buß 1985; Frissen, 1992; Gerbner & Gross, 1976; Jackson-Beeck & Sobal 1980; Peters, 1989). Non-viewers are, by definition, not directly exposed to this assumed 'cultivating effect' of television. It may therefore be expected that they will clearly distinguish themselves by their characteristics of cultivation from the rest of the population and from the category of heavy viewers in particular.

Not only theories about the consequences of media use, but also theories focusing on audience activity prove useful in the speculations about the characteristics of non-viewers. In this respect, particularly the recent approach to media behaviour based on the social action perspective (see Hunziker, 1988; Renckstorf, 1977; 1989; Renckstorf & Wester, 1992; see also Chapter 1) should be mentioned. This approach is based on the assumption that media use in industrialized Western societies has become an everyday activity. Most

---

4   According to Schulz (1986a:61), the category of non-viewers in Germany amounts to approximately 3 per cent and the category of heavy viewers, which watches television at least six hours per day, approximately 7 per cent.

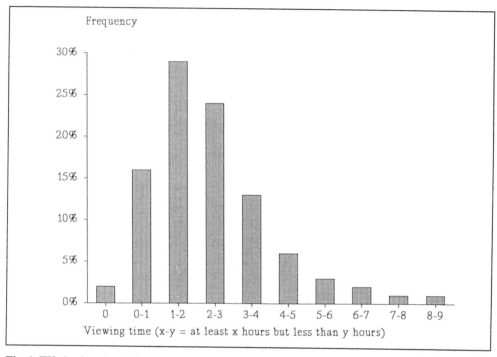

Frequency

Viewing time (x-y = at least x hours but less than y hours)

Fig. 1. TV viewing time in hours per day. Source: 'Media use in the Netherlands 1989' (MASSAT '89), n=943. Note: Percentages reflecting Dutch population 15 years and older.

people, with the exception of the structural non-viewers, spend a considerable amount of time simply watching television; see Fig. 1.

The common nature of media behaviour makes it possible to apply concepts for the description and explanation of everyday life to ideas and actions concerning the media and their messages (Hunziker, 1976:180; Renckstorf, 1977:12). Thus, findings of Kiefer (1987b) seem to justify the assumption that the organization of everyday life, leisure time in particular, plays an important role in the choice for more or less media usage. Kiefer differentiates, among others things, between light and heavy users of the media in her interpretation of the *Massenkommunikation 1964–85* time-series. For heavy users media are '*Begleiter des ganzen Tages*' (Kiefer, 1987b). In her *Polarisierungsthese* she states that heavy users clearly spend more and more time on media use, whereas light users spend less and less time on it, especially regarding television. According to Kiefer, these two groups differ significantly in their organisation of everyday life. This also goes for the number and structuralization of their leisure activities.

An Australian study involving families without television sets (Edgar, 1977) suggests more explicitly that not owning a television set is a choice people consciously make with their convictions and interests in mind. Most of the people in this study were well educated, belonged to the higher socio-economic strata and had an active social life. In their view 'television steals time, makes people lazier and more passive, and is addictive' (Edgar,

1977:74). Edgar (1977:76) also observes that 'it was felt that television conditioned people to accept mediocrity' In short, this study describes a socio-economic and cultural elite which consciously rejects television.

On the basis of these findings, using the social action perspective, a series of questions can be formulated regarding non-viewers. Thus, one may expect that non-viewers have deviating views on certain subjects, e.g. with regard to the function of spare time, and that their leisure activities are considerably more in number or of a totally different nature when compared to light and heavy viewers, e.g. a strong participation in clubs and associations. Furthermore, it may be useful to examine whether there exist any possible alternatives for watching television among non-viewers, e.g. extensive reading of newspapers.

Research methods

In order to find the answers to the questions underlying this study, data are used from the nation-wide survey 'Media use in the Netherlands' (MASSAT '89) carried out in 1989 by the Department of Communication at the University of Nijmegen. These data concern several media related subjects as well as attitudes, interests, activities, and a large number of background characteristics of the 956 respondents (see further, Arts et al., 1990b).

In the above summary of key questions, the main focus was on the presupposed differences between non-viewers, light viewers, and heavy viewers. The research population was therefore divided into four categories according to viewing time.[5] The first category consists of non-viewers in the population (n=20).[6] Using quartile scores, the remaining population is divided, following Schulz (1986b), into 25 per cent light viewers (up to 72 minutes per day; n=229), 50 per cent moderate viewers (72 up to 177 minutes per day; n=455) and 25 per cent heavy viewers (177 minutes or more per day; n=237). These four categories are subsequently compared with respect to a series of other characteristics.

It should be noted that the number of non-viewers in the sample survey was rather small. This often allowed only bivariate and relatively superficial analysis. For the same reason the differences between non-viewers and the other categories, which were quite considerable as such, sometimes were statistically insignificant. Nonetheless, these differences are presented here in order to illuminate the relative unknown group of non-viewers. It should be clear that, because of these limitations, the results of this study must be regarded as tentative, but nevertheless important as an initial step towards further research into non-viewing.

---

5   The variable average viewing time per day can be calculated for 943 television viewing respondents. This is done with the use of the following data: the number of working days on which the respondents watch television, the number of hours/minutes on Saturday and the number of hours/minutes on Sunday.

6   Twenty non-viewers amount to nearly 2 per cent of the research population. This low percentage is probably due to the fact that the survey was introduced to the respondents as dealing with media-related subjects. This may have led to self-(non)selection among non-viewers.

Table 1. Basic characteristics of TV (non-)viewers, mean values

	Non-viewers	Light viewers	Moderate viewers	Heavy viewers	Total
Age	42.3	37.4	37.9	40.7	38.6
Education	3.4	4.0*	3.5	3.1	3.5
Professional status	42.6	50.0*	45.2	41.0	45.2
Personal income	2.7	3.4	3.1	2.7	3.1
Household income	3.0	3.0	2.9	2.6	2.8
House size	4.3	3.1	3.2	2.9*	3.2
Size of town/city	52	99	103	110	103

Source: datafile MASSAT, '89.
*mean is significantly different from the mean of non-viewers ($\alpha = 0.05$ two-tailed).
Note: ages range from 15 to 73; education from code 2 (primary) to 6 (Master's degree); professional status determined on the basis of the professional codes of the Central Bureau of Statistics according to Sixma & Ultee (1983) and ranges from 13 (low) to 87 (high); personal and household incomes categorized in 7 and 5 categories respectively; household size ranges from 1 to 9; size of town/city represents number of thousand inhabitants.

Results

non-viewers as well as light, moderate and heavy viewers will now be discussed according to their background characteristics, their general attitudes to life, the extent and nature of their leisure activities and their media consumption, particularly the consumption of radio and newspapers. To what extent these four categories of the population differ from each other will not be discussed in any great detail. The main focus is on the differences, i.e. those differences between non-viewers and the three categories of viewers.

Basic characteristics

For a first description of non-viewers and light, moderate and heavy viewers, the background characteristics of these categories are presented in Tables 1 and 2.

Table 2. Basic characteristics of TV (non-)viewers

	Non-viewers	Light viewers	Moderate viewers	Heavy viewers	Total
Male	47	55	50	46	50
Wage-earning	89	89	92	95	92
Unskilled labour	39	18	24	31	25
Political preference:					
orthodox confessional	35	3*	3*	0*	4
Religion: Calvinist	39	14	10*	7*	11
Religion: Dutch Reformed	18	12	11	9	1
Religion: Roman Catholic	5	22*	27*	30*	26
Non-religious	24	50	51*	54*	51

Source: Datafile MASSAT '89.
*percentage significantly differs from the percentage among non-viewers. ($P < 0.05$ two-tailed).

Some variables were strictly speaking not measured at interval level, but, because they did come very close to this level of measurement, it was decided to calculate their means.

First of all, these tables show that a number of characteristics of non-viewers are clearly different from those of the viewers. Among non-viewers there are many Calvinists, but few Catholics or non-religious people. Moreover, the average number of inhabitants of a town/city where non-viewers live is smaller than that of the categories of viewers (although the difference is not significant). Also, non-viewing families contain at least one person more on average than the three other categories. Finally, among non-viewers there are clearly more followers of the small right-wing political parties (affiliated with orthodox confessional Calvinist religious groups) than among the other categories.

Furthermore, non-viewers differ considerably from light viewers in their lower level of education and professional status, but very little from heavy viewers in these matters. Also, compared to light viewers, they have on average a lower personal income, although the difference is not significant; a higher percentage of unskilled labourers is also found among non-viewers. The obvious conclusion, therefore, is that the socio-economic status of non-viewers is lower than that of light viewers. On the other hand, it is not very different from the status of heavy viewers. The fact that the average household income of non-viewers corresponds with that of light viewers does not alter the conclusion. This high household income can easily be explained by the difference in household size between the two categories, and the more persons there are in a household, the greater the chance that more persons in that household will have their own income.

There are also a number of characteristics that show no great difference between non-viewers and the other three categories. For instance, the difference between the number of males, in terms of percentages, is not very significant when we consider that the 47 per cent males among non-viewers would have become 53 per cent if this category had contained only one male more. It is also quite striking that the percentage of wage-earning, as opposed to self-employed, non-viewers does not differ from the other categories. Apparently non-viewers are not predominantly entrepreneurs.

In summary, two conclusions can be drawn from the above discussion, First, regarding non-viewers, they seem to differ from the rest of the population because of the relatively high percentage of Calvinists, preference for orthodox right-wing political parties, large families and small places of residence. Second, non-viewers are similar to heavy viewers, but differ from light viewers, because of their relatively low socio-economic status.

The first conclusion relates what might be considered a typically Dutch phenomenon: the influence of strict Calvinists living in relatively small towns situated in sections of the country such as the 'Veluwe' and the province of Zeeland. Quite a large number of these people do not watch television for reasons associated with their religious beliefs.

This conclusion raises the question as to whether the unique characteristics of these Calvinist non-viewers may have distorted the results. After all, the results concerning the socio-economic status of non-viewers are particularly prominent. Given Edgar's findings

(1977), one would sooner expect non-viewers to differ from heavy viewers in that they had attained a relatively high socio-economic status. Hirsch' findings (1980), in which non-viewers were merely a side-issue, also point in that direction. Hirsch asserts that, although non-viewers do not have such high incomes, they tend to be rather well educated. Moreover, they often come from the upper classes.

To ascertain a possible bias in our results, the analysis would have to be repeated separately for Calvinist and non-Calvinist respondents. However, the data were far from ideal for this task because of the small number of non-viewers. In order to secure some indication, this procedure was followed using a datafile from another study, conducted in 1985: 'Social and Cultural Developments in the Netherlands 1985' (SOCON '85); see Felling et al., 1987), which contained data on 97 non-viewers for the three available indicators of socio-economic status in this datafile.[7] See Table 3.

Table 3. Basic characteristics of TV (non-)viewers

	Non-viewers	Light viewers	Moderate viewers	Heavy viewers	Total
Calvinists					
Education	3.0	4.0*	3.6	2.4	3.5
Professional status	43.4	49.6	48.1	39.6	46.8
% unskilled labour	29.0	18.0	18.0	34.0	22.0
Non-Calvinists					
Education	4.4	4.2	3.6*	2.7*	3.5
Professional status	52.8	50.6	47.0	37.3*	45.6
% unskilled labour	19.0	14.0	20.0	37.0*	23.0

Source: datafile SOCON '85
Note: Means used for education and professional status, and percentages for unskilled labour. Education ranges from code 1 (primary) to 6 (university); professional status is based on the CBS codes according to Sixma and Ultee (1983) and ranges from 13 (low) to 87 (high).
*Mean differs significantly from the mean of non-viewers ($\alpha = 0.05$ two-tailed for education and professional status; percentage differs significantly from the percentage of non-viewers ($P < 0.05$ two-tailed for the per cent unskilled labour).

Table 3 suggests large differences between Calvinists and non-Calvinists: Calvinist non-viewers generally attain only a low level of education, have a rather low professional status, and often perform unskilled work. These Calvinist non-viewers are therefore much more similar to heavy viewers than to light viewers. However, non-Calvinist non-viewers, on the average, have attained the highest level of education and highest professional status, and the percentage of unskilled labourers among them is not particularly high. They are therefore very much like light viewers and do not resemble heavy viewers.

7   The members of the *Gereformeerde Bond* (Reformed Federation) were listed as Calvinist. Officially the *Gereformeerde Bond* belongs to the Dutch Reformed Church; it nevertheless tries to realize the same goals as the Calvinist groups that seceded from the Dutch Reformed Church and is therefore often seen as part of the Calvinist Church (see Dekker, 1981; Dekker & Peters, 1989).

In conclusion it seems there are two distinct categories of non-viewers: Calvinist non-viewers with a rather low socio-economic status, and non-Calvinist non-viewers with a high socio-economic status. The second category, interestingly, corresponds with non-viewers in Edgar's study (1977).

General attitudes to life

In order to get an impression of the attitudes to life and the world which non-viewers have, they were compared with several categories of viewers on a number of attitude scales. For example, the scales of traditional family attitudes and traditional achievement attitudes reflect respectively the (perceived) importance of marriage, family, children and of getting on in life or accomplishing something. The scale of hedonism reflects the degree of importance associated with enjoying life and having fun, while the social criticism scale expresses the promotion of social and financial equality (Felling *et al.* 1983). The scale of the work ethic expresses the importance of work in everyday life. The fatalism scale reflects a lack of trust in authorities and people in general as well as a certain helplessness and a lack of faith in the future. The scale of political interest contains items that indicate whether or not people keep themselves informed about politics and how important the world of politics is to them. Finally, the scales of social and cultural localism consist of items that measure the degree of identification with the immediate environment and the value assigned to the local community in general (Eisinga & Peters, 1989). The mean scores of non-viewers and the categories of viewers on these scales are reflected in Table 4.

Table 4. General attitudes to life of TV (non-)viewers

	Non-viewers	Light viewers	Moderate viewers	Heavy viewers
Traditional family values	0.09	−0.24	0.01	0.22
Traditional achievement attitudes	−0.63	−0.13*	0.05*	0.10*
Social criticism	−0.17	−0.08	0.07	−0.05
Hedonism	−0.59	−0.02	−0.03	0.11
Labour ethics	0.37	−0.09	0.03	0.03
Fatalism	0.15	−0.30	−0.04	0.37
Political interest	−0.49	0.24*	0.04	−0.26
Social localism	0.15	−0.19	−0.06	0.28
Cultural localism	0.06	−0.30	−0.03	0.36

Source: MASSAT '89. Note: Figures in columns are the means of the standardized sum of scores. *Mean is significantly different from non-viewers' mean ($\alpha = 0.05$ two-tailed).

Table 4 shows that, in general, non-viewers do not differ significantly from the other categories of viewers. The most prominent deviations are the low level of economic achievement attitudes and, though not significantly, the low level of hedonism as well as the strong work ethic. In these three areas, non-viewers distinguish themselves from all the categories of viewers.

These results raise a number of questions. Particularly the scores of non-viewers for fatalism and political interest do not correspond with, or are even the opposite of, the scores that one might expect in the light of Gerbner's cultivation thesis. Moreover, these prominent scores of non-viewers for economic achievement attitudes, hedonism and work ethics can easily be explained by looking at the (orthodox) Calvinist background of a number of non-viewers. Again, this finding raises the question as to whether this particular category may have distorted the overall picture emerging from the data.

To gain some insight in this matter, data from SOCON '85 were again examined, since that survey used the same scales as those shown in Table 4.[8] Table 5 reflects the results of the separate analysis of Calvinists and non-Calvinists.

Table 5. General attitudes of TV (non-)viewers

	Non-viewers	Light viewers	Moderate viewers	Heavy viewers	Total
		Calvinists			
Traditional family values	0.40	0.20	0.36	0.22	0.30
Traditional achievement attitudes	-0.57	-0.38	-0.16	-0.09	-0.26
Social criticism	-0.93	-0.28*	-0.25*	-0.52	-0.38
Hedonism	-1.34	-0.39*	-0.33*	-0.40*	-0.48
Labour ethics	0.54	0.01	0.34	0.47	0.29
Fatalism	-0.22	-0.26	-0.41	0.04	-0.28
Political interest	-0.21	0.07	0.19	-0.13	0.07
Social localism	0.20	0.04	-0.04	0.19	0.04
Cultural localism	0.42	0.17	0.08	0.51	0.20
		Non-Calvinists			
Traditional family values	-0.53	-0.27	-0.01*	0.20*	-0.03
Traditional achievement attitudes	-0.49	-0.11*	-0.01*	0.26*	0.03
Social criticism	-0.17	-0.10	0.05	0.17	0.04
Hedonism	-0.26	-0.02	0.05*	0.14*	0.05
Labour ethics	-0.38	-0.17	-0.01*	0.10*	0.03
Fatalism	-0.02	-0.33	-0.04	0.47*	0.03
Political interest	0.22	0.23	0.03	-0.33*	0.01
Social localism	-0.39	-0.21	-0.01*	0.21*	0.00
Cultural localism	-0.49	-0.27	-0.06*	0.32*	0.02

Source: datafile SOCON '85.
Note: Figures in columns are the means of the standardized sum of scores for all respondents.
*Mean is significantly different from non-viewers' mean (α = 0.05 two-tailed).

Again, the picture becomes clearer when a distinction is made along the line of religious belief. Among the Calvinists, when compared with all categories of viewers, non-viewers are socially not very critical and not at all hedonistic. Furthermore, they are quite different

---

8   For certain scales some of the items of SOCON '85 deviate from those of MASSAT '89. Regarding the content, the scales in both databases are quite comparable.

from light viewers, but resemble heavy viewers in their strong work ethic and, although not significant, in the great value they assign to small communities.

The results for the non-Calvinist are surprisingly unequivocal. For almost all characteristics, the means of non-viewers differ from those of heavy viewers, whereas there is a rather great similarity with light viewers. Although the scores on fatalism scale do not entirely fit this picture, these data seem to indicate that non-viewing is indeed an extreme form of light viewing.

Finally, these results demonstrate that Calvinist non-viewers and non-Calvinist non-viewers are quite different people. Save the shared non-achievement attitudes, both categories differ greatly in all characteristics measured. For the most part these differences are also significant.[9]

In conclusion, it can be said that these results justify separation of Calvinist and non-Calvinist (non-)viewers. Within both of these groups non-viewers distinguish themselves from the categories of viewers by distinct attitudes. Calvinist and non-Calvinist non-viewers are also two distinct categories. This conclusion has, of course, consequences for further research. The most important consequence is the need to distinguish between Calvinist and non-Calvinist respondents in any further analyses. But, in order to perform analyses on leisure activities and media consumption in the Dutch situation, the only source presently available is MASSAT '89. This means that in subsequent analyses eight Calvinist and twelve non-Calvinist non-viewers will be compared with three categories of Calvinist and non-Calvinist viewers respectively. Statements on the basis of such limited respondents should only be made with much reservation. This is particularly the case where insignificant correlations are concerned, as will become clear from the next subject: the leisure activities of non-viewers.

Leisure activities

The questionnaire of MASSAT '89 contained a considerable number of questions about leisure activities. Respondents could fill in for example how often they had engaged in certain leisure activities during the previous month. Other indications of leisure activities were found by checking the amount of time in the previous month that the respondents spent in clubs and associations, the number of action or interest groups of which they were members, the extent of their political activities and how often they went to church. Table 6 presents the mean scores of non-viewers and the categories of viewers in the Calvinist and non-Calvinist populations.

The following example may illustrate how dangerous it can be to make statements about insignificant differences between such a small number of cases. At first it seems as if non-Calvinist non-viewers distinguish themselves from non-Calvinist viewers by going out more often. On closer inspection of the data, however, it became clear that this high

---

9   Table 5 does not specify whether differences are significant because this would have detracted from the readability of the table.

Table 6. Activities engaged in by TV (non-)viewers

	Non-viewers	Light viewers	Moderate viewers	Heavy viewers	Total
	Calvinists				
Going out: bar/disco/restaurant, etc.	1.4	1.9	1.0	2.3	1.5
Visiting: cinema/theatre/museum/exhib.	0.2	0.8	0.5	0.2	0.5
Engaging in sporting activities (actively)	1.7	2.7	1.9	2.7	2.3
Going to see a sporting event	0.2	0.4	0.9	0.9	0.7
Hours spent in clubs/associations[1]	1.3	2.6	2.6	3.2	2.6
Political participation[2]	0.0	0.7	0.1	−0.3	0.2
Member action/interst group[3]	0.0	0.4*	0.1*	0.1	0.2
Church attendance[4]	9.7	5.5*	4.1*	3.1*	4.8
Visits to/from relatives/friends	25.0	12.3*	10.8*	13.6*	12.8
Walking/cycling/fishing/etc.	13.8	3.0*	4.2*	3.3*	4.4
	Non-Calvinists				
Going out: bar/disco/restaurant, etc.	3.8	2.7	2.5	2.1	2.5
Visiting: cinema/theatre/museum/exhib.	0.6	1.3	1.0	0.6	0.9
Engaging in sporting activities (actively)	0.3	5.3*	3.6*	2.6*	3.7
Going to see a sporting event	0.2	0.6*	0.6*	0.8*	0.7
Hours spent in clubs/associations[1]	1.6	4.3*	3.1*	2.0	3.1
Political participation[2]	0.7	0.2	−0.1	−0.2	0.0
Member action/interst group[3]	0.7	0.3	0.2	0.1*	0.2
Church attendance[4]	1.6	1.1	0.6	0.7	0.8
Visits to/from relatives/friends	14.8	14.7	13.5	15.6	14.5
Walking/cycling/fishing/etc.	14.3	5.2	5.3	4.7	5.2

Source: datafile MASSAT '89.
Notes: Figures in columns are the average number of times per four weeks for each activity. *Mean is significantly different from non-viewers' mean ($\alpha = 00.05$ two-tailed).
[1] No. of hours spent (according to respondents' own estimation).
[2] (conventional) political participation, standardized sum of scores;
[3] number of memberships of action/interest groups (no more than three);
[4] estimated church attendance, recorded on the basis of the original answers: up to 'several times per year': 0; 'once a month': 1; 'once a week': 4; 'more than once a week': 12.

mean was largely produced by only one of the respondents who went out rather frequently. This extreme case was responsible for 20/12 (times going out/number of non-Calvinist non-viewers) = 1.7 of the mean for this category. One look at Table 6 shows that the 'difference' between the non-Calvinist non-viewers and non-Calvinist viewers can be explained by the score of this one single non-viewer. Discussion of Table 6 concentrates therefore mainly on the significant differences.

Table 6 first of all reveals that Calvinist non-viewers differ significantly in other ways from television viewing Calvinists than non-Calvinistic non-viewers. Again, this result confirms that the two types of non-viewers are two very distinct categories.

Compared with all the categories of Calvinist viewers, the Calvinist non-viewers stand out because of their frequent church attendance and their leisure activities often conducted within a private setting, such as walking, cycling and visiting or entertaining relatives and friends. None of these non-viewers are members of any action or interest groups; in this they differ considerably from light viewers in their religious group.

Non-viewers among the non-Calvinists stand out because of their evident aversion to participate in sports, be it actively or passively. It is also rather striking that they are, on the average, often members of action and interest groups, particularly more often than heavy viewers. Surprisingly, they do not participate much in clubs and associations; in this they are more like heavy viewers than like light viewers. A possible explanation for this might be that many clubs and associations are active in sports.

Media consumption

In connection with media consumption there is one question which has been repeatedly studied, namely whether the extent of television consumption is directly or inversely proportional to the extent of the consumption of other media. In Germany, Schulz (1986b) has found that light viewers hardly read newspapers and do not listen to the radio very often in comparison with heavy viewers. Vierkant (1987) came up with similar results in the Netherlands. Peters (1989), however, has found that there was a strong connection between viewing time and the type of newspaper read. Moreover, Peters' research showed that people who do not read any papers at all are, on the average, the ones who watch television most frequently. On the basis of these findings he has placed the statements of Schulz and Vierkant into a more elaborate perspective as far as the link between newspaper reading and television viewing is concerned.

Questions such as whether certain types of media consumption are directly or inversely proportional to each other are particularly important when studying the presence of any compensation mechanisms at work during the absence or light consumption of a certain medium. Such questions are particularly interesting for an extreme category as that of non-viewers. In this case the question is whether non-viewers use newspapers and radios to compensate for the lack of television, and if so, to what extent this is done. Table 7 therefore not only indicates the average viewing time, but also the average listening and reading time for Calvinist as well as non-Calvinist respondents.

Table 7. Media consumption among Calvinists and non-Calvinists

	Non-viewers	Light viewers	Moderate viewers	Heavy viewers	Total
		Calvinists			
Viewing time TV	0	321*	859*	1754*	763
Listening time radio	321	670	1215*	1438*	1026
Reading time newspaper	147	250	262*	192	240
		Non-Calvinists			
Viewing time TV	0	328*	841*	1705*	934
Listening time radio	587	1041	1312*	1572*	1306
Reading time newspaper	287	253	233	225	237

Source: MASSAT '89. *Mean is significantly different from non-viewers' mean ($\alpha = 0.05$ two-tailed).

Table 7 shows that the two categories of non-viewers also listen to the radio less than average. In this respect, the means fit in with the fact that TV and radio consumption are directly proportional to each other. The picture with regard to the reading of newspapers is somewhat different. Calvinist non-viewers, on the average, spend less time reading newspapers than light and moderate viewers of the same persuasion. This does not correspond with the non-Calvinist non-viewers. The data suggest that these respondents spend even more time on reading newspapers than all other categories of non-Calvinist viewers. This difference, however, is not statistically significant.

It seems, then, that Calvinist non-viewers do not compensate their non-viewing by a greater consumption of radio listening or newspaper reading. non-Calvinist non-viewers do not seem to compensate their non-viewing by listening more to the radio, but their average consumption of newspapers seems somewhat higher and may therefore point to compensatory behaviour. This possibility, however, requires verification through additional research.

Conclusions

At the beginning of this chapter three questions were posed concerning non-viewers: (1) who non-viewers are, in a descriptive sense, (2) to what extent can non-viewing be considered as behaviour which induces social disintegration, and (3) can, methodologically and theoretically speaking, non-viewers and light viewers be combined into one category and compared to heavy viewers. Several concluding comments can be made regarding these questions.

As for the first question, there seem to be two distinct types of non-viewers. Non-viewers of the first type (approximately 40 per cent of non-viewer respondents) are Calvinist and mostly belong to the lower socio-economic strata. The most prominent characteristics of these non-viewers are their aversion to hedonism and lack of a well developed work ethic. These features refer largely to what Weber (1985) defined as the protestant ethic. Furthermore, these non-viewers have almost no social criticism, deduced from the fact that none of the Calvinist non-viewers are members of action or interest groups. Leisure time is to a large extent spent on maintaining relations with relatives and friends; other favourite pastimes are walking and cycling. They consume media messages very rarely: non-viewing is combined with a low consumption of radio and newspapers.

Non-viewers of the second type (approximately 60 per cent of the non-viewers) are non-Calvinist and mostly belong to the higher socio-economic strata. These non-viewers hardly distinguish themselves from the non-Calvinist light viewers in their general attitudes to life and the world in which they live; as opposed to the non-Calvinist heavy viewers, these two categories are neither family-oriented nor socially critical. These non-viewers do not combine an anti-hedonistic attitude with strong work ethics. They cannot be said to have an extremely fatalistic world view, but they do have a more than average interest in the world of politics. Furthermore, they are also not locally oriented. They dislike sports and, on the average, spend only little time in clubs and other associations. On the other hand, they are quite often members of action and interest groups. As far as media consumption is concerned, they behave less extreme than the Calvinist non-viewers. They do not listen to the radio very often, but spend more time than an average amount of time reading newspapers (although this difference is not significant).

Regarding the second question (the extent to which non-viewing relates to social disintegration), it is necessary to separate Calvinist and non-Calvinist respondents. Leisure activities indicate that Calvinist non-viewers like to engage in activities within the more private sphere, such as visits with relatives and friends, walks and bicycle rides. A strong involvement with the rest of the world could not be measured on the basis of the limited data. Still, the findings suggest that this group had almost no social criticism or participation in action or interest groups. Also, the low level of radio and newspaper consumption – apart from television, the two major sources of information – points to this.

These findings raise the question whether for these Calvinist non-viewers, non-viewing is part of a way of life which also involves withdrawal into small communities and shutting out of the outside world. If the answer is affirmative, this conscious avoidance of media use may be seen as part of a behaviour that will lead to disintegration where the society as a whole is concerned, and on the other hand, integration into the community in which these Calvinist non-viewers live. On the basis of these results this question cannot be satisfactorily answered and must be further explored in future research.

The results of the non-Calvinist non-viewers largely correspond with Edgar's (1977) findings on the socio-economic elite. However, her statement that they also form an elite in the sense that they actively participate in social and cultural life is supported only by occasional instances. For example, the number of non-viewers that are members of action and interest groups is above average. They also read more newspapers than average (although the difference is not significant). Furthermore, their aversion to sports fits the picture of a socio-economic elite. Contrary to this, however, they do not go to cinemas, theatres, museums and exhibitions more than average. They also spend less time in clubs and associations. In short, the question remains whether, for these non-viewers, non-viewing is a conscious part of a socio-cultural way of life which allows little space for television viewing. The same goes for disintegrative behaviour: on the basis of the data available, no firm statement can be made.

As for the third question – whether it is sensible to consider non-viewers and light viewers as a homogeneous group in comparisons between light and heavy viewers – two remarks can be made. The findings regarding non-Calvinist non-viewers seem to indicate that this category should be regarded as extremely light viewers. No distortions will therefore occur in the comparisons between light viewers and heavy viewers, if these non-viewers and light viewers are put together in one category.

For the Calvinist non-viewers the situation is somewhat different. This very specific category has not only its own unique characteristics (e.g. anti-hedonism, church attendance), but also has a great number of similarities with heavy viewers. Grouping this category together with light viewers would theoretically lead to distortion of the results.

In practice, this distinction may not be too great because the percentage of Calvinist non-viewers generally will be very small compared to the percentage of light viewers and Calvinist non-viewers put together. However, in some instances it may be a decisive factor generating or preventing significant results. Therefore, caution is required in grouping non-viewers together with light viewers.

7 Television viewing as social activity

Wilbert Mutsaers

Watching television usually takes place within the social context of family life. As a consequence, viewers generally must take into account the interests and preferences for particular programmes of other household members. programme selection is therefore seldom an individual affair, but the result of group interactions. This is one of the factors which may lead to different patterns in viewing behaviour and differences in the social uses of television between people who live together and those who live alone. The ways in which the domestic environment constructs people's use of television are considered in an examination of relevant literature and of data taken from two large scale surveys.

Soon after the introduction of television in the early 1950's, studies (for overview, see Schramm *et al.*, 1961) appeared concerning the effects of television viewing on the emotions, knowledge and behaviour of individual viewers. At the time, television broadcasts brought housemates, neighbours, friends and other acquaintances together in front of the television set. Nonetheless, the majority of these early studies generally did not consider television viewing to be a social activity of groups of viewers. Viewers, instead, were seen as isolated, and therefore defenceless and unrelated individuals. The image of man on which this was based, came from the 'mass society' concept which was rather common at the time (DeFleur, 1970).[1] In this first generation of studies on television, the context in which television was watched, and the possible influence of the context on the selection and interpretation of programmes played only a marginal role. Due to the then strong conviction that television had direct negative effects on its viewers, the social relations – normally valued highly in other areas such as education, – were considered of no substantial importance. Researchers did see a connection between isolated individuals and television, but failed to see one between the individuals themselves (Katz, 1961). They

---

1 'Mass society' is as said to consist of isolated, atomized individuals who have no contact with each other and therefore, at least potentially anomic, live without purpose, intentions or interests. Compare with Tönnies' (1887/1957) concepts of 'Gemeinschaft' and 'Gesellschaft'.

acknowledged that social networks existed, but did not consider them of any influence regarding television viewing.

However, later studies were unable to provide any empirical support for the ideas noted above. A number of investigators then decided to shift focus from the media to its users and the place of mass media in everyday life (see e.g. Katz & Lazarsfeld, 1955; Schramm *et al.*, 1961; Bauer, 1964). Theoretical notions developed by sociologists and psychologists proved useful in such research. For example, notions commonly used in psychology such as selective exposure, attention and retention, derived from the balance and selection theories of Festinger (1957), were later applied to investigations on the use of mass media (see Klapper, 1958). People, it was found, are confronted with such a large supply of information via the mass media that they are forced to make choices. The idea of selection is also evident in the uses and gratifications approach to investigating media behaviour. This approach assumes that recipients only choose those messages from the total number of messages that are 'useful' to them or that provide some form of gratification for their personal motives (see Katz *et al.*, 1974). Studies in this tradition often state implicitly that the choices of certain television programmes are entirely reducible to individual interests, motives and problems of the viewers (e.g. Greenberg, 1974; Darmon, 1976). From that point of view, people only watch television programmes which they have consciously selected on the basis of their personal interests.

Recent investigations, however, suggest that the selectivity of people watching television, as assumed by some researchers, is limited. Manschot and Van der Brug (1986) and Heeter and Greenberg (1988) suggest that viewing behaviour is only partly linked with personal interests of viewers. Such results suggest that viewers also watch programmes that are of no real interest to them and – possibly because of that – miss programmes that they would have actually liked to see. Evidently, television viewing cannot only be explained in terms of individual interests, as there are also other important factors and motives to be taken into consideration.

The literature across in the field of mass communication points to several factors which may interfere with selective television viewing. Some authors point to the 'unicity' of the television medium compared to other mass media; a unicity which may encourage non-selective viewing. The characteristics of television messages – passage of time, moving images and sound – may contribute to the fact that people can only determine after the fact whether the programmes were really worth watching (see Comstock, 1989; Hendriksen, 1979; Gerbner, 1973; Goodhardt *et al.*, 1975). It is therefore possible that people watch television programmes which – in retrospect – do not correspond with their interests or needs.

Apart from such medium-oriented explanations, the social context in which television is used may also be responsible for the differences between people's interests and the television programmes they watch. After all, viewers are not only interrelated through television, they also have unmediated connections with each other. These direct relations between viewers may have consequences for the use of television and the functions that people derive from watching television. As already mentioned, the idea that television has a direct influence on viewers lacked empirical support. Partly because of this, some of the researchers in the 1950's and 1960's integrated sociological notions such as 'primary group' and 'significant others' into their investigations on television viewing (e.g. Riley & Riley, 1959; Niven, 1960). In the early 1950s, Riley and Flowerman (1951) stated that, when receiving messages, people do not just react as isolated personalities, but also as members of the different groups to which they belong (see also Riley & Riley, 1951). Later, Schramm *et al.* (1961) followed this line of argument and stated that group relations may determine the use of the mass media in general. Forsey (1963) and Wand (1968) studied the social context in which people usually watch television. They found that a majority of people attend to television in a family context. According to Wand, this does not necessarily mean that the whole family is watching; sometimes, in fact, only the children or the parents watch television together.[2]

The presence of these co-viewers may be the reason that individual wishes are not always fulfilled. Housemates may want to see programmes which other housemates do not find particularly interesting (see Bogart, 1972; Brown & Linné, 1976; Gunter & Svennevig, 1987; Mutsaers & Vierkant, 1991; Mutsaers *et al.*, 1992; Verwey, 1986a; Zahn & Baran, 1984).

Another study which supports this assumption was conducted by Webster and Wakshlag (1982:453-455). Their research into the effects of watching television with others shows that the so-called 'programme loyalty' (watching programmes of the preferred type) is the strongest when people watch television on their own. When people watch television together, there is some decline in this loyalty towards preferred programmes. programme loyalty declines in particular when the composition of the group of viewers differs over a period of time. The decline is not very noticeable in groups that do not normally change in composition as, for example, families. According to Webster and Wakshlag, this is because that after some time the preferences of dominant people in the family will have come to represent the choice patterns of other family members. Such an interpretation implies that – in households of two or more people – not only the preferences for specific television programmes of certain housemates, but also the influential positions of these housemates in the group play an important role in the choice of television programmes (see also Forsyth, 1990).

Studies by researchers such as Fritz (1987), Morley (1986; 1989) and Lull (1978; 1980a; 1988; 1990) follow this line of argument. According to Morley (1986), specific patterns of television use may be a way of demonstrating patterns of dominance. Morley concentrates his research particularly on the relations between men and women inasmuch as he feels that the specific social roles of the sexes within the family will lead to rather different viewing styles. These differences not only become apparent in the choice of programmes, but also in other aspects of viewing behaviour such as the amount of time spent watching

---

2   Wand therefore uses the term 'peer group viewing', a notion also later employed by McDonald (1986).

television, how often television it watched, use of video and remote control devices, and watching together or alone. Like Morley, Lull considers media use as one of the means that people have to purposefully construct their social reality. From this idea, he developed a typology of 'social uses of television' (Lull 1980) which he suggests can indicate, among other things, how the use of television structures the social interaction within a family (see also Chaffee *et al.*, 1973; Lindlof & Copeland, 1982; Tims & Masland, 1985). In connection with this, Frissen and Wester (1990:165) comment that 'by emphasizing the social dimensions of viewing behaviour, Lull makes clear that television viewing behaviour cannot be isolated from the ordinary social relationships within people's lives.'

Problem formulation and method

If we regard watching television as a social activity – i.e. as something that people normally do together and is considered to be a form of social action (see Anderson & Meyer, 1988; Hunzinker, 1988; Renckstorf, 1977; 1989) – then this will have implications for theories and research on the use of television. Morley (1989) contends that from this perspective we can no longer regard television viewers as 'free' consumers who rationally, in a manner of gratification maximization, shop around in a cultural supermarket. Especially when viewers live together with others, they often have to comply with the programme choices of their housemates. This is particularly the case for members that occupy less influential positions within the family. Dutch research by Meier and Peeters (1988) and Meier and Frissen (1988), based on Morley's (1986) work, suggests that Dutch women occupy less influential positions within families than their male partners, as far as the choice of programmes is concerned.

This investigation therefore first considers how men and women evaluate their own influence on the choice of television programmes. The underlying question is whether possible differences in such influence can be related to the roles that men and women play and the resulting tasks they perform within their families.

The research focuses on the question whether the influence of the viewers on the choice of programmes becomes less when families are larger. For, the more members a household consists of, the larger the chance that the members will have different interests and preferences. This may lead to greater differences between individual interests of family members and their respective viewing behaviour. This supposition is, among other things, based on a study by Bosman and Renckstorf (1992; see also Chapter 4 in this volume) which states that there is a higher correlation between interest in information about certain subjects and the consumption of information about these subjects (e.g. via television) among people living alone than among people living in larger households.

The availability of video recorders and/or multiple television sets in a household provide people with an opportunity to withdraw from possible conflicts with their co-viewers about the choice of programmes. In this investigation, then, it is important to examine whether viewers who own video recorders and/or several television sets miss their favourite programmes less often than viewers who do not have these additional pieces of equipment.

The second part of this investigation is concerned with the effects that collective viewing has on the diversity of the television programmes and the types of programmes people watch. In other words, do people's viewing patterns (watching different types of programmes) vary according to the size of the family in which they live? Results from a study by Mutsaers and Vierkant (1991) show that the diversity of programmes watched by family members becomes smaller when families are larger. It may be expected that people in households with two or more people will sooner opt for programmes that most of their co-viewers like than for programmes appreciated by only a few of the viewers. Due to such group processes the individuals' unique viewing needs will more often be satisfied in small households than in large households.

Further, it is relevant to examine whether there are any connections between watching foreign television stations (such as English, German and French channels) and the size and composition of a family. The larger the families, the more people watch television together and the more likely it is that they will not watch foreign television channels because not all viewers present (e.g. children) will have adequate knowledge of these foreign languages.

Findings

For this research, data were used collected during the MASSAT '89 survey, a large-scale field study of media equipment, media exposure and media use in the Netherlands. This study was divided into two parts: a random survey among the Dutch population (n=956) (Arts *et al.*, 1990b) and a time budget study among a number of the respondents for a period of one week (n=583) (Arts *et al.*, 1990a). The data concerning the amount of time spent watching foreign channels and the total viewing time (in minutes per week) are from the time budget study. The other data are from the survey. Viewing time has been determined by means of the diary method.[3]

Influence of co-viewers on television use

On the basis of research conducted by Morley (1986) and Lull (1978), the present study examines the supposition that men and women have a different influence on the selection of television programmes within their families. Tables 1 and 2 show how men and women, living alone or together with others, evaluate their influence on the choice of television programmes.

---

3   For the time budget study, all respondents who participated in the survey were asked to keep a so-called time diary for seven consecutive days, starting with the day prior to the interview. In this time diary they could note down categorized activities, such as watching television, for every quarter of an hour between 6 am and 1 am each day. Within certain limits they could also list several activities for every 15 minute period, for example, eating and watching television simultaneously. For more information, see Arts *et al.* (1990a).

Table 1. Gender, living situation and TV programme choice. Question: When watching television together with others, how often do you yourself decide what to watch?

	Men living with partners/children (n = 300)	Women living with partners/children (n = 286)	Men and women living alone (n = 64)
Never, rarely, occasionally	40.7%	51.9%	24.1%
Fairly often	32.0%	29.7%	17.9%
Frequently, nearly always	27.3%	18.4%	58.0%

Table 2. Influence of partner on choice of TV programmes: Question: When watching television together with others, how often does your partner decide what to watch?

	Men living with partners (n = 323)	Women living with partners (n = 324)
Never, rarely, occasionally	56.0%	53.2%
Fairly often	32.3%	26.0%
Frequently, nearly always	11.7%	20.0%

Table 1 indicates that people living alone more often decide themselves what to watch when they have 'visitors' than people living in a family normally do. Men living together with their partners more often say that they decide themselves what to watch than women living together with their partners; see Table 1. Correspondingly, women more often say that their partners decide what to watch than the men; see Table 2.

The extent of 'zapping' as a method for choosing what programme to watch also gives an indication of the influence gender has on the choice of television programmes. Table 3 highlights the differences in 'zapping' between men and women living with partners and/or children. This data suggest that nearly 20 per cent of the women, compared to almost twice the percentage of the men, say that they zap frequently or nearly always.

Table 3. 'Zapping,' gender and living situation: Question: How often do you 'zap' to decide what programme to watch?

	Men living with partners/children (n = 323)	Women living with partners/children (n = 324)
Never, rarely, occasionally	32.0%	53.1%
Fairly often	28.4%	27.1%
Frequently, nearly always	39.6%	19.8%

The collective results of Tables 1, 2 and 3 seem to indicate that, within the family context, women are more willing to let others decide what programmes they will watch. Meier and Frissen (1988) came to the same conclusion and suggest state that women in a family context watch television in order to be sociable and not so much because they want to watch a certain programme. In connection with this aspect, there may also be another explanation for the fact that women in a family context miss more programmes they are interested in than men do, which may be related to the roles men and women usually have in family life. For men, the home is usually a place to relax, whereas for women it is often a place of work. This difference in household function may be the reason why some women, when others are watching television in concentration, only occasionally cast a glance at the television set, because they are doing other things at the same time. To examine this idea further, Table 4 lists the activities that men and women in families perform while watching television.

Table 4. Activities performed while watching TV

Activities during television viewing	Men (n = 424)	Women (n = 409)
Reading	44.8%	51.2%
Fetching food/drinks	83.2%	89.5%
Eating	56.6%	51.4%
Sleeping	35.8%	31.1%
Going to the toilet	83.5%	86.3%
Needlework	4.7%	50.5%
Looking after children	32.0%	46.4%
Housekeeping	29.8%	39.8%
Talking about TV programmes	76.7%	81.6%
Talking about other things	72.8%	71.5%

First of all, it appears that many people fairly often perform other activities while watching television. Second, the data in Table 4 show that women in particular combine watching television with other activities, which collaborates the central thesis of this study. The only things that men 'do' more often than women in front of the television set is sleep and eat. The other noted activities such as needlework, looking after the children, and housekeeping are mostly done by the women. As a as consequence, women may be less actively involved in choosing television programmes than men are (see Tables 1, 2 and 3). Men have a relatively dominant role within the households as far as the choice of television programmes is concerned. Nevertheless, they also fairly often watch programmes that they did not choose themselves, particularly when compared to people that live alone: about 40 per cent of them indicates that this is fairly often to nearly always the case (see Tables 1 and 2).

The more people there are in a household, the greater the chance that there will be conflicting preferences. It may therefore be expected that both men and women who live in larger households will miss their favourite programmes more often. Studies by Wand

(1968) and McDonald (1986) have shown that, in the family context, children often successfully determine what programme will be watched, particularly in the early evening hours; see Table 5.

Table 5. Missing favourite TV programmes and household size: Question: How often does it happen that you cannot watch a programme you like because others want to watch something else?

No. of people in the household: (n)	one (101)	two (260)	three (177)	four (257)	five> (140)
Rarely, never	80.0%	59.1%	47.8%	48.2%	47.4%
Occasionally	15.4%	34.0%	42.9%	36.8%	40.6%
Fairly often	3.3%	5.5%	7.3%	11.8%	9.4%
Frequently/nearly always	1.3%	1.5%	2.0%	3.1%	2.6%

Table 5 suggests that the more people there are in a household, the more viewers who miss their favourite programmes because of the preferences of others. It is rather striking that only half of the interviewees who live in households of three or more people (combinations of men, women and children) say that they rarely or never miss a programme because of other people. The percentages for households of one or two people are considerably higher (80 per cent and 59 per cent respectively). Evidently, children have an important say in the choice processes concerning television programmes: people from families with children more often say that they miss their favourite programme than people from families without children.

From this perspective, it might be relevant to distinguish between households that have one television set and multiple set households. After all, if a family has more than one television set, family members can watch television separately and each person can choose his or her own programme. It is therefore likely that members of households with multiple sets miss their favourite programmes less often because of deviating programme preferences of their housemates than people from families with just one television set; see Table 6.

Table 6. Missing favourite programmes, number of TVs and household size: Question: How often does it happen that you cannot watch a programme you like, because others want to watch something else?

No. of household members	one		two		three		four		five+	
TV sets*:	1	2>	1	2>	1	2>	1	2>	1	2>
Rarely, never	78.9	82.6	56.9	65.8	36.2	61.3	44.9	50.9	43.6	50.2
Occasionally	16.0	17.4	37.5	23.0	52.5	32.7	35.4	38.8	45.5	36.6
Fairly often	3.7	–	5.0	7.0	10.2	4.2	14.8	8.8	8.4	10.4
Frequently/nearly always	1.4	–	0.6	4.2	1.2	1.8	4.8	1.4	2.5	2.7
N:	90	6	197	63	93	84	130	125	66	73

*The variable 'number of television sets' is dichotomized in: one set (60.5 per cent of the respondents) and two or more sets (36.9 per cent).

The same argument holds for the connection between the availability of video recorders in the households and the possibility of watching favourite programmes. With the arrival of video recorders – which an increasing number of Dutch families have in their homes (Knulst & Kalmijn, 1988) – people living together obtained the possibility to record programmes that they were unable to see due to programming preferences of their housemates, and to watch them at a later time, for example, when their housemates are not watching television, see Table 7.

Table 7: Missing favourite programmes, VCRs and household size: Question: How often does it happen that you cannot watch a programme you like because others want to watch something else?

No. of household members:	one		two		three		four		five+	
VCR:	Yes	No	Yes	No	Yes	No	Yes	No	Yes	No
Rarely, never	77.1	81.1	63.6	54.9	54.4	39.1	48.3	48.0	52.4	42.9
Occasionally	19.9	13.6	30.4	37.2	35.3	53.1	38.7	34.1	36.9	43.9
Fairly often	3.0	3.4	4.7	6.2	7.8	6.7	10.3	14.1	5.2	13.2
Frequently/nearly always	–	1.8	1.3	1.7	2.6	1.2	2.7	3.8	5.5	–
N:	29	72	125	135	102	76	152	105	67	73

Exactly half the number of respondents (n=478) possess a VCR.

Table 6 shows that people in households with more than one television set miss programmes they like less often because housemates want to watch something else than people in households with just one set. It should be noted that at least 40 per cent of the respondents in households with three or more people and multiple sets say they fairly often miss programmes because their housemates prefer other programmes. Apparently, the availability of more television sets does not necessarily lead to the use of these sets every time members of the family disagree on what programme they should watch.

Table 7 suggests that, when a VCR is available, viewers miss their favourite programmes less often than people in households of the same size without a video recorder. It is remarkable, though, that also a considerable percentage of the people (at least 40 per cent) in the large households (three or more people) with a VCR say they occasionally, fairly often or frequently are unable to watch a programme because their housemates want to watch something else.

An obvious explanation for the data in Table 6 and 7 is that the availability of a VCR or second television set in a household of, for example, five people does not really increase the chance that people can watch their favourite programmes despite the conflicting interests of their housemates. This may be because the person who uses the VCR or second television set makes it impossible for his or her housemates to watch their favourite programmes.

There is also another possible explanation for the situation that multiple television sets and/or VCRs does not lead to a significant increase in watching favourite programmes. This may be found in the social functions which television viewing can have in a family.

Many families spend their evenings watching television. These are often the only occasions family members communicate and interact with each other. Lull (1980: 203) suggests that television viewing, in this way, can facilitate the communication between family members or serve as a potential for 'the construction of desired opportunities for interpersonal contact or avoidance'. Lindlof, Shatzer and Wilkinson (1988: 158) note that 'television is one of the few occasions when all family members gather, yet it is also used for separating oneself from other family members.' From this perspective, people do not only watch television because they want to see certain programmes, but also occasionally because watching television enables them to make or avoid contact with other members of the household. In such cases it is not really important what programme is on. As a result people may not want to use the second television set, which is usually in another room, or programme the VCR, because they would then miss contact with other household members.

Television may also have a similar 'contact function' for people living alone. Horton and Wohl (1956) and Charlton and Neumann (1986) see this as 'para-social interaction' between viewers and their television. By this concept they mean that television may create the suggestion of having company, which may compensate for the absence of social contact which people living alone may experience as suggested in studies by De Jong-Gierveld (1969), Woldringh and Knapen (1980), and Van der Aa and De Neeve (1983). See further Tables 8 and 9 below.

Table 8, Feelings of loneliness and household size: Question: How often do you feel lonely?

	People living alone (n = 106)	People living with partners/children (n = 849)
Rarely, never	57.0%	82.2%
Occasionally	34.8%	16.7%
Fairly often/Frequently	8.2%	1.1%

Table 9. TV viewing as remedy for feelings of loneliness. Statement: I watch television to feel less alone

	People living alone (n = 102)	People living with partners/children (n = 834)
(Totally) agree	24.5%	8.0%
Agree nor disagree	13.9%	12.7%
(Totally) disagree	61.5%	79.3%

Tables 8 and 9 generally support the central thesis of this study. Of those persons who live alone, 43 per cent occasionally, fairly often or frequently feel lonely, compared to only

17.8 per cent of those living with partners. For people living alone, television evidently plays a more important role in alleviating feelings of loneliness than for people living with their partners. Almost a quarter of the people living alone say that they watch television to feel less alone, whereas only 8 per cent of the people living with their partners agree with this statement.

Viewing different programmes types and social context

Co-viewers often tell viewers what programmes they should choose. This may have several consequences for the variation in types of programmes that people watch with others. As these people occasionally watch programmes that their co-viewers find interesting – although they themselves do not – they may develop more varied viewing habits than people living alone who chiefly watch programmes that they themselves find interesting. On the other hand, the opposite may also be true. People who live alone are entirely free to watch television according to their own preferences and do not have to take into account other people's wishes. This is not the case for people who share a television set with others. In such households they often watch programmes that the majority of the viewers present approve of instead of the ones that a single individual might find interesting. This may lead to a certain impoverishment in the types of programmes watched by people from large families. People who prefer programmes other than those preferred by the largest part of the television audience will usually not be able to watch these programmes under pressure from their housemates. Put another way, in large households individual variations in programme preferences can be levelled out in such a way that a collective pattern of viewing habits emerges in which individual preferences are only represented insofar as they correspond with the preferences of the housemates, which leaves only the greatest common denominator. It may therefore be expected that, due to the above mentioned group processes, so-called 'heavy' programmes on, for example, art or religion and programmes on foreign channels will not be watched by people in large households as much as by people who live alone or together with their partners. Results from studies by Mutsaers and Vierkant (1991) and Mutsaers et al. (1992) seem to support this. Mutsaers et al. (1992: 250) suggest that 'when comparing viewing patterns of sports and culture on television, the conflicting interests within a family have different consequences for the viewing behaviour of family members.' Mutsaers and Vierkant (1991) find that the larger the household, the less its members watch informative or art programmes and the more they watch films and entertainment programmes. Such results point to a possible connection between the number of people in a household and the viewing habits they develop.

Table 10 shows the relation between the total time that people spend on watching television and family size. Table 11 specifies this for the various types of programmes which people can watch. Table 10 suggests that the total time people spend watching television hardly varies with family size. The maximum difference in viewing time as indicated in Table 10 is rather small: 21 minutes per day between households of three persons and households of five or more. The correlation between viewing time and family size is not significant (= 00.05, two-tailed). Both men and women spend approximately two hours per day watching television. However, a comparison between the viewers in small and large households with respect to the specific types of television programmes they watch, reveals a number of differences; see Table 11.[4]

Table 10: Time spent watching TV and household size

No. of household members	N:	Viewing time per week	Viewing time per day
One	60	841.38 min	2h 0 min
Two	164	879.48 min	2h 5 min
Three	99	898.68 min	2h 8 min
Four	151	786.25 min	1h 52 min
Five–nine	91	748.40 min	1h 47 min
Total population	565	832.82 min	1h 59 min
Men	281	848.38 min	2h 1 min
Women	284	817.44 min	1h 57 min

'Viewing time' by 'people per household': Proportion explained variance (Eta sq.)= 1.3 per cent, F=1.830, Sig.F.=n.s. Source: MASSAT '89

Table 11: Viewing TV programme types and household size:
Question: How often do you watch the following types of television programmes? If a type of programme does not appear regularly on television, but you nevertheless watch it almost every time, answer 'nearly always'.

No. of people	Total n=936	One n=102	Two n=260	Three n=177	Four n=257	Five+ n=140	Eta sq.[‡]	F.	Sig. F
Watching programmes:									
Courses	1.33*	1.31	1.41	1.30	1.30	1.28	0.7%	1.66	0.156[†]
Religion	1.37	1.49	1.42	1.39	1.29	1.35	0.8%	1.97	0.097[†]
Art/Classical Music	1.57	1.94	1.71	1.45	1.43	1.39	3.7%	8.92	0.000
Children's programmes	1.76	1.48	1.47	1.91	1.96	1.91	5.3%	13.07	0.000
Pop music	1.87	1.69	1.58	1.89	2.11	2.07	3.8%	9.09	0.000
Dutch series	2.18	1.90	2.18	2.26	2.22	2.22	1.0%	2.36	0.052[†]
Quiz/Game Shows	2.25	1.96	2.29	2.48	2.18	2.24	1.4%	3.26	0.011
Talk shows	2.29	2.23	2.33	2.32	2.29	2.26	0.1%	0.27	0.900[†]
Foreign series	2.40	2.26	2.34	2.43	2.45	2.45	0.4%	1.12	0.452[†]
Commercials	2.41	2.47	2.37	2.48	2.41	2.35	0.2%	0.38	0.821[†]
Scientific/Medical	2.43	2.11	2.55	2.54	2.35	2.46	1.5%	3.55	0.007
Documentaries	2.60	2.63	2.71	2.65	2.52	2.42	0.9%	2.13	0.075[†]
Consumer info/hobby	2.61	2.25	2.70	2.74	2.61	2.51	1.7%	3.96	0.003
Sports	2.68	1.82	2.63	2.77	2.94	2.81	4.4%	10.76	0.000
Natural history	2.68	2.46	2.90	2.78	2.56	2.52	2.1%	4.94	0.001
Films	2.69	2.69	2.86	2.91	3.01	2.86	0.5%	1.43	0.357[†]

*Mean scores of respondent groups on a five-point scale: rarely/never (1), occasionally (2), fairly often (3), frequently (4), nearly always (5) (m.c.=20). [†]Not significant at alpha= 0.05, two-tailed. [‡] percentage explained variance (Eta sq.); Df1=4, Df2=924.

To facilitate interpretation of Table 11, programme types are divided into three categories: (1) programmes that people in small households watch more often than people in large

---

4   There were no available data from the time budget study with respect to people watching several types of television programmes. Instead, data from the survey were used.

households, (2) programmes that show no significant differences in this respect, and (3) programmes that people in small households watch less often than people in large households. Table 11 reveals that all households watch television programmes to the same extent in the following categories: 'scientific/medical,' 'commercials,' 'talk shows/discussions,' 'courses,' 'quiz/game shows,' 'Dutch series,' and 'consumer info/hobby'. On the average, people in large households watch more often programmes in the categories 'sports,' 'foreign series,' 'pop music,' 'children's programmes' and 'films' than people in small households. People in small households, on the other hand, watch more often 'art/classical music,' 'religion,' 'documentaries,' and 'nature films' than people in large households.

These results confirm on all points the basic assumption of this study, namely, that people in large households have different and less pronounced viewing habits than people in small households. After all, entertaining programmes as 'sports,' 'children's programmes,' 'foreign series,' 'films,' and 'pop music' are watched more often by persons from large families than by persons from small families. In comparison to persons from large families, those from small families watch far more 'informative' programmes such as religious programmes, art and classical music programmes, documentaries, and nature films (although some observers as, for example, Postman (1985) rightly state that every television programme is entertaining in some way or other). On the basis of tables 10 and 11 it can be concluded that – although people in all households spend approximately an equal amount of time per week watching television – the viewing behaviour of persons in small households is different with regard to the content of the programmes they watch from persons in large households.

Findings such as these in Table 11 make clear that a more modest attitude is called for when one is trying to statistically predict types of programmes watched by household size. The explained variance is not very high (maximum: 5.3 per cent). Furthermore, there are several types of programmes which have no significant results (= 0.05, two-tailed). The individual viewing behaviour with respect to several types of programmes can be predicted, then, only to a limited extent with the use of the variable household size. However, only one indicator of social context was included in this analysis, i.e. the number of people in a household, whereas other indicators are also important such as interests of housemates (see Mutsaers *et al.*, 1992) and the position of members within the family (see Morley, 1986). All things considered, the amount of the variance explained with a single indicator is far from disappointing.[5]

Foreign television channels (French, German or English) require more effort and concentration of the Dutch audience than Dutch programmes or foreign programmes with Dutch

---

5   The aforementioned study by Webster and Wakshlag (1982) suggests that – in a family context – the preferences of dominant family members gradually start to represent the preferences of less influential members. For example, when people are often 'forced' to watch certain programmes, they may become interested in such programmes. Such subtle long-term influences of the social context on the development of viewing behaviour and interests are not traceable by means of a single survey. This may also be an explanation for the small amount of variance found in Table 11.

subtitles, not to speak of the necessary command of the language in question (see Renckstorf & Hendriks Vettehen, 1992). If several people watch television together, it may therefore be expected that they will not directly choose a foreign channel, although some of them might have done so if they had been watching television alone. After all, the more members there are in a household, the greater the chance that there are people in that household who do not have any command of a foreign language (particularly children). Also, when watching foreign channels, the necessary concentration and silence may interfere with the communication between the viewers. This also does not encourage large households to watch foreign channels; see Table 12.[6]

Table 12. Watching foreign TV channels and household size

Number of people in household	N	Viewing time in mins per week (FC)*	Relative viewing time (FC) %[†]
One	60	90.70	9.47%
Two	164	86.86	7.85%
Three	99	69.75	6.10%
Four	151	46.26	5.86%
Five and more	91	37.64	4.44%
Total population	565	65.55	6.64%

Notes: FC = foreign channels. 'Viewing time FC' by 'number of people in a household:' Proportion explained variance (Eta sq.)= 1.7 per cent, F=2.467, Sig. F.= 0.044. *Foreign channels: BBC 1/2, Germany 1/2/3, France 1/2/3, ITV, RTL+, Belgium-French, and TV-5. Not included were the 'foreign' channels MTV, Super Channel and Sky Channel, because they predominantly broadcast music (in 1989) and therefore do not really require knowledge of a foreign language. [†]The relative viewing time is the viewing time spent on watching FC divided by the total viewing time multiplied by 100. Source: dataset MASSAT '89.

Table 12 shows that small families spend more time watching foreign channels than do large households, as measured in minutes per week. This remains the same when the time of watching foreign channels is related to the total time spent watching television. People living alone watch foreign channels for 9.5 per cent of the total time that they attend to television, whereas people in large households (five or more people) watch foreign channels for only 4.4 per cent. The correlation between watching foreign channels and family size is significant (Sig.F.= 0.044; $P = 0.05$, two-tailed). This confirms the hypothesis that large families watch foreign channels less often than small families.

Discussion

The above results correspond with the basic assumption underlying this study: to understand television use, viewers should not be considered as isolated individuals, but as members of social systems in which co-viewers can influence the viewing behaviour of 'individual' viewers in several ways and to different degrees.

---

6   Table 4 shows that people often talk while watching television, not only about the programme they are watching, but also about other subjects. Watching foreign channels may interfere with this 'social talk'.

On the basis of the above findings, several conclusions can be formulated. First, the results confirm the idea that selection of television programmes is normally not an individual affair, but often a collective activity. Because co-viewers often influence programme choice, viewers are occasionally forced to let the preferences of their housemates prevail over their own.

Within a family, men seem to play a more dominant role in television programme choice than women. This difference in influence may, among other things, correspond with the different roles men and women usually play in family life. More often than men, women combine television viewing with housekeeping activities and are therefore often less directly involved in choosing television programmes.

Second, the larger the household, the more often viewers must comply with choices of co-viewers. The availability of a video recorder and/or multiple television sets in the household basically enables viewers to avoid conflicts with co-viewers, and thus slightly reduces the correlation between missing favourite programmes and the number of people in a household. Nevertheless, it is also more common in households with several television sets and/or VCRs that people occasionally watch programmes which they personally are not interested in. The larger the family, the more often this is the case. Some interpretations and possible explanations for these results have been suggested. These interpretations correspond with the social functions that television viewing may have for family members, such as to make or avoid contact with housemates, apart from satisfying interests and/or information needs. People who live alone – and therefore have on average less contact with others in a household context – use television more often to alleviate feelings of loneliness than people who live together with partners and/or children.

Furthermore, we can conclude that there is a correlation between the variety of television programme types which people watch and the number of people in a household. Irrespective of family size, people overall spend an equal amount of time watching television. With regard to types of programmes, however, this amount of time is spent in entirely different ways depending on household size. The more people with which viewers have to negotiate when choosing a television programme, the more 'impoverished' the viewing behaviour of the entire family becomes. For example, persons in large families – compared to those living alone and those in small families – watch foreign channels and programmes about religion, nature, art and classical music less often.

A modest attitude is called for when trying to statistically predict this relation between types of programmes watched and household size. However, the low values of explained variances found do not necessarily mean that the basic assumption is wrong. As mentioned earlier, the influences of the household on the viewing behaviour of individuals are exerted in a subtle way and over a long period of time. Furthermore, only one of the possible indicators of influence of the social context on the viewing behaviour of individuals was employed, and from this point of view the amount of explained variance is more than encouraging.

To gain more specific insight in the ways in which – and to what extent – co-viewers exert influence on the viewing behaviour of people, further study is necessary which incorporates different techniques of data collection to 'uncover' the aforementioned subtle and long-term influences (see e.g. Ang, 1991; Jensen, 1987; Morley & Silverstone, 1991). Such additional studies may focus on the position of individual members within a family, on the rules and procedures governing the choice of television programmes, on the consequences watching television with others may have for the interpretation of television messages, and on the functions that television viewing and the participation in choice processes within a family may have for viewers at different times of the day. In this respect, Hasebrink and Krotz (1992) stress that the different use of television by viewers at different moments deserve specific attention. After all, viewers turn on and switch off the television set, switch over to other channels or choose a certain programme, watch the programme attentively or less attentively, and 'read' the message as it was meant or in some other way. According to these investigators, and in conformity with the basic assumption of this study, research concerning such aspects of television use should take into account the viewing context with respect to the home situation and the interaction between members of the household in order to better understand individual use of television.

8 Watching foreign TV channels

Karsten Renckstorf and Paul Hendriks Vettehen

The analysis presented in this chapter suggests that a preference for foreign television channels does not imply a greater interest in or appreciation of events happening outside viewers' immediate social environment. However, there does seem to be a connection between interest in particular content and preference for certain programmes.

As a result of the deregulation of the national and international communication markets and the arrival of cable and satellite television, the availability of television programmes in the Netherlands has increased tremendously as it has in most of the other Western European countries (Wilde, 1992). Frissen, (1992:190), in this regard, asserts that: 'since the 1980s there has been a spectacular growth in the number of television programmes. Nowadays, basically any hour of spare time can be filled watching television, a situation inconceivable in the 1970s.'

To some extent, this increase is the result of the introduction of three new Dutch television channels[1] (the public channel Netherlands 3 in 1988, and the commercial channels RTL4 in 1989 and RTL5 in 1993), and also of the fact that the Dutch public broadcasting companies acquired more broadcasting time during that period (Hammersma, 1990). However, the major increase in the number of television programmes available in the Netherlands has been the result of a huge expansion of foreign television channels since the early 1980s. In 1980 only 1 per cent of Dutch population could receive eight or more foreign television channels. In 1989 this percentage had increased to 50 per cent (Olderaan & Jankowski, 1988). Modern television sets with remote control devices have also made it easier for the viewer to switch channels and have thus further increased the accessibility of these channels (and programmes).

This rather substantial expansion of television programmes available to the Dutch population raises a number of issues with respect to the use of the medium. The total supply of programmes may have increased dramatically, but it remains uncertain whether this has

---

[1] RTL4 and RTL5 do not broadcast from the Netherlands. We nevertheless consider it a Dutch channel because its programmes are almost exclusively intended for the Dutch market and its 'foreign character' is merely a legal construction.

influenced viewing behaviour. Are more Dutch people watching television as a result of the increase in the general supply of programming as some observers have feared and others had hoped (SCP, 1990:232; see also Knulst & Kalmijn, 1988:9). Or are the Dutch now watching television in such a purposeful manner that only the viewing time of specific programming genres has increased? Can the recent phenomenon of zapping or switching channels be attributed to the fact that so many programmes are available simultaneously?

In this chapter we will discuss a number of questions related to an aspect of the above mentioned developments, i.e. the increase in the amount of foreign televisiaon channels that can be received in the Netherlands. One of these questions concerns the possibility watching foreign television channels: does the Dutch viewer watch foreign television channels more often than previously? This question is, among other things,[2] relevant within the context of the discussion on the cultural significance of the influx of foreign television programmes in the Netherlands (Heinsman, 1982; see also Knulst, 1982; Heinsman & Servaes, 1991).[3] The key issue in this discussion is whether this influx of foreign television channels and programmes, i.e. products of foreign cultures, should be regarded as a threat to Dutch 'cultural identity'[4] or, on the contrary, as a possibly important contribution to the development of mutual understanding among European cultures.

We hope to contribute to these discussions by examining the profiles of regular viewers of foreign television channels in order to find possible motives underlying their viewing behaviour. Do people watch foreign television channels simply because these channels are available? Does the supply actually create the demand or do people make a conscious choice, either because they have a (more general) interest in events happening outside the local context or because they have a (more specific) interest as regards the content of the programmes broadcast by these channels? To what extent does, for example, language decide whether people watch programmes on foreign channels?

---

2 An increase in viewing time of foreign networks may also have a negative effect on the viewing time of the Dutch public channels. Just like the commercial channels these networks largely depend on ratings which more or less directly determine funds obtained by advertising of both the commercial and public television channels, and they undoubtedly also determine in the long run the willingness of the government to continue financing the public channels (through radio and television licences).

3 Insofar as the increase in foreign television products (from complete television channels to individual programmes and series) also concerns American television producers and products, discussions held in Europe at the end of the 1960s with respect to Servan-Schreiber's *Le defi americain* (1970) may possibly be continued.

4 Authors do not seem to agree about the precise meaning of the term 'cultural identity'. Many use (working) definitions that contain one or both elements of Servaes' definition (1992:82): 'The term cultural identity refers to two complementary phenomena: on the one hand, an inward sense of association or identification with a specific culture or subculture; on the other hand, an outward tendency within a specific culture to share a common sense of what it has in common with other cultures and what distinguishes it from other cultures.' A more precise definition of this notion is difficult to formulate because its meaning largely depends on the specific historical context in which it is used (Brants & Van Zoonen, 1992).

Table 1. Viewing time per day of Dutch and foreign TV channels

Channels	Viewing time
1988:Netherlands 1,2 and 3	1h 18 min
Foreign*	15 min
1989: Netherlands 1,2 and 3	1h 12 min
Foreign*	13 min
1990: Netherlands 1,2 and 3, RTL4	1h 16 min
Foreign	12 min
1991: Netherlands 1,2 and 3, RTL4	1h 24 min
Foreign	15 min
1992: Netherlands 1,2 and 3, RTL4[†]	1h 26 min
Foreign	14 min
1993: Netherlands 1,2 and 3, RTL4 & RTL5[‡]	1h 27 min
Foreign	14 min

Source: NOS/KLO (1992b; 1994).
Notes: Channel viewing time was recorded between 6 p.m. and midnight for persons 6 years and older.
*Until March 1989, the figures for the category of 'foreign' also included watching videos. These figures have therefore been slightly adjusted on the basis of the relationship between the viewing times of the more refined categories devised after March 1989.
[†]Includes RTL4 from October 1989.
[‡]Includes RTL5 from October 1993.

The answers to these questions should provide relevant information for evaluating the increase in viewing time with respect to watching foreign channels. Furthermore, this information may also be important for policy issues, whether this concerns efforts by the public broadcasting companies to retain viewers or efforts from the cultural sector to preserve Dutch identity.

First, the increase in watching foreign television channels in the Netherlands across time is described. Next, we examine the kinds of people who watch foreign channels. For this purpose, a typology of viewers is constructed: those who exclusively watch Dutch channels, those who occasionally watch foreign channels, and those who watch foreign channels relatively often. These profiles may provide clues to help determine the motives people have for selecting foreign channels when watching television.

Unless stated otherwise, the data originate from a large scale study of media equipment, exposure and use in the Netherlands – MASSAT '89. This study consisted of a nation-wide survey of a random sample of 956 respondents (Arts *et al.*, 1990b) and an accompanying time budget study among 583 of the survey respondents during a week period (Arts *et al.*, 1990a). The data regarding viewing time of Dutch and foreign channels are from the time budget study; the other data come from the survey.

Findings

Absolute and relative viewing time of foreign channels

The first question is whether Dutch viewers actually watch foreign television channels more than sporadically and, if so, whether that behaviour is recent. Table 1 contains the viewing times per day for Dutch and foreign television channels between 6 p.m. and midnight during the last few years. It seems that the Dutch population has been consistently watching foreign television channels between 12 and 15 minutes per day, i.e. approximately one and a half hour per week, over the last few years.[5]

Table 2 contains the viewing time per week calculated on the basis of the MASSAT '89 time budget study for a number of channels clustered according to primary language used in broadcasts. The calculations in this study differ considerably from those performed by the Dutch broadcasting organization NOS/KLO. The data of these two studies are therefore not entirely comparable.[6] For this reason, the estimated total viewing time of foreign channels per week is approximately 15 minutes more than indicated by the NOS/KLO figures shown in Table 1. Furthermore, it appears that the Dutch population watches the Flemish television channel for 20 minutes per week on the average, which is hardly surprising. More significant is the fact that the Dutch population spends even more time watching English as well as German language channels (half an hour per week on each). By contrast, the Dutch population very seldom watches the French language channels.

Table 2. Weekly viewing time of Dutch and foreign channels

Channels	Viewing time
Netherlands 1, 2 and 3	11h 35 min
Foreign channels	1h 47 min
consisting of:	
English language channels[*]	30 min
German language channels[†]	31 min
French language channels[‡]	5 min
Flemish channels	20 min
Other channels	21 min

Source: MASSAT '89, n=583.
[*]BBC1 and 2, ITV, MTV, Sky Channel and Super Channel.
[†]Germany 1, 2 and 3. [‡]Belgium (French), France 1, 2 and 3, and TV5.

It appears, then, that Dutch viewers, on the average, attend to foreign television channels more than sporadically. However, watching foreign channels automatically involves attending to television in general. When studying the viewing behaviour with respect to

---

5   At first glance, recent NOS audience survey bulletins seem to reveal an alarming trend: the data of March 1992 show that the three Dutch television networks together had on average only a share of 55 per cent of the total viewing time. The remaining 45 per cent of viewing time was spent on foreign networks, including RTL4 (28 per cent) and watching videos (NOS/KLO, 1992:9). However, as already mentioned, we consider RTL4 to be a Dutch network (see also note 1, p. 109). From this view the share in viewing time of the Dutch networks amounts to 83 per cent.

6   The main differences include the following points: the data were collected for different times of the day (NOS: 18.00–24.00 hrs; MASSAT: 6.00–1.00 hrs), the data were collected in different periods of the year (NOS: January–December 1989; MASSAT: April 1989), the populations studied were different (NOS: aged 6 and older; MASSAT: aged 15 and older), and the measuring insruments were different (NOS: viewing meter; MASSAT: diary, activities categorised every 15 minutes).

foreign television channels this fact often causes problems. For instance, it may be argued that watching foreign television channels involves listening to foreign languages, thus suggesting a positive relation between watching foreign channels and the mastery of foreign languages. However, it may also be argued that watching foreign television channels presupposes watching television, which is know to be negatively related to educational level. Educational level, in turn, is positively related to the mastery of foreign languages. This line of argument suggests a negative relation between watching foreign channels and the mastery of foreign languages. In this instance, the interpretation of an observed statistical relation between the two concepts is difficult. One has to find a (statistical) way to disentangle the effects of the 'foreign' dimension from the effects of the 'watching television' dimension.

In the formulation of some questions this kind of problem can be avoided by using the relative share of foreign channels in the total viewing time instead of the absolute viewing time to foreign television channels. In this way, it is possible to concentrate on the question why some people, when they watch television, have a preference for foreign television channels whereas others stick to the Dutch channels. To answer this question we can use the relative portions of the foreign channels in the total viewing time. These portions are listed in Table 3. The channels are again clustered according to language.[7]

Table 3. Foreign channel viewing compared to total viewing time

Portion	English	German	French	Flemish	Other	Total
0%	77.6	71.4	92.6	73.7	86.3	42.2
≤5%	7.7	7.5	4.0	9.5	5.2	10.1
6–10%	4.5	8.6	0.9	9.8	3.3	11.6
11–15%	4.3	4.8	1.4	3.5	1.4	7.7
16–20%	0.8	3.6	0.0	1.0	2.0	6.2
21%	5.0	4.2	1.1	2.5	1.8	22.2

n=565

Some 42.2 per cent of the Dutch population does not watch any foreign channels. On the other hand, 22.2 per cent spends more than a fifth of the viewing time on foreign channels. French language and 'other' channels are the least popular, whereas English, German and Flemish language channels are the most popular. Approximately one of every four Dutch viewers watched one of these three groups of channels during the week of the time budget study.

Profile of foreign channel viewers

As already mentioned, many Dutch viewers spend a substantial part of their viewing time on watching foreign television channels. There are, however, differences regarding the

---

7   Some 18 respondents did not watch any television during the week that the time budget study took place. As we could not calculate their relative share of 'viewing time of foreign networks' in the total viewing time, they were left out of the remaining part of this study.

extent to which this happens. This leads to the rather obvious question: how and to what extent do viewers of foreign channels differ from those who only attend to Dutch channels. For this question, we constructed a profile of three categories of viewers: those who exclusively watch Dutch channels (N=238), those who moderately watch foreign channels (1-20 per cent of the total viewing time; N=202) and those who watch foreign channels relatively often (more than 20 per cent; N=125).

Table 4. Characteristics of (non-)viewers of foreign TV channels

	Mean scores relative viewing time, foreign TV				
	Non-viewing	Moderate viewing	Frequent viewing	Pop.	ETA
Age	38.6	38.2	37.9	38.3	n.s.
Household size	3.2	3.3	2.8	3.1	0.12
Household income	2.6	2.9	2.9	2.8	0.12
Professional status	42.9	45.5	45.2	44.4	n.s.
Passive language use	1.4	1.6	1.7	1.6	0.12
No. of receivable channels	8.0	10.1	10.3	9.3	0.32

	Percentage scores relative viewing time, foreign TV				
	Non-viewing	Moderate viewing	Frequent viewing	Pop	V
Sex: male	47.2	50.3	53.5	49.7	n.s.
Profession: white collar	57.7	59.2	59.0	58.6	n.s.
Higher education	56.0	48.1	55.1	53.0	n.s.
Cable TV system	68.3	83.6	90.1	78.6	0.22
Remote control device	50.3	65.2	61.1	57.9	0.14

n.s. = no significant correlation ($\alpha = 0.05$, two-tailed).
Notes: Age range: 15-72 years; Household size ranges from: 1-9 members; Household income ranges from: 1-5; household income is, strictly speaking, not measured at interval level, but because it is very near this level, we have nevertheless calculated averages scores.
Professional status is based on the professional codes of the Central Bureau of Statistics as used by Sixma & Ultee (1983) and ranges from 13 (low) to 87 (high);
Passive knowledge of language ranges from 0 to 3 and is the sumscore of the number of languages (English, French and German) reasonably well understood;
Range of the number of receivable TV channels: 0-16; Variables for which percentage scores have been calculated are all dichotomous.

As evident in Table 4, the three categories of viewers differ most regarding subscription to cable television and availability of remote control devices. Inasmuch as most foreign channels can only be received via the cable, the first difference is not surprising. Moreover, possession of remote control devices simplifies switching to other channels and thus also to foreign channels. Other significant differences are that frequent viewers of foreign channels live, on the average, in somewhat smaller households, and moderate and frequent viewers have slightly higher household income. Furthermore, viewers of foreign channels seem – not surprisingly – to have a better passive knowledge of foreign languages than those who exclusively watch Dutch channels.[8]

Most striking is that, on the whole, these three categories of viewers do not differ much in terms of demographic and socio-economic characteristics. Data from 1973, however, suggested that interest in more television channels was relatively strong among young people in the middle and higher occupational groups, among the higher educated, and among persons with higher incomes (NOS/KLO, 1975). One would expect that more than a decade later, in 1989, there would be an increase of viewers of foreign channels with these characteristics. Apart from a slight increase in viewers in the higher income brackets, this is not the case. If watching foreign channels was ever an occupation of a socio-economic elite, then this is apparently no longer so.

Given the issues sketched at the beginning of this chapter, the questions related to several subjective characteristics of foreign channel viewers are particularly interesting. One of these questions is whether foreign channel viewers are characterized by a somewhat broader spatial orientation. In other words, the question is whether a relative preference for foreign channels also implies a greater interest in or appreciation of events outside the viewers' immediate social environment. To gain insight into this, the three categories were compared on scales widely used in the social sciences regarding orientations of people towards themselves and their immediate social environment or towards the world at large.[9] For example, the scales of 'family attitudes' and 'social criticism' give an indication of the extent to which people are concerned with marriage, family and children, and societal change (Felling et al., 1987:273-275). The scales of 'personal matters' and 'worldly matters' provide an indication of the extent in which people worry about matters related to themselves and their immediate social environment, and society at large (Arts et al., 1990b:286-288). The scales of 'social localism' and 'cultural localism' indicate the extent to which people identify themselves with their immediate local environment and to which they appreciate living in a small community (Eisinga & Peters, 1989). The scale of 'political interest' indicates to what extent people keep informed about politics and find this important (Arts et al., 1990b:280). Finally, the 'range of interest' scale provides indication of the extent to which people are interested in information about geographically distant areas.[10]

8   The correlation between knowledge of language and watching foreign channels was even more pronounced in analyses for the separate language areas (English and German language channels separately; the French language channels werenot included because they were not watched sufficiently).

9   Also, on the basis of the items which constitute these scales, we presuppose that these scales give some indication of people's spatial orientation. This does not alter the fact that most of the scales are meant to measure something else than spatial orientation. The results must therefore be interpreted with great caution.

10 This scale was constructed by means of the scores on six items that measure interest in information about the neighbourhood, city, region, country at large, Europe, and the rest of the world. We summed the scores of the last three items and subsequently deducted the scores of the first three items. We finally calculated Z scores for the resulting scale (as well as for the other scales in Table 5).

Table 5 contains the mean scores of non-viewers, moderate viewers and frequent viewers of foreign channels on these scales. Watching foreign channels does not correlate with any of the scales. Although we have some reservations with respect to the weak operationalization of this concept (see also note 4), there does not seem to be any connection between the relative preference for foreign channels and viewers' orientation towards matters and events that happen outside their immediate social environment.

Table 5. Spatial orientations of (non-)viewers of foreign TV channels

	Mean scores relative viewing time foreign TV				
	Non-viewing	Moderate viewing	Frequent viewing	Pop.	ETA
Scales:					
Familial values	0.00	0.07	–0.12	0.00	n.s.
Personal matters	–0.02	–0.05	0.13	0.00	n.s.
Social localism	–0.00	0.03	–0.05	0.00	n.s.
Cultural localism	0.01	0.02	–0.05	0.00	n.s.
Social criticism	0.06	–0.04	–0.05	0.00	n.s.
Worldly matters	–0.06	0.04	0.06	0.00	n.s.
Range of interest	–0.05	0.02	0.06	0.00	n.s.
Political interest	0.04	–0.02	–0.06	0.00	n.s.

n.s. = no significant correlation ($\alpha = 0.05$, two-tailed).

Let us now examine the thematic orientation of the three categories of viewers. The question is whether a relative preference for foreign channels also implies an interest in certain subjects highlighted by these channels. First, we examine possible correlations between watching foreign channels and information interests in a large number of subjects; see Table 6.

Table 6. Information interests of (non-)viewers of foreign TV channels

	Mean scores relative viewing time foreign TV				
	Non-viewing	Moderate viewing	Frequent viewing	Pop.	ETA
Subject of interest:					
Relations/partner/familty	1.9	1.8	1.7	1.8	0.11
Agriculture/fishing	1.5	1.3	1.3	1.4	0.17
Religion/philosophy of life	1.9	1.6	1.6	1.7	0.17
Developments outside Netherlands	1.7	1.8	1.9	1.8	0.12
Sports events	1.9	2.2	2.3	2.1	0.18

n.s. = no significant correlation ($\alpha = 0.05$, two-tailed). Note: No significant linear correlations were found with watching foreign channels for the other 34 subjects.

Only for 5 of the 39 subjects is a linear correlation[11] present between preference for foreign channels and a subject. Furthermore, the correlations with 'relations, partner, family' and 'developments outside the Netherlands' are very weak. The finding that relative frequent viewers of foreign channels are, on the average, slightly more interested in information about developments outside the Netherlands is in contrast with findings in Table 5. This correlation is, however, so weak that we cannot draw any conclusions from it.

When we look at the somewhat stronger correlations we notice that there is a relatively large interest in 'sports events/results' among moderate and frequent viewers of foreign channels. Finally, we see that the same categories have relatively little interest in 'religion, philosophy of life' and 'agriculture, fishing'. With respect to the latter it should be mentioned that other audience survey findings (NOS/KLO, 1975) on the interest among viewers for expansion of television reception suggest that farmers, market gardeners and agricultural workers showed the least interest for such expansion. This might at least partially explain the relatively large interest in the subject 'agriculture, fishing' among non-viewers of foreign channels.

Apart from the possible correlations between the relative preference for foreign channels and information interests, we also examined the possible correlations with viewing behaviour in relation to certain programmes; see Table 7.

Table 7. programme selection by (non-)viewers of foreign TV channels

	Mean scores relative viewing time foreign TV				
	Non-viewing	Moderate viewing	Frequent viewing	Pop.	ETA
Programme types					
Dutch series	2.3	2.3	2.2	2.2	n.s.
Foreign series	2.3	2.6	2.5	2.5	n.s.
Arts/classical music	1.7	1.5	1.6	1.6	n.s.
Films	2.6	3.1	3.2	2.9	0.21
Info/consumer/hobby	2.5	2.8	2.6	2.6	0.11
Documentaries	2.5	2.6	2.7	2.6	n.s.
Sports programmes	2.4	3.1	3.0	2.8	0.22
Quizzes/game shows	2.3	2.5	2.1	2.3	0.12
Religious programmes	1.5	1.3	1.3	1.4	0.12
Children's programmes	1.7	1.9	1.7	1.8	0.10
Talk shows/discussion programmes	2.4	2.5	2.2	2.4	n.s.
Natural history	2.7	2.7	2.8	2.7	n.s.
Courses (Open University, etc.)	1.3	1.4	1.4	1.4	0.11
Scientific/medical programme	2.4	2.6	2.4	2.5	n.s.
Pop music programmes	1.8	2.0	1.9	1.9	n.s.

n.s. = no significant correlation ($\alpha = 0.5$, two-tailed).

---

11 For one topic (burglary and vandalism in the city, local well-known people, accidents') we found a weak, but significant, curvilinear correlation.

111

A preference for foreign channels correlates with about half of the programme preferences. However, most of the correlations are rather weak. Most striking is the rather strong preference for films and sports programmes among moderate and frequent viewers of foreign channels. The latter is in line with the findings of a NOS/KLO (1992b:17) survey: 'the audiences watching foreign channels are especially interested in entertainment programmes such as sports programmes, shows and films.' For example, many people in the Netherlands watch 'Die Sportschau' on one of the German channels.

Conclusions

In the introduction to this chapter we referred to a discussion which implicitly presupposed a relation between watching foreign television programmes and viewers' orientations. Watching foreign television might undercut the national 'cultural identity' or, put differently, might help to educate people and prepare them for 'world citizenship.' The limited results of this study do not point to a connection between watching foreign television channels and any form of such 'spatial orientation.' On the contrary, watching foreign channels seems to be a case of availability, general interest and programme preferences. It should be noted that only weak correlations were found. One possible explanation for this might be the following: if we take all foreign channels into account, regardless of the differences in programme supply, we get a complex which in terms of programme supply probably does not differ much from what the Dutch channels on average supply viewers. This makes it less likely deviating interests will be found or programme preferences among these viewers.

Given this, further research should consider viewing patterns of specific channels which have different programme content – e.g. sports, music and information channels. To gain an impression of the possibilities of such an approach, we analysed some of the MASSAT time budget data in relation to use of the Music Television channel (MTV). Given that only 18 respondents had watched MTV during the week of reporting, the results can only suggest possible differences. MTV viewers turned out to be, on the average, more than 15 years younger than the average age of all television viewers, and had a more than average preference for foreign series, films and – of course – pop music programmes. The profile of the MTV viewer seemed more clearly delineated than that of the viewer of foreign channels.

Subsequent research should examine further correlations between interests and watching certain channels, not only in terms of viewership profiles, but also through multivariate analysis. In this way, by eliminating the influence of extraneous variables (e.g. age) one may assess to what extent interest in a given subject (e.g. pop music) can indeed be a motive for watching a certain channel (e.g. MTV).

9 Viewership of information-oriented TV programmes

Leo Van Snippenburg

Taking Bourdieu's (1984/1979) three dimensional model of social inequality and the uses and gratifications approach to media use as points of departure, hypotheses are formulated relating demographic variables and predisposition towards television to the use of information-oriented programmes. Results suggest that income and age have positive, and education and membership of associations negative, effects on watching information-oriented programmes. The subjective factor 'information gratification' has a relatively strong positive effect on watching these programmes. It thereby hardly acts as an intermediary factor between the objective social position and viewers' exposure to programmes, i.e. it is an independent predictor of watching information-oriented programmes. General affinity for television and specific television programme preference also appear to have positive effects on watching information-oriented programmes. To some extent, however, these two subjective variables mediate the influence of objective social position, particularly education, on the dependent variable.

The dissemination of knowledge has a high priority in the politics of Western welfare states. Broadcasting information-oriented programmes appears to be an important tool for this objective. Television is, after all, a widespread and accessible medium, and information-oriented programmes basically reach all levels of the population. However, it is clear from much previous research that broadcasting such programmes does not necessarily lead to a situation in which all categories of viewers actually watch them. Moreover, it remains to be seen whether the categories of viewers who do watch will process the information offered in the manner intended. More information on television might just as well enlarge the existing social inequalities with respect to level of knowledge.

A possible difference between socio-economic classes in exposure to informational media content was one of the considerations which led to the formulation of the knowledge gap hypothesis. Other considerations concerned selective acceptance and retention. According to an early version of this hypothesis, an increase in the dissemination of information in society by means of mass media would enlarge instead of reduce the existing gap in knowledge between lower and higher socio-economic classes (Tichenor *et al.*, 1970:159-160). Attempts to test the knowledge gap hypothesis[1] showed contradictory results (Gaziano, 1983). And also for the opposite situation, i.e. increase in media information leading to a reduction of the knowledge gap, insufficient empirical support could be found.

These and similar considerations concerning social determinants of media use bring into question the extent need for, and the actual watching of, general information-oriented programmes are determined by social background. This is the focus of the research presented here. The theoretical model underlying the research is mainly based on Bourdieu's theory of social inequality (Bourdieu, 1984/1979). Notions from the uses and gratifications approach are also incorporated in order to provide the model with a broader conceptual basis. Empirical research was conducted on the basis of data from the nation-wide MASSAT '89 survey, a project of the Institute of Mass Communication at the University of Nijmegen in the Netherlands.

Three dimensions of social inequality

According to Bourdieu (1984/1979), regular behaviour patterns which distinguish people (their life styles) are to a large extent based on the possibilities and limitations inherent in their social position (see also Weber's (1987/1922) notion of 'life chances'). Bourdieu distinguishes three dimensions in the social structure: an economic, cultural and social dimension. He uses the term 'capital' for the possibilities, chances or resources that people have as a result of their position on each of these three dimensions. The nature of this capital differs in accordance with the dimension to which it pertains. The term 'capital' in this sense, therefore, denotes more than just material possibilities such as income and access to means of production. The extent to which one has these specific material forms of capital is entirely related to one's position on the economic dimension. Possibilities related to position on the cultural dimension constitute cultural capital. This last form of capital consists of all the cognitive skills acquired during one's childhood and youth, i.e. during the years of formal education, and the knowledge and wisdom acquired during the remaining lifetime. The position on the social dimension determines to what extent a person has so-called social capital. Social capital is related to the quality of the social networks to which one belongs.

---

1   In later versions of the hypothesis, and particularly in attempts to test it empirically, more precise formulations emerged. Additional specifications concerned aspects such as the type of mass medium (e.g. print media), the type of information (e.g. social *vs* scientific information) and the socio-political situation (e.g. conflict situation *vs* circumstances of social stability).

The three types of capital are used – invested – in everyday life particularly to maintain or improve one's societal position. Capital is invested to gain profit, analogous to investments in the production sector. Thus, people who already own a certain amount of cultural capital will be the ones who particularly benefit from watching information-oriented programmes. They can process and possibly use the information to maintain or improve their economic, cultural or social capital.[2]

Social position and viewing information-oriented programmes

On the basis of Bourdieu's theory of social inequality and the notion that income, education and age are relevant elements of the economic and cultural dimension, some basic assumptions can be formulated as to the effects of these factors on the frequency of watching information-oriented programmes. The third dimension, social inequality, is also included in this study. Bourdieu (1984/1979) is rather vague about the meaning of this dimension. He points to, among other things, the potential sources that relate to the nature of the social networks and also to the average economic or cultural capital of the circle in which one operates. The present study is mainly focused on the first aspect, i.e. the nature of the social networks, in order to examine to what extent the effects of the social dimension are essentially different from the two other dimensions.[3] In this study, the social dimension is considered the involvement in social networks existing outside the primary circle of family and friends as well as outside the real economic sphere; namely, involvement through membership in formal associations.

Regarding possible effects of education, age, income and membership of associations on watching information-oriented programmes, a number of comments should be made. In general, people with a higher level of education (more cultural capital in Bourdieu's terms) sooner turn to informational media content than people with a lower level of education because they are intellectually better equipped. It is also of greater importance for enlarging their cultural capital because this will provide them with better opportunities to rise up the social ladder than less educated persons. The latter are more interested in the training and perfection of skills needed for routine tasks and activities. In addition, higher educated people generally belong to status groups in which cultural capital and the expansion thereof is appreciated. Thus, they can gain more respect within these groups. These considerations lead to the expectation that higher educated persons will enjoy

2   Bourdieu's approach to social inequality is closely related to that of Weber and neo-Weberian theories (see Kerstholt, 1989), but also shows some essential differences. In Bourdieu's approach the political dimension is lacking and Weber's symbolic dimension is divided into a cultural and social dimension.

3   Note that the cultural and economic capital of the people with whom a person maintains a primary relation are usually on the level as those of the person concerned. This is because the status of friends and acquaintances are largely determined by one's own social status (see Jackman & Jackman, 1973). In general, the average status of acquaintances will therefore not contribute much to the explanation of behaviour patterns which are already explained by status characteristics of the person concerned. This seems to justify the conceptualization of social capital within the framework of the present study.

watching information-oriented programmes more than those with less education and that they will therefore also choose to watch such programmes more often.[4]

As people age they gradually acquire more general knowledge as a result of experience and further intellectual maturity. The cultural capital thus acquired broadens the cognitive basis and improves capacity to process information. Older people will therefore find more satisfaction in watching information-oriented programmes than young people.[5] It may therefore be expected that they will show a higher frequency of watching such programmes, independent of the average differences in educational levels between younger and older people.[6]

Maslow suggests that human needs are hierarchically structured. The more the basic needs (i.e. needs for physical safety and security) are satisfied, the more people will strive to satisfy higher needs, so-called 'growth needs'. Such higher needs are particularly related to further social and mental development (Miller & Buckhout, 1973:424-428). If it is assumed that satisfaction of elementary physical needs is more assured with an increase in income, then it should be expected that the higher income groups will generally have a stronger need for various information (to stimulate intellectual development) than lower income groups. It may therefore be expected that people with a higher income will receive more satisfaction from watching information-oriented programmes than those with a lower income. Further, it can be assumed that persons with a higher income will watch these programmes more often, independent of the differences in educational levels between higher and lower income groups.

Being a member of a social (formal) network outside the circle of family and friends may also contribute to the development of a broader range of interests. In such a network people have a better chance of meeting people who have other interests and come from other subcultures. People also find it easier to be a member of such a network if they can join in the conversation and are able to talk about a variety of subjects. This may stimulate their need to broaden their intellectual horizons even further. It is therefore expected that membership of associations will increase the satisfaction derived from watching information-oriented programmes and will consequently stimulate people to watch such programmes more often. Again, this is expected to be independent of possible connections between membership of associations, level of education, age and income.

These considerations about the factors underlying the effects of education, age, income and membership of associations on watching information-oriented programmes can be formulated as a research hypothesis as follows: *education, age, income and membership*

---

4   It should be mentioned that Verwey's (1986b:152) empirical analysis showed a positive effect of education on information interest. However, he did not interpret this effect in theoretical terms.

5   In some cases this may also be because older people try to uphold their reputation of knowing and understanding more of the world than younger generations.

6   Verwey (1986b:152) also found positive (partial) effects of age on information interest and watching current affairs programmes. These effects were not interpreted in theoretical terms.

of associations have independent positive effects on watching information-oriented tele-vision programmes.

Regarding the effects of income and education on television viewing, testing of this hypothesis may be particularly important for the knowledge gap hypothesis. Should positive effects be found, it will confirm that members of the higher socio-economic strata watch information-oriented programmes more frequently. This might be one of the reasons for a possible widening of the knowledge gap between the socio-economic strata in societies in which more and more information-oriented programmes are broadcast. Furthermore, empirical testing of the hypothesis may provide insight into the relationships between social inequality and watching information-oriented programmes, and allow assessment of the applicability of Bourdieu's inequality model to viewing behaviour.

Gratification and watching information-oriented programmes

It has been suggested above that education, age, income and membership of associations influence the general need for information and therefore also the gratification gained from watching information-oriented programmes. This statement actually represents introduction of the uses and gratifications approach into the overall conceptual model. This approach is based on the assumption that exposure to media content can particularly be explained by the fact that people seek gratification of certain needs (see Rubin, 1984; Renckstorf & Nelissen, 1989). In this case it involves gratification of the need to expand one's knowledge which watching information-oriented programmes may provide. In the model as presently formulated, the gratification motive does not play a crucial role. It only functions as an intermediary factor between social position and viewing information-oriented programmes. The uses and gratifications approach, however, does not regard the gratification motive as an intermediary variable. It considers seeking gratification as an important motive as such, usually leaving aside the objective position of the one who is to be gratified, as a possible determinant of it.[7] In this research the purpose is to specifically explore the role of the gratification variable between social position and exposure. The purpose may be formulated as a formal research question as follows: *to what extent is watching information-oriented television programmes determined by the gratification motive, and to what extent does this motive play an intermediary role?* To answer this question, the variable 'gratification from television information' is introduced into the research model. Insofar as it contributes to the explanation of the variation in watching information-oriented programmes, it is expected that the relation will be positive, i.e. the larger the gratification, the more frequently the specific viewing behaviour will occur.

Regarding the effects of the objective position on the gratification motive, the previous discussion of the effects of social position on watching information-oriented programmes make clear that positive effects are anticipated. This leads to the following hypothesis: *a*

---

7   There are, of course, authors who apply the uses and gratifications approach in a less restricted way. Blumler *et al.* (1985:260), for example, point out that media gratifications are also related to people's social position.

117

higher level of education, older age, more income and membership of associations lead to more gratification from watching information-oriented television programmes.

Data and operationizations

Data from the Dutch MASSAT '89 survey were used for this study. This material was collected in the first half of 1989 by the Institute of Mass Communication at the University of Nijmegen in the Netherlands. The survey involved standardized interviews with a random sample of Dutch residents between the ages of 16 and 73. Data were collected from 956 respondents. After checking combinations of the characteristics 'gender,' 'age group,' 'civil status' and 'degree of urbanization,' the sample was considered a reasonable representation of the national population for these characteristics. A brief description of the measurement scales used and other operationalizations is provided below; further information about the followed procedures can be found in Arts *et al.* (1990b).

Frequency of watching information-oriented programmes was determined by a Likert scale consisting of seven items concerning respondents' viewing habits of documentaries, current affairs programmes, scientific and medical programmes, hobby and consumer programmes, natural history programmes, talk shows/discussion programmes and news-casts. Prior to scale construction, a factor analysis helped determine whether these items could indeed be considered parts of a unidimensional concept. The criterion was satisfied (Cronbach's alpha = 0.73)

Gratification from television information was determined by a three-item Likert scale through which respondents could indicate to what extent 'being informed about various subjects,' 'being informed about important events in their social environment' and 'keeping in touch with what goes on in the world' were motives for them to watch television. Again, prior to scale construction a factor analysis was conducted to determine whether the items could be considered parts of a unidimensional concept. Again, this proved to be the case (Cronbach's alpha = 0.68).

Level of education was determined by constructing an index ranging from the lowest to highest form of education completed. Household income was measured as net monthly income, with five categories ranging from less than Fl. 1,500 to more than Fl. 5,000. Membership of associations was measured as the total number of associations to which a respondent was a member. The skewed distribution of responses on this variable was normalized by collapsing the higher categories, resulting in a scale ranging from 0 to 5.[8]

Results

Multiple regression analysis was conducted to test the hypotheses formulated about the effects of the social position characteristics on the gratification motive, and of both of these aspects on the frequency of watching information-oriented programmes. This

---

8   To decrease uncertainty about the validity of the findings, analyses were conducted with the skewed and normalized variables. The results of both analyses did not differ substantially.

technique allowed estimation of the direct effects, i.e. the effects of each of the independent variables controlling for all other independent variables in the model. Missing data were handled according to the procedure of 'listwise deletion' (see Nie *et al.*, 1975:283). In this manner, the number of units for analysis was reduced to 762.

Table 1 indicates the results of the regression of frequency of watching information-oriented programmes on education, age, income, membership of associations and gratification from television-based information. The first column contains the non-standardized coefficients 'b' of the regression equation with only the social position characteristics as independent variables. The *t*-values are listed in brackets next to the coefficients. A *t*-value larger than 2 or smaller than –2 (depending on the sign of the effect predicted by the hypothesis) means that the coefficient concerned is significant (one-sided test, alpha 0.025).

The effects of age and income on watching information-oriented programmes are significant and have signs as were predicted by the hypothesis concerned.[9] These findings support this research hypothesis. This is, however, not the case with the effects of education and membership of associations on watching information-oriented programmes. Both variables appear to have negative effects instead of the expected positive effects. Possible interpretations of these deviating findings, as well as additional analyses for empirically supporting the alternative interpretations, are discussed later.

Continuing examination of the findings in Table 1, the amount of explained variance in the basic model is rather small ($r^2 = 0.091$). The social position variables selected according to Bourdieu's and Maslow's theoretical notions do not appear to have much explanatory power, although the effects cannot be neglected.

Table 1. Frequency of viewing information-oriented TV programmes and respondent characteristics

	b*	β*	b	β
Education	−0.64 (−3.9)[†]	−0.12	−0.81 (−4.6)	−0.15
Age	0.09 (6.8)	0.24	0.07 (6.1)	0.20
Income	0.57 (3.3)	0.12	0.56 (3.6)	0.12
Membership associations	−0.39 (−2.4)	−0.08	−0.36 (−2.4)	−0.08
Gratification TV info			1.11 (12.6)	0.40
Intercept	18.90 (18.5)		7.29 (5.6)	
R^2		0.091		0.249

n = 762;
*non-standardized coefficients are listed in column 'b'; standardized coefficients are listed in column β.
[†]*t*-values of the coefficients are in brackets. An absolute t-value larger than 2 indicates a significant effect (one-sided test, α < 0.025).

9   In many studies, the relations between age and (reported) behaviour variables appear to be curvilinear. The presently applied regression technique assumes linearity of relations. To check whether the assumption of linearity was plausible with respect to the effects of age, polynomial regression was performed on all models. The added polynomial terms were not significant. In other words, the assumption of linearity with respect to the effects of age in the present study can be considered as plausible.

119

The second column of Table 1 contains the standardized regression coefficients (beta) of the social position variables. These coefficients can be regarded as the expression of the relative importance of these variables in predicting the frequency of watching information-oriented programmes (in relation to the other predictors in the model and within the research population concerned. It is clear that age is the most important predictor. In terms of the theoretical model, this means that it is particularly the knowledge cumulatively acquired during one's lifetime which leads to watching information-oriented television programmes, as opposed to knowledge acquired in formal education. The negative coefficient of education shows that this variable leads to a lower frequency of watching information-oriented programmes. Education which contributes to exposure to informational content will probably manifest itself by exposure to other media. Further research on, for example, reading of information-oriented books and articles may provide evidence for this possibility.

The third column in Table 1 contains the non-standardized coefficients 'b' of the regression model with the social position characteristics and gratification from television-based information as predictors of frequency of watching information-oriented programmes. Comparing these coefficients with those in column 1 (comparing the basic model to the model incorporating the independent variable 'gratification from television-based information') is a good method to ascertain to what extent and in which way the subjective characteristic 'gratification from television-based information' influences watching information-oriented programmes. The amount of explained variance (0.249) of watching information-oriented programmes increases considerably by incorporating this subjective factor in the model.

Furthermore, the direct effects of the objective social characteristics do not change substantially. This not only means that gratification from television-based information contributes much to the explanation of variance in watching information-oriented programmes, but also that this contribution is almost entirely independent of the other predictors in the model. In other words, gratification from television-based information only plays a minor intermediary role between the objective factors and viewing frequency. The importance of gratification from television-based information in explaining viewing behaviour with respect to information-oriented programmes also becomes evident when we compare the standardized coefficients (beta) in column 4. The coefficient of this variable has a far greater value than the coefficients of the other predictors, including the coefficient of age. Incorporation of the uses and gratifications component in the model is therefore much more than simply a supplement to explaining the watching of information-oriented programmes; it is, in fact, the central predictor.

To further illustrate the independent role of the gratification from television-based information variable in the model, the coefficients were estimated of a model with this variable as a dependent variable and the social position characteristics as independent variables. The estimates are shown in Table 2. The explained variance of only 1.4 per cent reveals that the subjective characteristic 'gratification from television-based information' is hardly dependent on the objective characteristics. Education and age do have effects with the predicted signs, but these are barely significant. The effects of income and membership of associations are not even significant and therefore of negligible value in the model.

The findings in Table 2 indicate that the social inequality approach is not very productive when studying the degree of gratification related to watching information-oriented programmes. Possibly, stronger explanatory factors of this gratification can be found in the characteristics of the primary groups (communities) people belong to, in their value orientation and in their specific life histories. Further research may focus on these aspects. Such matters fall outside the scope of this study, however, inasmuch as it was not designed to explain gratification from television-based information.

Table 2. Gratification from TV-based information and respondent characteristics

	b*	β*
Education	0.15 (2.0)[†]	0.08
Age	0.02 (2.9)	0.11
Income	0.01 (0.1)	0.01
Membership associations	−0.03 (−0.06)	−0.02
Intercept	10.52 (18.5)	
R^2		0.014

n=762. *non-standardized coefficients are listed in column 'b'; standardized coefficients are listed in column 'beta.'[†]*t*-values of the coefficients are in brackets. An absolute *t*-value larger than 2 indicates a significant effect (one-sided test, alpha 0.025).

Returning to Table 1, the level of education and membership of associations seem to decrease instead of increase the frequency of watching information-oriented programmes. This does not necessarily mean that the higher educated and members of associations have a tendency to expose themselves less to information-oriented media content. It may well mean that they are not quite so involved with television, that this medium is not their major source of information.[10]

Other data in the survey allow exploration of this possibility. Affinity for television in general (variable 'television affinity') was measured as well as the extent to which respondents prefer television to other (media) communication forms as sources of information on a variety of topics (variable 'TV-info source'). These data may help to determine to what extent affinity for television and television as a source for information play a role in the negative effect of education, and of membership of associations, on watching information-oriented programmes.

The variable 'television affinity' was constructed as a Likert scale consisting of four items by which respondents could indicate to what extent they considered television viewing as

---

10 The negative effect of membership of associations might be, at least partially, caused by the fact that such memberships demand considerable time, so that respondents do not have much additional time to watch information-oriented programmes. This possibility could not be tested with the available data, however.

'important,' 'enjoyable' and 'difficult to do without'.[11] The variable 'TV-info source' was operationalized by the relative number of times that respondents selected the alternative 'television' when asked which source was most useful to them when they wanted information on specific topics. A total of thirty topics were presented. Among those on the list were: health and illness, hobbies, politics, economics, theatre and concerts. The respondents could indicate for each of the thirty topics whether they found radio, television, newspapers, conversations or books and magazines most useful.[12]

Three regression analyses were performed in order to determine the extent to which negative effects of education and membership of associations on frequency of watching information-oriented programmes are mediated by the subjective characteristics 'television affinity' and 'TV-info source.' In the first analysis, only television affinity was incorporated in the regression model as an independent variable. In the second, only TV-info source was incorporated as such. In the final analysis both television affinity and TV-info source were included. The results of the three regressions are shown in Table 3.

Table 3. Viewing frequency of information-oriented TV programmes and respondent characteristics

	b*	b	b
Education	−0.55(−3.0)[†]	−0.60 (−3.1)	−0.46 (−2.4)
Age	0.07 (6.2)	0.08 (6.0)	0.08 (6.0)
Income	0.58 (3.8)	0.47 (3.0)	0.47 (3.0)
Membership associations	−0.31 (−2.1)	−0.38(−2.5)	−0.35 (−2.4)
Gratification TV info	1.05 (12.0)	0.98 (10.0)	0.95 (9.8)
TV affinity	0.37 (5.3)		0.25 (3.4)
TV info source		6.50 (6.7)	5.71 (5.8)
Intercept	4.04 (2.8)	6.26 (4.4)	4.30 (2.8)
R^2	0.277	0.295	0.307

n=762. *non-standardized coefficients. [†]t-values of the coefficients are in brackets. An absolute t-value larger than 2 indicates a significant effect (one-sided test, alpha 0.025).

Table 3 suggests that television affinity and TV-info source have significant positive effects on watching information-oriented programmes in all of the models analyzed. If the non-standardized coefficients in the third column of Table 1 (model without television affinity and TV-info source) are compared with those in the first column of Table 3 (television affinity incorporated in the model), it appears that the coefficient of education has become weaker (from −0.81 to −0.55), due to the incorporation of the independent

---

11 Also, previous to this scale construction, factor analysis was performed in order to determine whether the items could be considered representatives of a unidimensional concept. This was ascertained; Cronbach's alpha = 0.76.

12 The categories 'don't know' and 'not interested' were also included. For more information, see Arts *et al.* (1990b).

television affinity variable.[13] This means that the negative effect of education on watching information-oriented programmes proceeds, at least partly, via a negative effect of education on television affinity and a relatively strong positive effect of the latter on viewing behaviour (0.37; see Table 3, column 1).

If the second column of Table 3 is compared with the third column of Table 1, we see that the same conclusion can be drawn with respect to TV-info source. This characteristic also appears to intermediate part of the negative effect of education on watching information-oriented programmes via a negative effect of education on TV-info source and a positive effect of TV-info source on watching information-oriented programmes (6.50; notice that this large figure is the result of the relatively small range of the variable 'TV-info source' which was measured as a proportion).

The last column of Table 3 shows what happens when television affinity and TV-info source are both incorporated in the model. The coefficients do not change much more. The effect of education is, for example, only slightly lower than that in which only television affinity was incorporated. The coefficients of the other variables hardly change. From this it may be concluded that television affinity and TV-info source are characteristics which partly stand for the same thing. They both measure 'involvement with television'; television affinity in a more general way and TV-info source more specifically in relation to information.

Further empirical exploration of the negative effect of education on the frequency of watching information-oriented programmes is possible by incorporating other relevant intermediary (subjective) factors. However, the original findings concerning the total (gross) effect of education on viewing frequency will not be affected by this: the total effect remains negative. It may, however, help to reveal the ways in which this negative effect comes into being.

Conclusions

The hypothesis regarding the relations between socio-structural characteristics and watching information-oriented television programmes was only confirmed regarding the positive effects of age and income. The findings contradicted the expected positive effects of education and membership of associations. These proved to be significantly negative. As for the second part of the formulated problem, i.e. the question about the possible intermediary role of the subjective factor 'gratification from television-based information,' it plays a very important, but hardly an intermediary role. It contributes independently to watching information-oriented programmes. This contribution is strong and positive, as was assumed theoretically.

---

13 The coefficient of membership of associations was also somewhat weaker. However, the difference was so small that it could be justifiably neglected. It may be interpreted in a way analogous to the interpretation of the reduced effect of education.

In the previous section, possible interpretations for unexpected results were discussed, additional analyses performed and suggestions for further research presented. In this section, the findings will be placed in a somewhat broader context. First, the over-simplified way in which the notion of 'social class' is often used (or vague variants such as 'socio-economic strata' and 'status group') in formulations of the knowledge gap hypothesis is discussed. Next, some speculations are made about possible consequences of the findings for the knowledge gap hypothesis.

The results show that statements about the relation between socio-economic position (social class) and media exposure – in our case watching information-oriented programmes – are often imprecise and over-simplified. Several aspects of social class can be distinguished and placed on multiple dimensions. This may seem a superfluous observation, but in actuality it is not. Take, for example, the notion of 'social class' as well as many of its variations, often formulated in general terms regarding the knowledge gap hypothesis. This study shows that education and income as aspects of the socio-economic position have opposite effects on watching information-oriented programmes. This indicates, once again, that education (cultural dimension) and income (economic dimension), although they are often empirically connected, are essentially different characteristics which cannot simply be combined in a theoretically and analytically vague notion such as 'social class' (see also Ganzeboom *et al.*, 1987).

With respect to the knowledge gap hypothesis, the findings concerning the effects of education and income on watching information-oriented programmes lead to the following consideration. Insofar as frequency of television viewing is important in relation to this hypothesis, an increase in the number of information-oriented programmes might widen the knowledge gap between people with higher and those with lower incomes, but not between people with higher and those with lower levels of education. This is because income has a positive and education a negative effect on frequency of watching information-oriented television programmes.

The knowledge gap between people with higher and lower levels of education might even become smaller when more information-oriented programmes are broadcast. Especially when we take into consideration the prevailing opinion that the higher educated are more capable of processing complex material than the lower educated, it may be less relevant for watching information-oriented programmes. Generally, the presentation of subject matter in television programmes is not very complex. Practically all information in Dutch television programmes is provided in a rather popularized form.[14] The lower educated are generally quite capable of processing such content. From this perspective, the results of this study indicate that information-oriented television programmes may be sources of knowledge for the less educated which should not be neglected, and that these programmes

---

14 It may be that higher educated people watch less information-oriented programmes has much to do with this aspect. Perhaps the popular mode of presentation of many programmes does not form a cognitive challenge for them.

can be important in reducing the knowledge gap between people with higher and those with lower levels of education.

But, as already mentioned, watching information-oriented programmes does not say anything about the 'success' of the communication (see Fauconnier 1990:23-25), in this case the transfer of knowledge. Differences in interpretation and retention of programme content by people with different incomes or levels of education also play a role here. These processes first need to be studied before more can be said about a possible reduction of the knowledge gap between people with different levels of education as a result of watching information-oriented television programmes.

10 Issue involvement and viewing TV news

Niek Hietbrink

In communication research the motivation by the public for viewing television news is often measured in terms of gratifications. Recent theoretical and empirical work has shown that people have different information needs on specific issues rather than a general need for information. Instead of using the 'information need' gratification to predict information use, it might be more useful to measure and use the personal relevance of issues as a concept in audience research. In this study personal relevance is conceptualized as 'issue involvement'. The purpose of this exploratory study is two-fold. First, the relationships between the audience's involvement in a number of typical news issues and their television news viewing activities are assessed. Second, the relationship between the audience's issue involvement profile and the gratifications they derive from watching tv news are examined. The results of this investigation suggest that the concept of issue involvement can be applied to describe and predict audience activities in more detail. Furthermore, it seems that people who are involved in issues like politics and pollution focus more on the informational dimensions of news, whereas people who are involved in crime news and disasters watch news in a more diversionary manner.

In the Netherlands, 57 per cent of the population state that the Dutch public broadcasting newscast, *NOS journal*, is their most important news source (Peeters, 1990). In another recent study in the Netherlands, 66 per cent of the respondents claim to view the *NOS journal* seven days a week (Arts *et al.*, 1990b). But in spite of the great popularity of news programmes, there is still relatively little insight as to the motivations people have for watching news.

Theoretical background

Engaging in news viewing activities is one of a variety of actions an individual can initiate in order to relate to the outside world. As Dahlgren (1988) points out, there is more to watching news than just the transfer of news or information from communicator to receiver. If we consider watching news as a form of human action, we may gain insight into how people plan and evaluate their news viewing activity. According to the social action perspective (Bosman *et al.*, 1989; Anderson & Meyer, 1988), people act upon their environment according to their subjective image of reality. More specifically, the structuring elements of the individual's image of reality are her/his own goals, motives and relevance structures (Schütz, 1970). Another central theme of the social action perspective is the importance of interpretive processes in human action. Both of these aspects are addressed in this study.

Changing conceptions of audience activity

In recent years, conceptualization of the mass media audience has changed considerably (see e.g. Chaffee & Roser, 1986). In early research, the mass media audience was thought to be a passive target of media messages. Exposure to mass media was considered sufficient to elicit media effects. Later, in uses and gratifications research, researchers took the opposite viewpoint, presuming that audience members are purposefully active in their use of the media. Today, audience activity level is more often thought of as a variable concept, reflecting the intensity with which an activity is performed by an audience member (Chaffee & Roser, 1986). In other words, in some situations audience members are more active than in others. It is assumed that different levels of activity are followed by different kinds of consequences of media use (Blumler, 1979; Greenwald & Leavitt, 1984; Petty & Cacioppo, 1986).

In spite of the centrality of audience activity in gratifications theory there have been few empirical investigations which have focused on such activity. According to Blumler (1979), audience activity should not be treated as an 'article of faith,' but should be empirically investigated. Levy and Windahl, (1984) and Perse (1990a, 1990b) have operationalized audience activity as a multidimensional concept. They show that the audience can be more or less active on several dimensions of the television news viewing experience, such as selectivity of programme and content, intentionality, time spent with a medium, amount of attention paid, engaging in other activities, talking about message content, mental elaboration on message content, and using media content. From the social action perspective, these dimensions of audience activity are more important for predicting the consequences of television news viewing than just the amount of time spent watching (Nelissen, 1992). However, exposure is very often the only dimension of media use that is measured. Empirically, Chaffee and Schleuder (1986) demonstrated that attention measures are more valid predictors of the amount of learning from news media content than exposure measures.

The meaning of gratification measures

Motives for watching television news are commonly conceptualized and measured as gratifications. Perse (1990a) considered television news viewing gratifications in terms of both informational and diversionary motives. In recent years, several studies have used

127

gratifications to predict the amount of time people spend watching the news as well as other dimensions of audience activity (Perse, 1990a; 1990b). They show that groups with different television news viewing gratifications differ regarding audience activities.

However, the concept of gratifications and the way it has been used has three important shortcomings in the areas of both theory and methodology. First, gratifications are measured at a general level. The gratifications tradition thus only considers a general need for information. From the social action perspective, an individual's need for information can only be fulfilled with information on the specific issues that have personal relevance to that individual. Second, rather than just focusing on the need for information one should also examine the factors underlying this need. The determinants of a need for information on specific issues are embedded in the individual's image of reality and the subjective relevance of different knowledge domains which are part of that image (Bosman & Renckstorf, 1992). Third, it is unclear whether the gratification measures should be considered as causes (motives), or as consequences (evaluations) of media use (Swanson, 1977). This shortcoming is most serious when no distinction is made between gratifications sought (motives) and gratifications obtained (evaluations). Taking this fact into account, one should be careful to use gratification measures as motives, in order to predict audience activities. Therefore, gratification measures will be considered in this study as qualifying descriptions of media use. They represent the extent to which the individual describes his or her television news viewing as an informational, or a diversionary process.

The concept of issue involvement

Several studies on tv news have shown that a significant amount of variance in viewers' recall of news stories is accounted for by the issues presented in news stories (Findahl & Höijer, 1985; Renckstorf, 1980a; Robinson & Levy, 1986). People differ in their levels of involvement with different issues (Van Westendorp, 1981). Furthermore, the rate and amount of diffusion of a news event is demonstrated to be highly dependent on the relevance, importance or interest the audience attaches to the issue (Hanneman & Greenberg, 1973). These findings suggest that we need to measure issue-specific motivational concepts in order to understand more completely the way people choose, watch, and use television news.

For reasons mentioned above, researchers from different disciplines have used the motivational concept of 'involvement' to predict communicative actions. Levy and Windahl (1984) (re)introduced involvement into gratifications research. They assert that involvement has two different meanings in communication research: 'We understand audience involvement to be, first, the degree to which an audience member perceives a connection between himself or herself and mass media content and, second, the degree to which the individual interacts psychologically with a medium or its messages' (Levy & Windahl, 1985:112). In the present study, involvement is considered a motivational variable reflecting the 'perceived personal relevance' of an issue, as stated in the first definition. By contrast, Levy and Windahl (1985) and Perse (1990a; 1990b) choose the second definition of involvement. In their opinion, involvement is a behavioural dimension and the consequence of personal relevance of an issue. These two types of involvement can be labelled 'issue involvement' (Petty & Cacioppo, 1986) and 'audience involvement' (Greenwald & Leavitt, 1984), respectively.

Issue involvement and the nature of news viewing

The knowledge domains that are relevant for an individual are part of his or her subjective image of reality. People are motivated toward reducing uncertainty or toward solving problems they may perceive in areas that are relevant to them (Bosman *et al.*, 1989; Schramm 1968). One way to reduce the negative consequences of uncertainty is to gather information. A certain kind of information on public affairs and other news issues is provided by television news. Therefore, watching television news can be instrumental in reducing uncertainty people may have on certain issues. To the extent that people watch television news for informational reasons it will be, according to the approach followed here, partly due to their involvement with news issues.

People may also have 'problems' that can be solved by the process of watching television news as such, and/or the emotional dimension of news content. At that moment, the information provided in the news is of secondary importance. These problems may have to do with the wish to be entertained, to have something to talk about, or problems that have to do with filling time, escaping reality and similar activities.

Similar to the above mentioned two ways of viewing news, Schramm (1968) proposes that there might be two different ways of 'news reading:'[1] news reading with a 'delayed reward' and news reading with an 'immediate reward' respectively. He reasons that people can process the news in order to use the information for decisions in the future, in other words a delayed reward. People can also process the news because they focus on the experience of watching news itself – an immediate reward, which is often pleasurable and possibly reduces tensions. Schramm (1968) hypothesizes that these two ways of processing news would generally be linked to different types of news issues. He considers 'public interest' issues (e.g. politics) to be 'hard news' of the 'delayed reward' type, and human interest and sensational news issues (e.g. disasters and criminality) to be 'soft news' of the 'immediate reward' type.[2] Applying the concepts of emotional and cognitive involvement might allow further investigation of these two different ways of news viewing.

Using the theoretical frame described above, an analysis is to be made of issue involvement, news viewing activities, and television news gratifications. As for Schramm's hypothesis, the present study is only exploratory in nature. Here, the main hypotheses are: first, that issue involvement is related more to informational than to diversionary ways of news viewing; and second, that people who are more involved with typical news issues,

---

1 Schramm uses the word 'reading' to indicate processing or interpretation of printed news contents. His notion, it is argued here, can be applied to television news viewing as well as to reading.

2 Schramm (1968:169) stresses that '... while the division of categories holds in general, the predispositions of the individual [which may include issue involvement, N.H.] may transfer any story from one kind of reading to another, or divide the experience between two kinds of reward'.

such as politics, public policy, environmental issues and crime are more active in their news viewing behaviours than people who are less involved in these issues.

Research procedures

The data for this study were compiled in a large scale survey project carried out to investigate media equipment, media exposure and media use, in the Netherlands, called MASSAT '89 (see Arts *et al.*, 1990b). The data were gathered in face-to-face interviews using a questionnaire. The interviews were conducted by 80 experienced interviewers during the spring of 1989. A two-stage random sample was drawn as follows: first, 68 municipalities were chosen. The cities were proportionate to regional distribution and degree of urbanization. Second, from every city a proportionate number of people was randomly chosen. The respondents were contacted a maximum of three times. A total of 956 (43 per cent) of the 2223 individuals contacted expressed willingness to participate in the survey.

Television news gratifications were measured using a multiple item instrument. The items were selected from those commonly used to measure television news gratifications (Levy & Windahl, 1984; Perse, 1990a; 1990b) and were translated into Dutch. The respondents were requested to indicate whether the items, formulated as statements, applied to their own news watching experience (on a five-point scale). Using factor analysis with oblique rotation, two underlying factors emerged: (a) a diversionary gratification factor (= 0.71; 4 items) and (b) an information gratification factor (= 0.74; 5 items).

As other researchers have suggested (Perse, 1990a; Van Westendorp, 1981), involvement has a cognitive and an emotional dimension. The cognitive dimension was measured in this study as the amount of interest people have in a particular issue. The emotional dimension was measured by the amount of concern people have with respect to that particular issue. Although cognitive and emotional dimensions of knowledge and relevance are never fully separable (Zajonc, 1980), the concern measured can be considered (see Van Westendorp, 1981) to tap a more emotional relation of the viewer toward the issue. Concern about an issue – and interest in an issue – will usually go hand in hand, but to some degree they will indicate different dimensions of involvement, i.e. a more emotional and a more cognitive dimension. One can be interested in an issue, without being concerned about that issue, while one can be concerned without being interested.[3]

Interest and concern were measured with respect to a number of issues frequently occurring in the news: politics, education, health(care), disasters, criminality, science (and technology), environmental pollution, employment, and housing. Interest was measured using a four-point and concern with a five-point scale.

Respondents are considered interested in the news issues when their responses were either 'quite interested' or 'very interested' on the four-point scale. They are considered concerned about the issues when their responses were 'regularly,' 'often' or 'always'

---

3   Bosman & Renckstorf (1992) argue that concern ('extrinsic motivation') only influences information consumption indirectly, via interest ('information need').

Table 1. Interest and concern as indicators of involvement with news issues

	% of high involvement	
	Interest (Cognitive)	Concern (Emotional)
News issues	%	%
Housing	41.5	7.0
Politics	49.0	18.1
Science and technology	58.6	12.9
Employment	72.9	29.1
Education	80.2	12.2
Health	84.0	24.5
Disasters	73.0	41.7
Criminality	71.6	50.4
Environmental pollution	89.5	70.5
Average %	68.9	29.6

concerned as measured on the five-point scale. In the correlation analyses in Tables 2 through 4, the categories of the scales have not been combined.

The percentage of individuals involved with housing was the lowest: 41.5 per cent claimed to be interested and 7 per cent concerned. The highest percentages were found regarding environmental pollution: 89.5 per cent interested and 70.5 per cent concerned. The issues can be roughly divided into three groups: (a) housing, politics, and science and technology which elicit low interest and low concern; (b) employment, education, and health which elicit high interest but low concern; (c) disasters, criminality, and environmental pollution which elicit high interest and high concern.[4]

Five different television news viewing activities were measured. The amount of *television news exposure* was measured by asking how many days per week people usually watch the news (M = 5.9). Two-thirds of the respondents watch the news everyday. *Intentionality* was measured using a four-item scale (= 0.76) to assess the extent to which people plan their news viewing in advance. Intentionality ranged from 4 to 20 (M = 13.7). The amount of *attention* paid to the newscast was measured on a five-point scale (M = 3.8). Respondents were asked to rate how important it is for them to see the entire newscast. *Distraction* was operationalized with an index of three items measuring how often people engage in potentially distracting activities while watching the news.[5] The scores on this index range from 3 to 7 (M = 4.3). Another activity in addition to attention which is directed toward

---

4 Although, on average, none of the issues elicits a low level of interest combined with a high level of concern. This average does not, of course apply to the individual level.

5 Activities undertaken while the news is on include such things as 'eating their evening meals', fetching something to eat or drink', and 'talking about other things'. These activities are not very closely related, but because these activities are likely to have the same result, i.e. distraction from the news, they can be combined legitimately in an index for distraction.

Table 2. Zero-order correlations between gratifications and issue involvement

		Gratification information	Gratification diversion
Grat. information			0.48
Grat. diversion		0.48	
Politics	I	0.32	*
	C	0.27	*
Pollution	I	0.24	*
	C	0.24	*
Science	I	0.14	*
	C	*	*
Employment	I	0.19	0.10
	C	0.13	*
Education	I	0.13	0.08
	C	*	*
Housing	I	0.23	0.15
	C	*	*
Health	I	0.17	0.16
	C	0.10	0.11
Disasters	I	0.11	0.20
	C	0.20	0.12
Criminality	I	*	0.20
	C	0.16	0.14

I= interest/cognitive involvement; C= concern/emotional involvement. $r = 0.09$, $P < 0.01$. * = not significant

the content of the news is the amount of mental *elaboration* regarding the content that people engage in. Elaboration represents the amount of thinking about, or the amount of interpretation or decoding of media content.

The average amount of elaboration on television news content was measured on a five-point scale. Respondents were asked to indicate to what extent they usually think about the things they've seen and heard on the news (mean = 3.2). The analysis took place in two phases. First, Pearson coefficients of correlation were calculated to assess bivariate relationships among the variables. Second, three-order partial correlation analysis was carried out to diminish the likelihood that relationships found would be spurious, i.e. that both variables are influenced by the same third variable. Based on previous television news research in the Netherlands (Kleinnijenhuis *et al.*, 1991) education, age, and gender are considered relevant control variables.

Results

Issue involvement and television news gratifications

A statistically significant correlation ($r = 0.48$; $P < 0.01$) was found between the two different gratifications, which indicates that the two empirically most important general descriptions of watching television news are not mutually independent. See Table 2.

Looking, in Table 2, at the coefficients of correlation of issue involvement measures and information gratification, a differentiation among issues is revealed. Involvement with politics as well as involvement with environmental pollution show a statistically significant relationship with information gratification ($r = 0.32$ and $r = 0.27$; $r = 0.24$ and $r = 0.24$ respectively; all at the $P < 0.01$ level). Furthermore, there was no relationship found between involvement with politics, pollution, and science and the diversionary gratification scale.

Involvement with the issues of health, disasters and criminality is statistically significant as related to both gratification dimensions. This indicates that the level of involvement with these issues may affect diversionary news viewing to a greater extent than the level of involvement with politics, environmental pollution and science.

Table 2 also shows that involvement with the issues of education, employment and housing have a statistically significant relationship with watching the information content of news as well as watching the news in a diversionary way. This was more often the case with cognitive involvement which was measured as interest. Emotional involvement with these issues was most often unrelated to informational or diversionary ways of viewing. Controlling for education, gender and age revealed little differences in the results of the analysis. Therefore, these relationships generally hold for different levels of education, age, and gender; that is, they can be considered non-spurious.

Issue involvement and audience activity

Tv-news exposure. Exposure is the audience activity which is most commonly measured in surveys related to public affairs (Chaffee & Schleuder, 1986). The amount of exposure to news, showed a statistically significant relationship at the $P < 0.05$ level with both involvement measures of the issues politics and health ($r = 0.11$ and $r = 0.13$, and $r = 0.11$ and $r = 0.09$, respectively; see Table 3). Exposure to television news was also significantly related to cognitive involvement with employment ($r = 0.11$).

Intentionality. Table 3 shows that issue involvement is more often related to the intentionality of people towards television news, than to exposure. This indicates that the more people are involved with news issues, the more they plan their television news viewing. The kind of involvement, related to audience activities, i.e. emotional or cognitive, differs somewhat between issues. Particularly concerning issues such as disasters and criminality, emotional involvement is important for intentionally watching television news, whereas cognitive involvement is not. For the issue of pollution, the case is less clear cut. With this issue intentionality is also related to cognitive involvement. It is important to note that these were the three issues which elicited high levels of emotional involvement (see Table 1). For most other issues cognitive involvement seems to be more firmly linked to intentionality.

Attention and distraction. More than half of the involvement measures are related to the amount of attention people say they usually pay to television news. In the case of politics, environmental pollution and criminality both emotional and cognitive involvement are

Table 3. Issue involvement and news viewing

Involvement with:		Exposure	Intentionality	Attention	Distraction	Elaboration
Politics	I	0.11	0.26	0.20	*	0.29
	C	0.13	0.22	0.16	*	0.25
Pollution	I	*	0.14	0.12	0.11	0.22
	C	*	0.18	0.12	*	0.22
Science	I	*	0.11	*	*	0.19
	C	*	*	*	*	0.16
Housing	I	*	0.17	0.17	*	0.19
	C	*	*	*	0.11	*
Employment	I	0.11	0.11	0.11	*	0.18
	C	*	0.08	*	*	0.20
Education	I	*	0.09	*	−0.09	0.17
	C	*	*	*	*	0.08
Health	I	0.11	0.12	0.12	*	0.16
	C	0.09	*	*	*	0.09
Disasters	I	*	*	*	*	0.13
	C	*	0.14	0.13	*	0.20
Criminality	I	*	*	0.09	*	0.12
	C	*	0.13	0.14	*	0.16

Notes: partialled out for age, education and gender. I= interest/cognitive involvement. C= concern/emotional involvement. $P < 0.01$. * = not significant

related to attention ($r = 0.20$ and $r = 0.16$; $r = 0.12$ and $r = 0.12$; $r = 0.07$ and $r = 0.14$, respectively). Negative relationships with the distraction measure were expected. First of all, the relationship between involvement and distraction reaches significance in only three cases. Surprisingly, though, there are positive relationships between distraction and extent of cognitive involvement with pollution ($r = 0.11$) and between distraction and emotional involvement with housing ($r = 0.11$). Cognitive involvement with education is, as expected, negatively related to the distraction index ($r = -0.09$).

Elaboration. Elaboration shows statistically significant relationships with all issue involvement measures except one: emotional involvement with housing. Respondents who are involved with news issues tend to invest a greater amount of mental activity in these issues than people who are less involved. This may indicate that they process the information they acquire from television news more thoroughly. In other words, they make greater effort to interpret the information they see, as well as scrutinize the information more critically than people who are less involved. The partial coefficients of correlation are strongest in case of politics, $r = 0.29$ and $r = 0.25$, and environmental pollution, $r = 0.22$ and $r = 0.22$.

In general, relationships between audience activities and interest and concern measures attain statistical significance at the $P < 0.05$ level in approximately the same number of occasions. This indicates that both may be important predictors for these types of audience activity. For most issues the interest measure of involvement is more strongly related to audience activities. However, for the issues disasters and criminality, emotional involvement – which was operationalized as concern – seems to be the stronger predictor of television news viewing activities.

Conclusions

The first hypothesis of this study focused on the relationship between issue involvement and informational and diversionary ways of viewing. High issue involvement was found to be related to news viewing directed toward the informational content. This relationship was most explicit for the issues of politics, environmental pollution, and science. Involvement with the remaining issues was related to both informational as well as diversionary news viewing. Involvement with disasters and crime seems to have the strongest relationship with diversionary use of television news. Concern for these issues, partly indicating the emotional dimension, also seems to be the major indicator of involvement and a better predictor of audience activities than interest (see Table 3). This seems to be consistent with Schramm's (1968) hypothesis that issues of this nature are more likely to give immediate (emotional) rewards, while 'hard news' issues, such as politics and environmental pollution are more likely to provide delayed rewards in terms of being better informed in the future. Our results have also shown that informational and diversionary ways of viewing are not independent. Both ways of viewing may be instrumental for the same person in different situations for different purposes.

In line with the second hypothesis, it was found that people who are involved with typical news issues are more active in their news viewing behaviours than people who are less involved. These results are also in line with the assumption of the social action perspective that people plan their actions, at least partly, according to their own image of reality which is structured by personal relevance structures (Bosman *et al.*, 1989).

Issue involvement seems to be most often related to intentionality and elaboration and less often to exposure and distraction. This could be due to the fact that elaboration and intentionality are highly determined by individual variables, like involvement, whereas exposure and distraction are more likely to be dependent upon situational and social influences present in the news viewing environment (Mutsaers, 1993; see also Chapter 7).

The relationship between involvement with the issues housing and pollution and the distraction index was contrary to prior expectations. Although no satisfying explanation was found, it is theoretically possible that people who are more involved tend to combine their news viewing with potentially distracting activities, because they watch the news more selectively. This does not explain, however, why these relationships were found only with the issues of pollution and housing.

The fact that the relationships found are, in most cases, not particularly strong is probably determined by the general level at which news viewing activities were measured. For example, respondents were not asked how much attention they paid to *specific* issues in the news (Chaffee & Schleuder, 1986). Instead, we asked how important it is to them to see the entire news programme. Measurement of involvement and audience activities at the same level, the issue level, will probably show stronger relationships in an analysis like the present one. The general descriptions of news viewing, in terms of the gratification measures, have a stronger link with the audience activities than the individual[6] issue involvement variables; compare Table 4 with Table 3.

Table 4. TV news viewing activities and news gratifications (third-order partial correlations)

	Exposure	Intention	Attention	Distraction	Elaboration
Information gratification	0.35	0.52	0.50	−0.07	0.54
Diversionary gratification	0.24	0.32	0.32	*	0.31

Partialled out for age, education and gender. $r = 0.07$, $P < 0.05$; *=not significant

It should be stressed that, with the benefit of hindsight, the above finding is not surprising because gratifications and audience activities were measured at the same general level, whereas issue involvement was measured at a specific level. Another possible explanation is that both audience activity measures and gratification measures explicitly focused on television news viewing. The words 'television news' are mentioned in all the items, which could possibly result in higher correlation coefficients. The involvement measures are not stated in terms of television news.

General discussion

A number of theoretical and socially relevant questions relating to the results of this investigation are considered in this section. A large number of television news studies show that, on average, recall and comprehension of television news issues is poor (Robinson & Levy, 1986; Findahl & Höijer, 1985). This study offers two possible explanations for this finding. First, many people who watch the news are not highly involved in a number of prominent news issues, in fact, hardly anyone is highly involved in all news issues. As a result, people are not likely to actively process all the issues presented and consequently will not remember important parts of the content.[7] The second possible explanation for low learning rates of television news is that people partly watch the news for diversionary reasons. Though the officially stated aim of television news agencies is to inform people, news is not watched just for information. In fact, many people may watch the news primarily for reasons other than information gathering in a narrow sense (Dahlgren, 1988).[8] News viewing directed at diversion and, by consequence, the individuals' passive attitude towards important parts of the content, may prohibit the elaboration on and learning of central information (Perse, 1990b).

6   The combined influence of the 18 issue involvement measures was not tested. This is expected, however, to be well above the individual influences.

7   A striking example is politics. It is the most prominent news issue in Dutch television news (Kleinnijenhuis et al., 1991), but half of our respondents are not interested in political issues and 80 per cent of them are hardly ever concerned about the political future of their country.

8   Besides diversion, there are a number of ways of viewing which are not directed toward information, such as: personal identity motives (Blumler, 1979), drive reduction (Schramm, 1968), habitual news viewing (Perse, 1990b), and ritual news viewing (Dahlgren, 1988).

The findings presented here are consistent with the assumption that television news viewing is related to the image of reality viewers have, indicated by the personal relevance of different aspects of reality. Our data do not allow an assessment of the direction of the relationships. According to involvement theory, it was assumed that involvement causes audience activity. A high level of issue involvement makes an individual process the information presented actively, which in turn results in intentional learning of that information (see Greenwald & Leavitt, 1984). The results of this study show that high involvement is indeed related to more intensive processing and interpretation of news content. Other research shows that (political) involvement or personal relevance[9] is a major predictor of active learning from news media (Robinson & Levy, 1986; Kleinnijen-huis *et al.*, 1991; Hanneman & Greenberg, 1973). We have recently been able to replicate these findings; see Chapter 12.

In the low involvement condition, however, the causal effect is likely to be directed the other way. Passive reception of television news would result in little intentional learning but could affect aspects of peoples' images of reality via incidental learning processes (Hawkins & Pingree, 1983). A low level of issue involvement is linked to lower levels of intentional learning[10] (Petty & Cacioppo, 1986; Greenwald & Leavitt, 1984). Low involvement may also prohibit careful consideration of information and induce incidental or peripheral learning of fragments of information (Kraus & Davis 1976, Chaffee & Roser 1986, Petty & Cacioppo 1986), while the repetitive character of television news content and of viewing could even amplify this process (Blumler, 1979; Dahlgren, 1988).

For example, Kazee (1981) and Iyengar *et al.* (1982) found that less involved viewers tend to change their evaluations more often, and more in line with television news content than involved viewers.[11] The results of a study conducted by Perse (1989) show that low involvement learning may be connected with acceptance of television's images of reality. Only at the most superficial level of the interpretation process (i.e. the 'attention level') does watching television news relate to people's image of reality, conceptualized as 'perceived personal risk.' O'Keefe and Reid-Nash (1987) show that such processes are more likely to be found in watching television than in reading newspapers. Use of the concept of involvement could lead to more profound insight in the ways people learn, actively as well as passively, from television news.

In harmony with these findings and with theories of active and passive learning from television content, Blumler (1979) hypothesized, from the perspective of the uses and

---

9 Findahl & Höijer (1985) report that the 'psychological distance' of news issues has a major impact on news comprehension. This concept resembles closely what we have called issue involvement or personal relevance.

10 Low levels of involvement result in a low level of attention and shallow processing of information. This prohibits integration of information into existing knowledge. Therefore, learning and remembering the information will be poor.

11 Evaluations of objects, or attitudes, are an important part of the images people have of reality and of their knowledge structure. Further, Kraus en Davis (1976:135) report a number of studies that show similar results to those suggested here.

gratifications tradition, that 'cognitive motivation' for media use will facilitate information gain, while viewing for reasons of diversion and/or escape will favour audience acceptance of images of reality constructed in media content.[12] This in turn is in line with Schramm's (1968) hypothesis that information processing of the immediate reward type (like diversion) is the mechanism through which society might affects us, and that we can affect society through the mechanism of information processing of the delayed reward type.

The contribution of this study to an overall understanding of television new viewing is that the concept of issue involvement can be applied to describe and predict audience television news viewing activities more precisely. Issue involvement can also be used to predict different consequences of news viewing. Furthermore, it could also be applied as an indirect measure for audience activity, more specifically as an indicator of cognitive effort, in research situations where no other measures of audience activity are available.

Future studies of audience activity should also focus on the relationship between the social position of audience members, as antecedents of their involvement profile, and consequently of audience's news viewing activities. If we can assess more precisely in which situations watching television news is instrumental, we will be better able to explain interpretation, learning and use of television news as well as television news viewing patterns. In this respect special consideration should be given to the situations in which diversionary or ritualized news viewing can be instrumental, and the consequences this way of viewing has for members of the audience, as well as the knowledge and attitudes they use in daily life.

The measurement of issue involvement can be used by producers of television news to determine which issues are relevant to the audience. One of the main goals of Dutch news broadcasts is to provide the public with socially relevant information. In our view, news broadcasters can make a better choice of what is socially relevant when they combine their own subjective judgement of relevance with the audience's judgement of relevance. This certainly does not mean that television news should only give the people what they want or that news should be packaged as entertainment. But news makers should take audience's ways of viewing, and audience's relevance structures into account in their attempt to inform that same audience.

---

12 See Weaver (1980) for some empirical support of these ideas, as well as the low involvement or incidental learning hypothesis.

11 Women's use of TV news

Liesbeth Hermans and Leo van Snippenburg

Although most people watch television news regularly, little is known about the meaning they attach to the genre as a whole or to the various issues reported. This study explores Dutch women's use of the news (exposure and rendered meanings), and relates it to their background characteristics. Analysis of in-depth interviews conducted suggest that – in addition to commonly cited variables like educational level and employment – type of employment and the cultural climate within the respondent's childhood family are also related to exposure and involvement with television news programming.

Television news is of special interest to almost everyone. In large sections of the population it is an important source of information on current affairs. People see with their own eyes the latest developments on the television screen and they experience these as real and nearby (Dahlgren, 1986). Until now, audience research into the relation between viewers and the television news supply focused mainly on the extent to which a transfer of information take place by, for example, checking what viewers are able to remember and what they understood of various news items (Gunter, 1987; Findahl & Höijer, 1985; Renckstorf, 1980a; Robinson & Levy, 1986; Ruhrmann, 1989). The results of these studies, however, differ considerably and fail to provide a consistent picture. Nevertheless, they reveal that, especially in the short run, in terms of 'recall,' 'retention' and 'comprehension,' audiences are not becoming very informed by watching television news, at least not in a standard rational or cognitive sense. A possible reason for this might be that the impact of television news may lay beyond the transfer of information. In this regard, according to Dahlgren (1986; 1988), television news should be treated as a cultural form. Through social embedding and conventions in programming production – such as structure, language use and composition – it produces and convey meaning.

Television news should be regarded as a social institution with diverse social and political functions for people in their roles as citizens and consumers of news. It is not a transmitter of information in which society is mirrored, but television news represents in a symbolic way the constructs of social reality produced by the broadcaster (Adoni & Mane, 1984;

Anderson & Meyer, 1988; Jensen, 1986). These constructs/representations of reality are perceived and interpreted by the individual within the framework of his/her stock of knowledge and relevance structure (Renckstorf, 1994). This common knowledge gives the individual all kind of clues to understand the world around him and sets boundaries on how to act in different situations. Media are embedded in these daily routines. As part of everyday life, media use can be seen and should be studied as a form of social action (Anderson & Meyer, 1988, Renckstorf, 1994).

Individuals often watch television with their families in the domestic sphere. An increasingly number of researchers are conducting audience-oriented studies within this context (Lull, 1988; 1990; Morley, 1986) In Morley's (1986) study of television viewing of 18 working class families, one of the interesting results was the gender differences he found in viewing preferences. Men prefer to watch factual programmes – news and sports – while women prefer to watch fiction – soap operas and drama series. Morley argues that these patterns are not based on biological differences between men and women or on a natural authority possessed by men. Rather, they are the effect of the particular social roles that men and women occupy within the home (see also Ang, 1991). It is crucial to acknowledge that gender differences were especially found in traditional nuclear families. Morley (1992) suggests examining the social position of men and women in the family in further research.

In his study on 'how viewers process and use the genre of television news,' Jensen (1986:17) interviewed 24 men. His supposition was that social status and level of education where of vital importance for the reception of television news.[1] One of his reasons to include only men in his study was the consideration that (television) news is a typically masculine genre, i.e. a genre in which predominantly men are interested. Results of a recent Dutch radio and television audience survey (NOS/KLO, 1991) question this point of departure, at least as far as Dutch society is concerned. The news broadcast by the NOS (Dutch Broadcasting Foundation) is a television programme with very high ratings and is watched by equal numbers of men and women. It is therefore valuable to investigate how women use television news as an elaboration of some of Jensen's findings. This study constitutes a preliminary initiation of this objective. Jensen stresses the importance of a better understanding of the viewers/readers/listener needs and uses of (television) news. It is common sense that mass media and news media in particular play an (important) role in the process of shaping consciousness and of defining social reality. But until now this process has been remain largely unexplored.

As part of an on-going research project at the Institute of Mass Communications at the University of Nijmegen, this study addresses the use of television within the social context of everyday life. The main motivation behind this project was to better understand how

---

1   Jensen questioned 24 men working at a university in the United States by means of in-depth interviews. He made a distinction between academics who work with information as university teachers (highest category of education) and people who have 'lower' positions at the university. The men belonging to the latter category had a differentiated level of education (comparable with the middle and highest categories of education in this study).

viewers – particularly women – process and use television news. The research question of the study was formulated as follows: *What is the position of the news in the daily routine of married women and how do news items affect the constitution of meaning of their social reality.* This general question is further specified by the following sub-questions:

(1) How do women use television news; i.e., with what frequency do they watch news programmes, under what conditions, and what is the relation between situational factors and viewing habits?

(2) Does watching television news relate to using other news sources?

(3) What news subjects are of concern to women and why?

(4) To what extent are socio-structural characteristics, such as level of education and working in or outside the home, of importance in the use of and involvement with the news?

Research method

Little is known of the role played by the news in the everyday life of women. This situation lends itself, then, to an interpretative research strategy where the respondents' experience of daily life is taken into account as much as possible. For this reason, the interviewing did not include standardized questionnaires, but only a topic list containing subjects considered relevant.[2] In order to solicit useful responses and to enable respondents to tell their personal stories, interviews were held in the familiar surroundings of the respondents' homes. The interviews were recorded and subsequently transcribed. These transcriptions served as the source material for the interpretative analysis.

The interviews consisted of two parts. Questions in the first part concerned the women's social background characteristics. The second part dealt with subjects related to the use of television news. Using the topic list, women were interviewed about concrete subjects, such as viewing frequency, at what time of the day they watched the news, the conditions that determined whether they watched the news, other activities during viewing and the environment in which they watched. Furthermore, a number of topics were added concerning the use of other informational media such as newspapers, radio, free local publications and current affairs programmes. The involvement of the women with various news items became apparent after interviewing them about the following topics: motives for watching the news, discussion of news items, perceived objectivity and reliability of the news, and interest in concrete subjects and the relation between these subjects and the women's experiences of events in their immediate environment.

---

2 The procedure was pre-tested in two interviews. These pre-tests led to only one alteration of the original interview schedule. In the first interview, it turned out that the use of television news was often linked to the use of other informational media. As a result, questions about the use of other news sources were added.

The group of interviewees consisted of 14 married women[3] who lived in a family context and had at least one child of about 10 years old. The sample varies according to socio-economic characteristics such as the level of education and employment.[4] Level of education was divided into three categories: low, middle and high. A low level means that the respondent had completed no more than primary school or a few years of secondary education. Middle level means that the respondent had completed a secondary education, and high level means an occupational or university education degree was completed; see Table 1.

Table 1. Educational level and employment of respondents

Level of education:	Low	Middle	High	Total
Paid employment				
No	2	3	3	8
Yes	1	3	2	6
Total	3	6	5	14

The interpretative procedure followed was based on the grounded theory approach developed by Glaser and Strauss (1967) and consisted of four phases (see also Jensen, 1987). First, to obtain an overview of the phenomena under investigation, the material was carefully examined without looking specifically for relations or explanations. In this exploratory phase, special attention is given to concrete references that are related to the original research themes and questions. Subsequently, key words were placed in the margins of the text to give the material additional structure. The text, in this manner, was divided into smaller units to facilitate analysis. Next, a comparison was made between the units to which the same key words were assigned. The aim here was to discover and describe patterns underlying statements from respondents. Finally, the findings were related to the original research questions.

Results

Using television news

Some 11 of the 14 women interviewed watch the news everyday. They do so in the domestic sphere, together with their husbands and/or their children. They all prefer the

---

3   The group of interviewees was assembled according to the so-called 'snowball' method. In this study only a small group of women was interviewed. They were selected on account of specific characteristics and not because of statistical representativeness. Statements and conclusions, therefore, refer to the group of interviewees and are not generalizable to a larger population. Generation of such generalizations was not the objective of this exploratory study; the primary objective was to gain insight into a number of problems not yet studied in any great detail.

4   The two higher-educated women in the category of working women were employed full-time; both in secondary education, one as a teacher and the other as a principal of an institution for adult education. The working women from the lower and middle category of education were employed for 20 hours a week. The women in the middle category of education were employed as an office clerk, and as a group leader, whereas the woman from the lower category of education was working in a cafeteria.

NOS[5] news, particularly the 8 o'clock evening news. Moreover, these women also watch a news programme designed for young people[6] together with their children almost everyday. They approve highly of this newscast, because it 'is easy to understand,' 'gives background information,' and 'brings positive news.' Their comments about the evening news are usually less appreciative. As may become clear from remarks such as 'milked dry,' 'negative news,' and 'half of it consists of repeats.' Despite these clearly negative comments, they consider the NOS news as their most important source of information. Apparently, watching the news is not only related to the appreciation that the women have of the genre; from remarks such as 'if possible,' 'almost every night,' 'when I'm home,' and 'we do try,' it becomes clear that watching the news has taken on the form of a habit. Under normal conditions, the women do not ask themselves explicitly whether they really like to watch the news. It has become a fixed item in the planning of their daily events: '...clear things up, Joop takes the dog out, then we watch the news and go to bed.'

The women deviate from their normal daily routine only for exceptional circumstances. It may be that there is someone on the telephone, that guests have arrived or that they have obligations elsewhere. In those cases they usually watch one of the later newscasts.

The interviews indicate that a number of women combine watching the news with other activities, such as ironing, folding the linen, making coffee or playing with the children (cf. Morley, 1986). According to the women, these activities can be easily combined with watching the news: 'I don't stop working, I simply turn the ironing board around and go on while watching.'

It appears that there is a relationship between the use of the NOS news and the level of education. The higher the level of education, the more often the women watch the news. It is predominantly the women with a higher level of education that combine watching the NOS news with other activities. It is especially remarkable that the women who do not have a job outside the home, do other things while watching. For all 11 women, watching the news is a habit or routine that has become part of everyday life.

Television news and other news sources

The remarks and arguments of the women in this study reveal that the use of television news cannot be regarded as an isolated event. It has to be investigated within the wider context of the total use of news sources. In an earlier study, Jensen (1986) compared respondents' television news habits with their use of newspapers. He found that 'confirmed non-viewers were also confirmed non-readers' (Jensen, 1986:254). This study, however, does not fully support his conclusion. Two of the three women who do not watch the news also do not read any newspapers. They have a lower level of education and do not work outside the home. This seems to corroborate Jensen's findings, but an important

---

5   The NOS news is the newscast prepared for a general audience in the Netherlands by the public
    broadcasting associations.

6   A special newscast prepared by the NOS for children under 12 on Dutch public service television.

difference is that he finds this connection in the category of those with the highest level of education. In this study, however, one of the women with a higher level of education who does not work outside the home and does not watch the news, does read the national newspapers and news magazines extensively. And this is precisely why she does not feel the need to watch the television newscasts.

Most women who watch the news also read a newspaper. Only three women, all from the middle category of education, watch the television news, but do not read a newspaper. They find it 'too expensive' or have 'no time' or 'no patience' for it. To them, watching the news is an alternative to reading a newspaper.

Whether women read a newspaper or not, one should also make a distinction between the different kinds of newspapers read. The women who read a regional newspaper are from the lower and middle categories of education. To them, the regional newspaper is the source of information for local and regional news, because it keeps them informed about what goes on in their neighbourhood. They use television news as their *main source* of information for the national and international news. They find that they are thus sufficiently informed about important events and practically never use any other information source.

The only exceptions to this general rule are two women, one from the category of those who work outside the home with a lower level of education and one from the category of those who do not work outside the home and with a middle level of education. They differ from the other women in their respective categories because they frequently use information oriented television programmes. Although they use several sources of information extensively, they also differ from the higher educated in that they prefer television news more than newspapers. It seems that, apart from level of education, habits developed in the use of television news are important. Both women mentioned the special stimuli they received in their youth from their father to watch informational programmes. The results suggest the importance of this factor in later use of news programmes by women.

Women who predominantly read national newspapers have a higher educational level. They use television news as well as newspapers as sources of information for national and international news. Apart from these media, the higher educated women also read weeklies and watch current affairs programmes regularly. Television repeats the most important news items for them. Because of this recall of information, it is also easier to comprehend the news messages. The women use television news as an *additional source* of information, in particular for current affairs: '...I often work at night, so watching the news is the only way for me, besides reading the papers, to keep informed and I think it also has something to do with the fact that it's so easy...it is presented to you in a fast and consumptive way.'

In this manner, the higher educated women all prefer printed media. The main reasons mentioned for this preference are the possibility of selective accessibility, presentation of more news items and the fact that print media provide more background information on certain topics than television programmes. Moreover, it is very important for them that

144

they can decide for themselves when they want to be informed. Jensen (1986:208) also notes that higher educated persons prefer print media. He suggests the background of these persons as a possible explanation. An academic education is primarily based on print media. To this we may add that print media are in general more accessible to those with a higher education, as far as language use and subject matter are concerned, than to less educated persons.

Involvement with television news

Motives for watching television news

The most important reason for watching the news is, according to all of the women: 'the wish to stay informed about important events that take place in the world.' To 'stay informed' does not only imply acquisition of information. From some of the comments that women made about the news, yet another aspect becomes apparent: the news plays an important role as an *institutionalized source of information* which people can use for maintaining social contacts. The women say that they watch the news because they feel they need the information in order to participate in certain social contexts: '... if you don't know anything about anything, then you're just stupid and simple ... You don't always have to talk about it, but if they talk about something, you also want to put a word in. When you don't have a television set or a radio or a paper, you've got nothing, you might just as well be a dog.'

Apart from this social use, the women also mention a number of other reasons for watching television news.[7] These can be divided into two categories. The first category contains those reasons that have something to do with the acquisition of 'practical' information about certain items such as the weather and sports, but also with being able to answer questions that their children ask. The second category contains those reasons that have something to do with using the news as a 'routine.' For instance, to satisfy one's curiosity or to arrange a regular pause in the daily schedule.

Talking about television news

Watching the news in the domestic sphere often leads to discussions within the family. The women make brief remarks to their husbands, usually while watching, to express their irritation or surprise. A more elaborate conversation ensues when the item or event concerns them personally. Watching the (young people's) news together with their children may also lead to discussions about certain items. The women have different views on the effects that watching television news may have on the family: 'Sometimes [when they are watching the news] I find the thing so unsocial, you're forced to listen and can't talk any more.' 'Sometimes it triggers all kinds of discussions. At a moment like that I think that you can watch television in a very social way, at least if you're not yelling "shut

---

7 In this study no indications were found that television news might also function in lieu of social contacts, as other authors have suggested (e.g. Levy, 1979; Charlton & Neumann, 1986).

up" or something similar all the time. And it often provides an opportunity to discuss all kinds of subjects with the children, particularly when they're a bit older.'

Outside the family, the news also provides an opportunity to talk about certain subjects. Important events are often discussed in school, in the street or at work. It usually takes the form of exchanging information and does not involve any deep discussions about basic ideas or opinions. The latter normally take place in more familiar surroundings as, for example, in a family setting or with friends. In these surroundings women find it more easy to express their ideas and opinions: '... at birthday parties and such we talk about them [news items]. Nowadays that boils down to arguing about politics.'

Objectivity and reliability of television news

Almost all the women regard the news as an important source of information with respect to current affairs. It may therefore be assumed that women are of the opinion that television news presents these affairs in an objective and reliable way (Kaiser, 1989:21). Their remarks, however, reveal that this assumption needs some modification. For instance, they are quite critical about the selectivity and partiality of the news coverage: 'you've got to take the information with a pinch of salt,' 'one-sided information,' 'doubts about the reliability of the information,' and 'certain things are hushed up.' These objections, however, do not provide them with a stimulus to look for additional information about specific topics which the news, in their opinion, did not cover correctly or sufficiently. In other words, their critical attitude does not lead to active information seeking behaviour. The women from the various categories of education do not look for additional information for different reasons. The higher educated state that, by using several sources of information, they are sufficiently informed and that they then have less biased opinions. The women from the lower and middle categories, who consult fewer sources of information, are aware that the news does not always give an objective and reliable representation, but they merely observe that 'there isn't much you can do about it.'

Interests and world of experience

All the women who participated in this study said that subjects which directly relate to their own world of experience are very important to them. They pay particular attention to these subjects when they are featured in the news. In addition to such direct involvement with their own environment, they also have a preference for subjects in which human aspects are prominent as, for example, the relationships between people. This genre is sometimes referred to as the human interest story. 'Human interest' should not be confused with the interest in sensational stories about important people, like 'the poor health of President Bush.' All of the women disapprove of such news reports and find the endless repetition of them annoying.

The results of this study point to a possible relationship between employment and the way in which women are able to distance themselves from certain subjects. For instance, the women who do not work outside the home have difficulty watching starving people. They tend to identify themselves with the mothers of the dying children. In this way they relate the news to their own environment and become emotionally involved. The feeling of helplessness they experience when watching such misery is something they rather want to avoid; they therefore either switch to another channel or turn off the television set: 'I often don't watch because it's all so horrible what they show you. Then I think to myself, let's not watch, it makes me sick.'

The women who have a job tend to distance themselves somewhat more from such subjects than the women who do not work outside the home. Those from the lower and middle categories of education show a tendency to put the events into perspective: 'you've got to get it out of your mind, if you become too involved with all the misery it'll drive you round the bend.' 'I watch it and don't do anything with it.' In contrast, the higher educated working women are also able to appreciate the confrontation with these images: '...it makes you think of human existence and the terrible misery elsewhere and about the very special position we're in. I think it's good to get such a slap in the face now and again.'

In relating the interest in news items to aspects of the women's immediate environment, one should distinguish between different forms of interest. On the one hand, there is a *general* interest which stems from the social importance attributed to these subjects. General interests can be associated with socially accepted norms in our society, e.g. one ought to be interested in one's fellow human beings, the environment or the Third World. Subjects featured in the news often appeal to these interests. On the other hand, one can distinguish *special* interests which stem from personal circumstances and experiences. General and specific interests in subjects are not static notions. A general interest in a subject, for example, can become a specific interest at the moment that the involvement with the (social) subject is intensified by personal experiences (see the second observation described below).

The following three observations, drawn from the interviews, illustrate the different forms of interests in certain subjects. The first observation concerns a specific interest: education. The women participating in this research were all interested in education. This specific interest arises from their personal situation: they all have children who go to school. Three of the higher educated women hold or used to hold positions in secondary education. Two of them also held non-paid positions on the board of an educational institution. They were therefore particularly interested in educational policies and practice. To obtain information about these subjects they would usually consult print media. In order to be informed about recent developments concerning policy making they would turn to the television news. Two other women who were also particularly interested in education had a lower level of education and were unemployed. They were both members of the parents' council of the primary school which their children attended. Personal contact with the teachers and other parents was an important reason for them to be actively involved in education. They only use information from the media when they hear from other persons that there are developments in education which might affect their own situation. In such cases, they use television news as their main source of information and seldom, if at all, consult the print media. Although there is a specific interest in the same subject – education – the information which these less educated women are interested in is determined by practical situations. The involvement with education is at the micro-level, related to the immediate environment. The information on education spread by the media is often not relevant to them. The higher educated women are more interested in aspects such as policy making, which takes place at macro-level, and this information is usually provided by the media.

A second observation shows that a general interest may become a specific interest through personal experience. An example of such a general interest in a subject, at the time that these interviews were conducted, was interest in the dire situation of the Kurds in Turkey. Most of the women made remarks about the terrible images they saw on television. Few, however, had examined the facts or knew exactly what was going on – with the exception of two women. These two had become interested in the subject because of certain events in their own lives. A recent holiday in Turkey induced one of them to make all kinds of remarks about the news coverage of the relief actions for the Kurds. The other woman had already been involved with the subject for years because she belonged to a church which tried to help persecuted Christian Kurds. As a result of this specific interest, these two women were clearly more interested in and better informed about developments in Turkey. They paid special attention to information about this subject on the newscasts and in the newspapers.

Finally, another observation shows that the actual subject does not always have to be the focus of attention. Sometimes people are more interested in matters related to the topic. Politics as a general theme is a regular ingredient of the news. The women initially said that politics as such was of no interest to them. This political disinterest was, however, not always as pronounced as might be expected. Several levels of (dis)interest could be distinguished. Some of the women did not have any interest at all in political subjects. There was, however, also a category of women who initially said not to be interested in politics, but from the examples given, it became clear that they considered politics tied to certain matters in which they were interested: 'No interest in politics whatsoever....of course that's what it's all about, I mean the Kurds and the Gulf War have everything to do with politics. That is important to me, actually... everything is tied up with politics. That's what it's all about, come to that, you can't get round it'.

These women were not directly concerned with political affairs such as parliamentary debates on policies, or with gathering information about the views of politicians, but they did find it important to know what the consequences of certain political events would be for ordinary people and their relationships. Finally, three women were really interested in information about political developments and policy making. These three, incidentally, were all employed. The examples they gave of political affairs in which they were interested were often connected to their work situation and, as such, with their immediate environment.

Conclusions

Three-quarters of the women who participated in this study watch the news regularly. Watching the news has become a part of their daily routine. Their use of television news is related to their use of other information oriented media. In addition to television news, the higher educated women extensively use other sources of information (newspaper dailies and weeklies, and current affairs television programmes). To get informed they prefer printed media. As mean reasons they mention the specific characteristics of the medium like selective accessibility and the amount of background information. They use television news predominantly as an *additional* source of information. The women from the lower and middle categories of education use fewer sources of information. Television news is for them the most important and their *main* source of information for national and international news. Although half of the women from this category read newspapers, they are primarily interested in local and regional news. Apart from the television newscasts and newspapers, other sources of information are seldom used and, in most cases, only if there is a special reason to do so. Thus, education seems to be an important decisive factor in the use of various sources of information. The higher educated women have 'learned' to use more sources, to compare pieces of information and to relate these to one another (see further Van Snippenburg, 1991; and Chapter 9).

The results of this study show that, apart from the level of education, another characteristic may be important in using information oriented media, i.e. the *cultural climate within the family during childhood*. There were two women who distinguished themselves from the other women with the same education and work situation as far as their use of television news and involvement with the topics were concerned. One working woman with a lower level of education watched the news several times a day and also watched current affairs programmes regularly, in contrast to the other women with limited education. She explained that she did so out of 'sheer curiosity' in order 'not to miss anything.' From her responses during the interview it appears that her father always encouraged her to watch informational programmes. Her upbringing probably laid the foundation for her interest in information oriented programmes. A woman from the middle category of education who did not work outside the home showed similar behaviour. She also distinguished herself from the other women in the same educational category as far as news consumption was concerned. In contrast with the others, she was very interested in informative programmes broadcast on foreign channels. She said that this probably could be explained by the fact that she was encouraged to watch foreign programmes as a child. These findings suggest that stimuli in the family during childhood to watch informational programmes play an important role in media use in later life. This characteristic, which is directly related to socialization processes, should be incorporated into future research on media use.

Furthermore, there seems to be a relation between the women's level of education and their interests in a variety of subjects. The more education they have received and the more general knowledge they have obtained, the more interested they are in subjects related to society as a whole. This might have been reinforced by the fact that these women often have a position and social contacts which encourage such a broad range of interests. They are possibly more capable of making connections between general social information and their personal circumstances, so more news items are recognized as relevant to their own situation. The women from the lower and middle categories of education are primarily interested in subjects related to the personal situation in their immediate environment. It is difficult for them to understand news items and to recognize the importance for their own lives. Should they want to be informed about important events in the world, they feel they receive sufficient information from television news.

Whether women are employed also determines interest in news subjects. Those who work outside the home have, next to their position in the family, also a position in society as a working person. This gives them other responsibilities and interests, and therefore more subjects become important to them. The working women are particularly interested in subjects that in one way or another relate or are relevant to their work situation. In this manner, the employment level is also a relevant factor. The higher their positions, the more important it becomes to keep informed about developments in social, political and economic fields.

Compared to other women in this study, the two working women from the higher education category occupy a special position, both in their families and in their jobs. They work full-time, in contrast to their spouses, and have a rather important position in society. Moreover, they are the main financial providers for their families. Socially, they take on the role usually played by men, i.e. as 'head' of the family. Thus, they have responsibilities normally ascribed to men (see Morley, 1986). Almost complete changes of social roles between men and women in the family is a rather new phenomenon in Western society and until now frequently neglected in social research.

For audience research on the use of (television) news and the process of rendering meaning to news subjects, it is important to consider characteristics as the dominance of social roles within the families and social position of people in society. This position follows from assumptions Morley (1986) made regarding the contribution of social roles in the house to a better understanding of gender differences regarding family television viewing. Regarding gender preferences, we can conclude that (television) news is not a specific masculine genre.

12 Differences between men and women in recalling TV news

Paul Hendriks Vettehen, Niek Hietbrink and Karsten Renckstorf

One of the most consistent findings of news research is that men on the average recall television news items better than women. Attempts to explain these findings, however, have seldom been undertaken. In this chapter hypotheses are tested in a laboratory setting regarding differences in prior knowledge and personal relevance between men and women. The findings suggest that prior knowledge does have a mediating effect on recall. Men, in other words, do not necessarily recall all news better, inasmuch as recall depends at least partially on prior knowledge of items presented.

Most of the Dutch population regards television news as a very important source of information about societal events. They also consider it to be a reliable and objective source of information (NOS/KLO, 1992a). In this respect ideas of the Dutch about television news hardly differ from ideas about television news that people in other Western countries have (Dahlgren, 1988; Robinson & Levy, 1986). These observations certainly look good against the background of a democratic ideal in which well-informed citizens determine the course of their society by means of discussion. Television news apparently has an important function within a democratic system by providing the citizens with socially relevant information.

In communication studies, several questions have been raised with respect to this ideal through the years. Possibly the most frequent question was to what extent people are able to remember the content of television news broadcasts.[1] More specifically formulated, this question is: *who* remember *which* television news reports under *which* conditions?

---

[1] However, the objective of news service is not so much that viewers and listeners will be able to remember a number of separate news facts, but far more that they will be able to see the connection between these facts; in other words, that they will be able to *understand* the news. The question concerning the *understanding* of television news reports is therefore certainly not less important than the question concerning the recall of them.

Some findings that regularly recur in this research tradition concern differences between men and women with respect to recalling television news. The results of a number of field experiments reveal that men are able to remember more of television news than women (Brosius & Berry, 1990; Robinson & Levy, 1986). For field experiments that could only be partly controlled, the occurring differences might be traced back to possible different viewing situations for men and women. For instance, it might be the case that women more often combine television viewing with household chores, which might interfere with the intake and processing of news reports (Hermans & Van Snippenburg, 1993; Wittebrood, 1992; see also Chapter 10). However, in completely controlled laboratory experiments such explanations cannot be expected. The results of some experimental studies nevertheless reveal differences between men and women (Findahl & Höijer, 1985; Renckstorf, 1980a; Renckstorf & Rohland, 1980). The question concerning the *explanation* of such differences, however, usually receives little attention. For us, though, this question is the starting point for this investigation.

Research question and hypotheses

The central theme here is recollection of two news reports from the Dutch NOS news, broadcast at 9 a.m. on February 25, 1994. The first report concerns the attack on a mosque in Hebron, Israel, which took place several hours earlier that day. The second report was about plans for a confederation of Muslims and Bosnian Croats.[2] In this study we first attend to the question as to whether there are any differences between men and women with respect to the extent in which they are able to remember these two news reports in the short term, under identical viewing conditions. Furthermore, we are concerned with identifying factors which might be responsible for possible differences between men and women in this regard.

The first hypothesis concerning recall of the two television news reports on the attack in Hebron and the confederation of Muslims and Bosnian Croats can be formulated rather easily. Practically all reported differences between men and women with respect to recall of television news suggest that men have a higher degree of recall (Findahl & Höijer, 1985; Renckstorf, 1980a; Renckstorf & Rohland, 1980). This finding applies to the recall of knowledge acquired in the short term (e.g. as a result of one news broadcast) as well as recall of knowledge acquired over a longer period of time (Al-Menayes & Sun, 1993; Graber, 1984; Lo, 1994). We expected therefore a similar difference in recall of the two news reports in our study. The hypothesis was formulated as follows:

Men remember more of the television news reports on Hebron and Bosnia than women do.

2　The news broadcast, which lasted six minutes, featured a total of three reports. Apart from the two 'experimental' items, there was also a brief report on a police raid on a small factory in which the illegal drug Ecstasy (XTC) was produced. Primarily due to the brevity of this report and the limited amount of preparation time for the data collection in this study, we were not able to collect sufficient data on this report in order to study the recollection of this report in the same way as the recollection of the two other items.

If this hypothesis is confirmed, then the second part of the research question becomes relevant. As already mentioned this concerns factors which may explain these differences between men and women. The formulation of hypotheses about relevant explanatory factors is based on two theoretical perspectives which emphasize cognitive and motivational aspects.

Some communication studies, for example, have used information processing theories of cognitive psychology to explain recollection of television news (Abrahamson, 1993; Berry, 1983; Findahl & Höijer, 1985; Woodall *et al.*, 1983). Such studies emphasize the *cognitive aspects* and particularly the key role of specific *previous knowledge* in the processing of incoming information. According to Woodall *et al.* (1983), existing networks of associated bits of knowledge form the background of information processes in which separate units of incoming information are understood and stored on the basis of their interrelatedness. The authors refer to the whole of these knowledge networks as episodic and semantic memory. In this theory, episodic memory is constituted particularly by the actual memories (of separate episodes from, for example, a news report), whereas semantic memory contains memories associated with already existing knowledge and feelings.[3] Woodall *et al.* state that people generally have a better retention as well as a better understanding of news features when their semantic memory as a whole is more extensive. This hypothesis can be specified for the retention of one given news item. Thus, we may state that the extent to which people can reproduce interrelated facts of a television news item about a given subject depends on the amount of previous knowledge they have about the subject concerned.

Furthermore, research has shown that men have on average more knowledge of foreign affairs than women do (Kleinnijenhuis *et al.*, 1991). We also expected a similar difference with respect to previous knowledge of the news reports on Hebron and Bosnia, i.e. knowledge of the (political) situation in the Middle East and Bosnia. This expectation, together with the presupposed influence of previous knowledge on the recall of news items, led to formulation of a second hypothesis:

If men, compared to women, recall television news reports on Hebron and Bosnia better, then this is caused, among other things, by the fact that they have more previous knowledge of these subjects.

Apart from studies which emphasize the cognitive aspects of news processing, there are many studies that highlight *motivational aspects* in news processing (Hietbrink, 1993; Levy & Windahl, 1984; Perse, 1990a; Renckstorf, 1980a; Renckstorf & Wester, 1993). In these studies various concepts are discussed such as problems, interests, motives, involvement and intentions. These concepts all have in common that they are related to the *personal relevance* that a message has for the individual actor and subsequently for the motivation with which he processes the message. Studies on the recollection of

---

3   This process of attributing meaning to incoming information can, for example, take place through associations according to subject or a certain time sequence.

153

television news which emphasize motivational aspects assume that the more relevant television news is to the actor, the better he will process and remember this television news. This hypothesis can also be specified for the recollection of one given news item. We suggest that recall of a news item will be better if the news item is more relevant to the person concerned.

Furthermore, we know from other studies that men are especially interested in news items concerning foreign affairs, wars and violence (Gunter, 1987). We expected therefore that particularly men would find reports on Hebron and Bosnia relevant. This expectation, together with the presupposed influence of relevance on the recollection of news items, led to the third and last hypothesis:

If men, compared to women, recall television news reports on Hebron and Bosnia better, then this is caused, among other things, by the fact that they find these subjects more relevant.

Research procedures

In the Netherlands, little research has been conducted until recently on the recall of television news.[4] For this reason extra attention is given to describing this study: its organisation and the operationalization of key concepts.

Data for this study were collected during a lecture on television news for first year students (n=83) of sociology and communication studies at the University of Nijmegen in the Netherlands. At the beginning of the course we asked students to complete a short questionnaire which contained questions about the use of news media as well as questions about the personal relevance of various subjects. Subsequently, we showed them a NOS news broadcast taped earlier that day (9 a.m. on February, 25, 1994), as an introduction to the lecture. At the end of the lecture, we asked the students again to fill in a questionnaire. This time the instrument contained a number of questions with respect to recall of the broadcast and general knowledge questions about the Middle East and Bosnia. After data processing and removal of 'suspect' records[5], 79 respondents remained in the database.

This group of people had been exposed to a stimulus (a news broadcast) in a controlled environment (a classroom) and asked to remember the news afterwards. This set-up, then, has certain advantages in making causal judgements comparable to the conditions of laboratory experiments. The causal sequence between exposure to the broadcast and recollection afterwards became particularly clear thanks to this procedure.[6]

---

4   A field experiment within the context of the audience survey by the NOS (Dutch Broadcasting Foundation) should be mentioned here (NOS/KLO, 1975). Also important are the laboratory experiments performed by Heuvelman (1989), although it should be noted that these did not involve newscasts, but other info rmative programmes such as an adapted series of Teleac courses.

5   Although the anonimity of the respondents was explicitly guaranteed during the collection of the data, it remained possible for students to copy each others' answers. On comparing patterns in scores, we decided to remove four 'suspect' questionnaires from the database.

To safeguard the causal sequence between relevance and recollection, it was important that the news broadcast could not influence the measurement of relevancies. This was achieved by dividing the collection of data into two parts. The first part of the data was collected before the news broadcast was shown and the second part of the data afterwards. To safeguard the causal sequence between previous knowledge and recall, we could have asked questions concerning previous knowledge with respect to the Middle East and Bosnia in the first part of the data collection. However, we decided not to do this because we were afraid that these measurements of previous knowledge might influence[7] measurement of recall. In order to safeguard the causal sequence between previous knowledge and recall, we therefore formulated questions concerning previous knowledge in such a way that they could not be answered on the basis of information acquired by watching the news broadcast. The correct answers to these questions could therefore only be given on the basis of knowledge which had been acquired prior to the news broadcast.

Another point of concern was the six hour interval between time of the original broadcast of the news and moment of data collection. This made it possible for some respondents to be already familiar with the news, which might lead to alterations in previous knowledge, relevance or recall. To control the observed relations between previous knowledge and relevance on the one hand and previous knowledge and recall on the other, we therefore included questions concerning respondents' media use earlier that day. With respect to the main news event, i.e. the attack in Hebron, we asked whether the respondent had already heard about the attack. Analysis showed that there was practically no disturbing effect from media use earlier during the day or from having heard about the attack.

Furthermore, there was also the possibility that disturbances might occur by the method of data collection itself. After completing the first questionnaire or after having seen the news broadcast, respondents might acquire some idea of the research procedure and subsequently might adapt their answers to it. To control for such an effect, we asked respondents whether they, while watching the news broadcast, had reckoned with the possibility that they would be asked to answer some questions about it. Although analysis showed that 27 per cent of the respondents expected this, the score patterns of this category hardly deviated from those of other respondents. We therefore assumed that the data collection method did not have substantial influence on answers given by respondents.

This study on the recall of news items by men and women had a number of limitations, mainly related to time, finances and organisational resources. First, the research population was limited to a group of first year students. In terms of age and education, this is a

---

6 Questions concerning recall were chosen in such a way that it was not, or hardly, possible to answer them solely on the basis of general knowledge or intuition. We therefore did not have to include a control group which did not view the news broadcast. In this way we were able to deviate from a strict experimental design.

7 In comparison to the measurement of relevance, measurement of previous knowledge is more extensive. The measurement error we were afraid of was the possibility that respondents, by first answering the questions regarding previous knowledge, would become more alert and would react more strongly to the news broadcast on these subjects.

homogeneous category of people. Second, the research was limited, as specified in the problem statement, to recall of two separate television news items, both dealing with foreign affairs. Third, the research was limited to recall in the short term, i.e. not more than half an hour after viewing of the news broadcast. Finally, the investigation was limited to a laboratory situation.

It should be clear that these limitations have consequences for the generalisation of the results. On the other hand, the same limitations enabled us to control a number of variables which might have influenced the relations mentioned in the hypotheses[8] and as such improved the validity of the results.

Apart from the variable *sex*, three other concepts were operationalized per news item: the concept which we tried to explain, i.e. 'recollection,' and the concepts that might intervene in the relation between sex and recollection, i.e. 'personal relevance' and 'previous knowledge.'

Recall of the news items about the attack in Hebron and the possible confederation in Bosnia was measured by respectively four and two open questions regarding certain facts and, insofar as possible, about the connection between various facts, regarding the respondents' understanding. The answers were coded as 0 (incorrect) and 1 (correct)[9] and were subsequently indexed for both subjects. This resulted in an index of 'recall item: Hebron' ranging from 0 to 4, and an index of 'recall item: Bosnia' ranging from 0 to 2.

Personal relevance of the 'problems in the Middle East' and of 'the war in Bosnia' was measured on a scale of 6, ranging from 1 (unimportant) to 6 (important). Furthermore, we measured the personal relevance of five other news subjects[10] so the respondents would not focus their attention too much on the subjects of the Middle East and Bosnia which might have affected the measurement of recall.

Previous knowledge of the 'problems in the Middle East' and the 'war in Bosnia' was indicated by 3 items. These consisted of two multiple choice questions and one open question.[11] After (re)coding the answers into 0 (incorrect) and 1 (correct), indices were

---

8 An example of this is the possible connections between variables such as 'age', 'education' and 'viewing context' on the one hand, and variables such as 'sex', 'previous knowledge', 'relevance' and 'recall' on the other.

9 Assigning a code to questions was relatively easy. If one or both coders were uncertain about an answer, then the final code was incorporated into a checklist to make sure that a similar answer given by other respondents would be coded in the same way.

10 The five other subjects were: national politics, crime, sports, art and culture, and foreign affairs.

11 The questions concerning previous knowledge of the 'problems in the Middle East' were: (1) Who is the leader of Syria? (4 options) (2): What position was held by Anwar Sadat? (4 options) and (3) Who is Israel's Minister of Foreign Affairs? (open question).The questions concerning previous knowledge of the 'war in Bosnia' were: (1) Who is the political leader of the Bosnian Serbs? (4 options); (2) Which of the following areas was not part of former Yugoslavia?'; and (3) Of which republic is Franjo Tudjman the political leader? (open question).

constructed, ranging from 0 to 3 for both the 'problems in the Middle East' and the 'war in Bosnia'.[12]

Analysis

The data were analysed in two phases. We first examined the connections between the variables mentioned in the hypotheses at a bivariate level. This enabled us to answer at least the first hypothesis. Next, we examined by means of multivariate analysis to what extent the second and third hypothesis were valid. A description of these analyses with respect to the news report on the attack in Hebron and the news report on the possible confederation in Bosnia is given in the following sections.

Item: Hebron

The four variables involved in the hypotheses with respect to this news report are sex, previous knowledge of the situation in the Middle East, personal relevance of the problems in the Middle East and recall of the news about the attack in Hebron. Table 1 contains the zero-order correlations between these variables.

Table 1. Correlation matrix of variables with TV news item Hebron

	1	2	3
Sex: male			
Previous knowledge of Middle East	0.30*		
Relevance of Middle East	0.11	0.28*	
Recall of item on Hebron	0.39*	0.31*	0.25*

*$P < 0.05$ (one-tailed); n=79

Table 1, first of all, shows a significant correlation between sex and recall of item on Hebron 0.39. This means that men were able to remember more of the news report than women. The first hypothesis is thus empirically supported as far as this news report is concerned.

Table 1 also shows that there is no significant correlation between sex and relevance. This means that the influence of sex on recollection does not take place via relevance. The third hypothesis is therefore not valid as far as this news report is concerned. There is a correlation between relevance and recall, and given the research procedure we might even speak of influence, however, we cannot prove that influence mediates between sex and recall.

---

12 The questionnaires had to be constructed in just a few hours which made it impossible to test the questions beforehand. The scaleability of items according to Likert or Mokken procedures was therefore not entirely satisfactory. The indices of previous knowledge and recollection subsequently constructed on the basis of content should therefore be considered as rough measures.

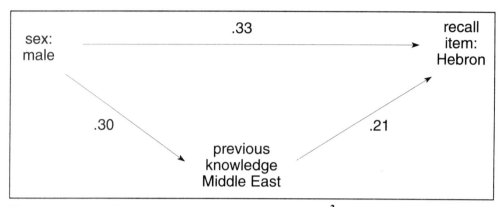

Fig. 1. Path model of recollection of TV news item Hebron. $R^2 = 0.19$; n = 79; one-tailed test

Finally, Table 1 shows that there is a significant correlation not only between previous knowledge and recall (0.31), but also between previous knowledge and sex (0.30). This may mean that previous knowledge is indeed the intermediating factor between sex and recall as stated in the second hypothesis. However, it may also indicate a spurious correlation between previous knowledge and recall as a result of the fact that they both are connected to sex.

To test the second hypothesis, we carried out a path analysis of the three variables involved. The results represented in Fig. 1 show that previous knowledge mediates part of the influence exerted by sex. This supports the hypothesis. This mediating effect is nevertheless rather limited: the direct effect of sex amounts to 0.33, whereas the effect through previous knowledge amounts to only: 0.30 * 0.21 = 0.06.

A spurious effect of previous knowledge on recall is not very prominent: the ß coefficient of previous knowledge decreases from 0.31 to 0.21 and remains significant.[13] Finally, the whole model explains 19 per cent of the variance of recall, which is not a bad result considering the fact that the model contains only a limited number of variables and relations between these variables.

Item: Bosnia

The four variables involved in the hypotheses with respect to the news report on Bosnia are sex, previous knowledge of Bosnia, personal relevance of the war in Bosnia and recollection of the news about the possible confederation in Bosnia. Table 2 shows the zero-order correlations between these variables.

---

13 The bivariate correlation coefficient from Table 1 equals, after all, the β coefficient in a regression equation in which prior knowledge is the *only* predictor of recall.

Table 2. Correlation matrix of variables with TV news item Bosnia

	1	2	3
Sex: male			
Previous knowledge of Bosnia	0.22*		
Relevance of Bosnia	0.06	0.18	
Recollection of item on Bosnia	0.31*	0.36*	0.11

*$P < 0.05$ (one-tailed); n=79

Also in Table 2 we see a significant correlation between sex and recall, this time 0.31. This means that the male respondents could also remember more of this news report than the women. This constitutes another empirical support for the first hypothesis.

Table 2 also shows that relevance does not correlate with recall nor with sex. The third hypothesis is therefore, also in this instance, not valid. Finally, Table 2 reveals that there is a significant correlation between previous knowledge and recall (0.36) as well as between previous knowledge and sex (0.22). On the basis of the correlations, it was also in this case not possible to determine to what extent the second hypothesis was supported. We therefore carried out another path analysis.

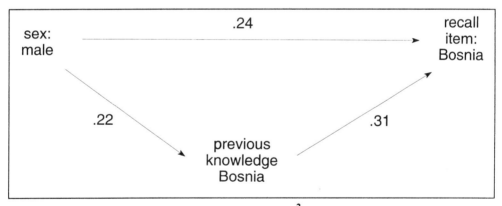

Fig. 2. Path model of recollection of TV news item Bosnia. $R^2 = 0.19$; n = 79; one-tailed test (T > 1.67).

Figure 2 shows that also in this case previous knowledge mediates part of the influence exerted by sex. This supports the second hypothesis. This mediating influence is also very small: the direct effect of sex amounts to 0.24, whereas the effect through previous knowledge is only: 0.22 * 0.31 = 0.07.

A spurious effect of previous knowledge on recollection is even less prominent here than it was in the Hebron case: the β coefficient of previous knowledge decreased from .36 (see Table 2) to 0.31 and remained significant. The explained variance of the model is exactly the same as it was in the Hebron model: 17 per cent.

Conclusions

The hypothesis that men will remember more of these two television news reports than women cannot be refuted on the basis of the results of these analyses. The same goes for the hypothesis that this difference in recall is partly mediated by a difference in previous knowledge. However, previous knowledge has only a weak mediating function between sex and recall. The hypothesis that a difference in recall is partly mediated by a difference in relevance of the news themes can be dismissed on the basis of these results.

The fact that men remember more of the news does not necessarily indicate that this is a general phenomenon, as recall is at least partly dependent on the previous knowledge men and women have of the various news themes. Thus, it remains to be seen whether men will remember more of certain news subjects of which women on the average have as much or even more previous knowledge. An example that seems to underline the influence of news themes on recall concerns a third item shown during the news broadcast which was about a police raid on a small factory that produced Ecstasy (XTC). For this item we could not test all three hypotheses because we did not have enough information to formulate suitable previous knowledge and relevance questions. In contrast with the news reports on Hebron and Bosnia, this report was better remembered by the female respondents.

As formulated in the research question, these results are only valid for a *short-term recall of only two items* by *first year students* in a *laboratory context*. This means, among other things, that more systematic research is needed before it is possible to generalize these results to a larger population and context. For example, the first year students were 'trapped' in a classroom. Apart from the news broadcast, they had fewer alternatives to focus their attention on than they would have had in a natural situation. Furthermore, the educational setting might also have increased their level of attention. This might mean that they were already watching very attentively on the average. As a result, the extra motivation through personal relevance of the theme might have had only a weak influence. The rejection of the hypothesis on relevance may therefore be caused to some extent by the laboratory-like research situation, which might to some degree have been associated with an exam situation.

And, due to the relatively small size of the group (N=79), the correlations had to be rather high to achieve statistically significance. Particularly, the relations between personal relevances and the other variables remain below the accepted limit. These relations tend to go in the direction that theoretically might be expected, but it is not possible to draw conclusions on the basis of these non-significant relations. Replication of this research among a larger population might lead to more significant relations.

The items on Hebron and Bosnia were considered separate subjects. However, qualitative research has shown that each individual defines his or her themes (Jensen, 1992). It is therefore possible that some of the students interpreted the items on Hebron and Bosnia as one single item, i.e. as foreign affairs. It is obvious that this may have consequences for the measurement of previous knowledge, relevance and recall.

One last comment is worth mentioning regarding measurement of previous knowledge and relevance. With respect to the questions concerning previous knowledge, the issue remains to what extent they measure the part of the 'memory' respondents used to process reports on Hebron and Bosnia. Given that theory concerning the nature and substance of memory and previous knowledge used to process media messages is still in its infancy, it is conceivable that the three questions concerning previous knowledge do not measure previous knowledge sufficiently. For example, it is possible that these questions measured to a large extent aspects of episodic memory, while semantic memory might be more important for answering questions concerning previous knowledge. A similar problem may occur in measuring personal relevance. Personal relevance per subject was measured by one item. This is, of course, a very rough estimate of personal relevance and one might even ask whether it is indeed possible to index a multidimensional theoretical construction as personal relevance in such a way (Hietbrink, 1993; Van Westendorp, 1981). Further research should, therefore, focus on development of suitable operationalizations of previous knowledge and relevance.

Discussion

The differences between men and women in remembering television news could only partly be explained by differences in previous knowledge and relevance. Are there any additional explanations that can be found in the literature? In addition to the variables of previous knowledge and relevance, one might also examine the process of information processing itself. One example of such an explanation is the theory that makes a distinction between processes in the left hemisphere of the brain and processes in the right hemisphere (McLuhan, 1978; Dahlgren, 1986). One of the elements of this theory, which is not entirely undisputed, is that the co-ordination of the functions of the left and the right hemisphere are somewhat different in men and women (Vroon, 1992). In men, the more rational, cognitive and sequentially oriented functions of the left hemisphere are said to dominate the more affective (emotional), associative and holistically operating right hemisphere. In women, both hemispheres of the brain are claimed to interact better, which, for example, might explain why women in general are more able to express their emotions, not because they have 'more' emotions, but because they are more aware of them (Vroon, 1992). Research has shown that women perform (particularly auditive) verbal tasks better (Robinson & Levy, 1986; Gunter, 1987) and they are better in interpreting facial expressions (Lanzetta *et al.*, 1985). McLuhan states that Western culture is characterized by an overestimation of the functions of the left hemisphere of the brain, but that television appeals more to the functions of the right hemisphere. Dahlgren (1986) formulated a similar hypothesis: 'Thus, tv-viewing, as an activity, is largely a "right brain" phenomenon, while reading is "left brain."' He explicitly applies this hypothesis to television news. Television news should in this way – at least formally – correspond more with the processing preferences of women than those of men. On the other hand, there are many who state that the choice of subjects and manner of presentation make television news a typically male genre (Jensen, 1986; Hermans & Van Snippenburg, 1993; Van Zoonen, 1991).

Given this, the differences found between men and women in remembering television news might possibly be explained by differences in content and form of presentation of the items, in interaction with sex. Gunter (1987) mentions three studies which revealed that, compared to men, women are less able to reproduce information from news items in which violent scenes are shown. When the violent images were left out, there was no difference in recall between men and women. In one of the experiments, women remembered significantly more of the 'non-violent' items than men. These findings are consistent with those in the present study: the items about the attack in Hebron and the war in Bosnia were rather shocking and both items were illustrated by images of blood and violence. A conceivable explanation might be that women focus their attention more on emotional aspects than on cognitive aspects. Despite emotional cues, men seem to focus more on cognitive aspects in processing the item. On the other hand, the item about the police raid on the Ecstasy factory was not of a violent or emotional nature at all. Perhaps that is why the cognitive aspects of this report were also processed by the women and why they on average recalled it better.

The questions concerning previous knowledge and recall in this research might 'favour' men because these questions measure cognitive knowledge that is based on spoken and written (subtitled) texts. We did not ask questions related to recall on any information given by images, which might point to a one-sided, possibly male-oriented, conceptualisation of the notion of recall. Also, the appreciation of the news items, which is a more emotional aspect, does not play a role in this research.

In short, the meaning of the differences between men and women in remembering television news reports, as often found and as also highlighted in this study, should be interpreted with the utmost of care. A broader interpretation of the concepts of 'knowledge' and 'recall' in further research is certainly desirable.

13 Information needs of the elderly

Gerrit van der Rijt

Why individuals seek information and how they go about doing this are important research concerns. Understanding these matters may offer insight which could assist us in designing proper strategies to reach people more adequately with information campaigns. This chapter provides empirical evidence for the supposition that two main types of information seeking behaviour patterns can be distinguished, namely a process of information seeking with a more routine character and a process of information seeking more specific in nature. The first type is a more general orientation adopted to accumulate information in a certain domain, while the second type is characterized by a specific orientation to seek out specific information on a topic. It is probable that each type of process has different roots or determinants: the first type by social position or professional interest and the second by 'problematic' problems which people experience.

Not only concretely experienced 'problematic' problems underlie the need for information and information seeking behaviour of people, as suggested by Bosman *et al.*, (1989), but that more routine needs for information evolve from the social position people have or the professional role they perform. This statement is based on a secondary analysis of data from an investigation among elderly people in Rotterdam, combined with the results of a study for determinants of interest in health information (Van der Rijt, 1990). First, the theoretical point of departure of the investigation is discussed and conclusions presented from the above mentioned study. Second, results from the secondary analysis are presented and interpreted in light of this theoretical perspective. Finally, a discussion about the significance of the results of both studies follows, and a proposal is outlined for further research.

Audience as theoretical focus

During the past decades a paradigm change has taken place among theories of mass communication. There has been a shift from a model in which sender and media were seen as central in the communication process to a model in which the audience has taken on a central position, and is seen as composed of intentional and meaningful actors. The consequence was not only a shift in the field of attention, but also and especially a shift in theoretical perspective – in the direction of an action theoretical approach (see Chapter 1).

The medium centered model of effects was based upon a number of dubious assumptions, such as:

- that media are able to reach (nearly) everyone in society effectively;
- that receivers of media messages are willing to accept the messages without criticism;
- that media messages in this manner constitute a direct and sufficient reason for the actual behaviour of audiences;
- that, therefore, audiences act according to the intention of the senders of media messages (Renckstorf, 1977).

In brief, audience members were seen as rather passive, uncritical consumers of media messages. This traditional paradigm of the omnipotent media, however, has been re-peatedly questioned. Klapper (1960), for one, demonstrated the limitations of this para-digm as early as 1960, and suggested that the media on their own accord seldom are a necessary and sufficient condition for the appearance of audience effects.

Since then, many studies (e.g. Atkin, 1973; Donohen & Tipton, 1973; Blumler, 1979) have demonstrated that the concept of the receiver as a rather passive, automatically reacting individual, does not justify his/her actual role in the process of communication. In fact, the receiver should be seen as an active, conscious, purposive and meaningful actor in a social setting who uses media products for the benefit of his/her own wishes and needs.

This audience-centered paradigm has given rise to a large number of alternative ap-proaches, of which the uses and gratifications approach (Katz *et al.*, 1974) became the prototype. In this approach the assumption was made that the receiver *uses* the media in order to *gratify* his own *needs*. Whereas concepts like information needs and information seeking behaviour were of no significance at all in the medium centered paradigm, these concepts have now become the focus of interest in recent work, like the 'sense-making approach, in which information seeking behaviour is accepted as the attempt by the individual consumer to bridge the gap between his/her knowledge of reality and proble-matic experiences with that reality (Dervin, 1989).

Bosman *et al.*, (1989), inspired by the sense-making approach, argue that one of the methods people use to tackle and solve problems which cannot be handled in a routine manner, is to search for information. Accordingly, 'A demand for information generally arises from an individual question, which is preceded by an individually subjectively experienced problem' (Bosman, *et al.*, 1989:141). Bosman *et al.* postulate a difference between problematic and non-problematic problems. In contrast with non-problematic problems, for which routine solutions already exist, the problematic ones are without such routine solutions. The experience of non-routinely solvable problems is therefore seen as the most important and sole direct determinant of the demand for information. And, although the question remains if the mentioned factor is the only one, it certainly must be valued as an important determinant for information seeking behaviour.

Several theories use a comparable point of departure, like the dissonance theory of Festinger (1957) and Dervin's (1989) sense-making approach. In addition to experienced 'problematic' problems, factors like curiosity, interest in a certain field of knowledge, and professional need to keep in touch with developments in one's professional field, can also be seen as determinants for a more or less routine information seeking behaviour (Van der Rijt, 1990). This implies the existence of a (type of) routine information seeking behaviour which is mainly independent of concretely experienced 'problematic' problems. Next to the two already mentioned processes (Bosman *et al.*, 1989:142), the possible existence of such routine orientation towards information suggests at least a third type of communicative process deserving investigation. All three categories can be formulated as follows:

(1) processes in which observed information leads to a 'real' problem and causes an individual demand to arise, and

(2) processes in which such individual demand causes a search for information in order to solve a problem,

(3) processes in which individuals are inclined to search routinely for information on a certain field because of interests caused and specified by professional, social and psychological factors.

Such routinely based interest can be described as a general information need for a certain domain of knowledge. This concept suggests a rather permanent motivational condition and intention to search for information in a specific domain of knowledge (for instance, the health domain). Whether such a permanent motivational condition exists and whether this condition indeed leads to permanent information seeking behaviour must still be established empirically.

An audience-centered frame of reference, as indicated above, is of great importance for health education interventions. A health education intervention is defined as 'a (mass)communicative intervention with the aim to promote the health of an individual and/or of the society as a collective' (Van der Rijt, 1990:150). The audience-centered approach, in particular, offers opportunity to study and identify factors which determine a need for information (or, in other words, a demand for health information) and the information seeking behaviour. In this sense, the same approach is appropriate to serve as a conceptual framework for so-called target group research intended to assist in the design of health information campaigns.

It is generally accepted that in order to conduct effective campaigns, it is necessary to understand the needs, wishes and customs of the target group regarding its already existing information supply. Only in this manner is it possible to adjust the campaign design to those needs, wishes and customs properly. Research into how people deal with health information and how the demand for information in this domain comes about is thus of fundamental importance in order to design a good target group campaign. This means that an audience-centered approach can exercise an important conceptual task on behalf of the campaign design. This is reference to so-called 'formative research' (Atkin & Freimuth, 1989). Here, the study among elderly people presented can be seen as a pre-campaign investigation.

This chapter also deals with the question as to what degree individually experienced problems lead to a demand for health information among the elderly. Attending to this question provides opportunity to test the central hypothesis of the theoretical frame of reference developed by Bosman *et al.* (1989). The question also has considerable social relevance. It is a commonly accepted thesis that an adequate health information (educational) policy should be developed for the elderly (Driest, 1986; Van Linschoten & Van den Heuvel, 1989; Beliën & Kanters, 1990).

Elderly people (65 years and older) constitute, in both relative and absolute terms, the fastest growing segment of the population in the Netherlands. The number of persons 80 years and older is also increasing. In addition, these senior citizens have – relatively speaking – many specific social and health problems. The idea that prevention or health promotion through information is unnecessary for much of this group because many of these persons are approaching the end of their lives is unjustified. Health information may not only lead to a healthier life-style during this period and so extend these persons lives, it may well contribute to a more fulfilling life-style. Good health information can help solve certain problems (e.g. solitude), lessen infirmities due to old age and reduce some inevitable forms of suffering. It is therefore relevant to determine which types of 'problematic' problems with which the elderly have to contend could be distinguished, and to what degree need for information arises from these problems.

Previous research

Earlier research (Van der Rijt, 1990) suggests that women in particular have interest in health information. Both age and social economic status were not, surprisingly, related to interest in health information. From the same investigation it appeared that of the four distinct health orientations (harm avoidance, unconcern, fatalism and locus of control) only harm avoidance could be seen as a determinant of interest in health information.

Apparently, women have more need for health information than men. The same goes for persons who have a preventive (harm avoiding) orientation towards health. Both socio-economic status and age were not related to these (general) needs in this study. As for the role of sex, because of the traditional division of roles between sexes in society in which women generally have to fulfil the caring tasks to which they are socialized from childhood, health information belongs to the domain of women's 'professional' interest and is an essential requisite for the performance of these caring tasks. In this sense, the (third) process of routine information seeking behaviour on the basis of professional interest is supported by the results of this study. This in contrast with the (second) process of information seeking behaviour on the basis of experienced 'problematic' problems.

However, it is likely that in the last case there exists a very specific demand for information and not an unspecified general interest; notably, a demand that is especially addressed to the domain in which the problem arises. For instance, the experience of problems in the domain of heart or vascular diseases will promulgate a search for specific information about (the handling of) these diseases. Consequently, the assumption is that routine interest leads to a rather general unspecified demand for information, while experienced 'problematic' problems generate a very specific demand for information.

On the basis of this discussion of theoretical issues and results from previous research, it is possible to formulate the research question and hypotheses to be tested in this investigation among the elderly.

Research question and hypotheses

The research question to be investigated is: *to what degree are experienced 'problematic' problems and social position determinants of the need for (health) information among the elderly?* On the basis of the theoretical frame of reference developed by Bosman *et al.* (1989) and results from previous research, it is possible to formulate the following hypotheses:

(1) The more a person experiences problems in a certain domain, the greater the demand for information will be regarding this domain. In addition, it is expected that the experience of 'problematic' problems will be a determinant of the demand for information in a certain domain, and hence the relationship of information demand with 'problematic' problems will be the strongest.

(2) Women will be more interested in health and safety information, while men will be more interested in financial information. It is also expected that SES and age will hardly relate to interest for information about health and safety. In all likelihood, SES will be related negatively to interest in financial information, as 'problematic' problems will rather occur in lower SES groups.

(3) Of the health orientations especially harm avoidance (a preventive orientation) will be related to interest in information about health and safety.

(4) The subjectively experienced state of health (the extent to which one feels healthy) will also be an important factor for determining one's interest in information about diseases. This hypothesis is based on the assumption that someone who feels less healthy will experience more 'problematic' problems in this domain.

Research method

The hypotheses were tested through secondary analysis of data from research on the relevance and feasibility of a special health information programme for elderly people on local television in Rotterdam (Cleophas & Vermeulen, 1990). The objective of this research was to gain insight into the wishes of elderly people with regard to the desired content of such a television programme. Questionnaires were administered to a random sample of 600 elderly, between 55 and 76 years. The questionnaire contained items about the need for (health) information and its determinating factors. Of the 600 elderly, 428 eventually responded (response: 71 per cent). However, it appeared that only 319 (53 per cent of the sample of 600 elderly) of the questionnaires were completed satisfactorily. Therefore, only data from those 319 respondents could be analyzed.

Measures were collected on the following variables and concepts:

- Interest in information about problems that particularly relate to ageing;
- Experience of social, financial and physical problems connected with ageing;
- Health orientations: preventive orientations (harm avoidance), unconcern, fatalism, and internal control (locus of control);
- Subjectively experienced state of health;
- Socio-structural variables: sex, age, marital state and SES.

Operationalizations and scale constructions

Interest in information

Interest in information was measured by asking respondents to indicate the topics, selected from a predetermined list, on which they liked being well informed. The topics from the list and the related percentage responses are presented in Table 1. Although some topics are not specifically relevant for elderly, they are presented within the frame of problems encountered by this age group. In this manner, each topic gained a specific character relevant for senior citizens.

A factor analysis was performed to determine whether clusters of related topics could be found. Topics mentioned by less than 10 per cent of the respondents were excluded from the analysis as well as topics with low communality. After oblique rotation, the factor analysis showed six well interpretable clusters of topics covering specific domains of information interest. Factor scores were then calculated with regard to each of these six clusters and the outcome was further used in the analysis as (six) dependent variables. One topic, which formed no clear cluster with the others, was also included in the analysis because of its special theoretical relevance.

The six scales and the single topic, the numbers of which correspond with those in Table 1, are noted below.

1. *Interest in Information about Safety* (IIS). This scale refers to the following topics (ranked in order of the factor loadings given in brackets):
9 (0.72), 7 (0.50), 14 (0.46), 5 (0.44), 1 (0.43). The reliability of this scale (α) is 0.63.

2. *Interest in Information about physical and psychological symptoms of Aging* (IIA). This scale includes topics: 10 (0.77) and 3 (0.75); $\alpha = 0.74$.

3. *Interest in Financial Information* (IIF), formed by topics: 15 (0.79) and 4 (0.44); $\alpha = 0.49$.

4. *Interest in Information about Leisure time* (IIL).

This scale includes topics: 8 (0.61) and 11 (0.49); $\alpha = 0.46$.

168

Table 1. Interest in elderly specific information

No.	Topic	Percentage
1	Provisions for elderly living independently	52
2	Healthy food and diet	43
3	Physical symptoms and aging	38
4	Social benefits and compensations	35
5	Housing and lodging	31
6	Holiday opportunities	31
7	Fear of crime	30
8	Physical training	29
9	Safety in and around the house	28
10	Psychological symptoms of aging	26
11	Leisure time and hobbies	25
12	Patient's rights	23
13	Use of medicine	21
14	Safety in traffic	20
15	Sufficient income	20
16	Aid and odd job services	16
17	Legal arrangements	16
18	Provisions for the handicapped/disabled	15
19	Admission to institutions/homes	15
20	Social contacts and solitude	14
21	Disease/illness	11
22	Hospitalization	11
23	Courses and education	8
24	Sexuality	5
25	Handicaps	4
26	Employment opportunities	4
27	Drinking problems	2

Note: The original categories were dichotomous (do/don't like to be informed about the referring topics)

5. *Interest in Information about Patient's rights and legal conditions* (IIP).

The topics are: 12 (0.68) and 17 (0.59); $\alpha = 0.56$.

6. *Interest in Information about Diseases and use of medicine* (IID).

The scale includes topics: 13 (0.49), 21 (0.45) and 2 (0.34). $\alpha = 0.51$.

7. *Interest in Information about (social) Contacts and solitude* (IIC). This particular topic (20) is employed in the analysis as a single item.

Health orientations

With a factor analysis involving items from a previous study (Van der Rijt, 1990), four factors were found after oblique rotation: *Fatalism* (FA), *Preventive Orientation* (or harm avoidance) (PO), *Internal Control* (IC) and *Unconcern* (UC). The highest loading (0.45) items of the factor 'Fatalism' (FA) were:

*   'staying healthy is purely good luck' (0.79);
*   'good health is a matter of having all go well' (0.76);

- 'having good health is determined mainly by accidental circumstances' (0.73);
- 'illness comes by fate' (0.69);
- 'most illness is a matter of bad luck' (0.65);
- 'most illness cannot be prevented' (0.59).

For the factor 'Preventive Orientation' (PO) the following items were loaded (0.45):

- 'as much as I can, I avoid all that might damage my health' (0.79);
- 'I always follow advice for a healthier life' (0.77);
- 'I pay a lot of attention to my health' (0.75);
- 'I do much to stay fit' (0.70);
- 'regularly consulting my physician is for me the best way to prevent disease' (0.52).

The highest loading (0.45) items on 'Internal Control' (IC) were:

- 'when feeling ill I know I wasn't careful enough' (0.79);
- 'if something goes wrong with my health it is my own fault' (0.75);
- 'I can prevent most diseases when I care for myself well' (0.48).

Finally, the next items loaded higher than .45 on the factor 'Unconcern' (UC):

- 'I am not afraid to become ill' (0.68);
- 'I hardly worry about my health' (0.62).

The reliability of the first three scales is reasonably high: is respectively: 0.83 (FA), 0.81 (PO), 0.78 (IC). The reliability of the last factor, however, is only 0.56 (UC). This can be explained by the fact that this scale is constructed from only two items.

Experienced problems

Respondents were asked to what extent they had to cope with a number of problems believed to be related to aging. They were given several statements, which could be answered with the help a five-point scale (highly agree to highly disagree). After oblique rotation the factor analysis resulted in four clusters of problem areas:

(a) *Psychological and physical problems of aging* (AP)

The highest loading items were:

>'I become forgetful (absent minded)' (0.77);
>'I become tired quickly' (0.75);
>'I get infirmities of old age' (0.74);
>'My eye-sight gets worse' (0.69);
>'I become a bad walker' (0.68);
>'My sense of hearing gets worse' (0.63). = 0.86.

(b) *Financial problems* (FP)

Here, the highest loaded items were:

>'I have to economize on many things'(0.90);
>'I have financial worries' (0.82);

'My income does not really allow me to make both ends meet' (0.82);
'I cannot afford extra expenses' (0.81). = 0.90.
(c) *Problems of spending leisure time – Time Problems* (TP):

'I like to do a lot in my leisure time but I don't know what and how' (0.81);
I don't know what to do' (0.76);
'I often feel bored' (0.75);
'I hardly have hobbies'(0.73). = 0.83.

d) Feeling unsafe / problems of safety (UP):

'I feel defenceless' (0.84);
'I don't feel safe at home' (0.75);
'I hardly dare to walk in the streets' (0.69)
'I don't feel safe in traffic anymore' (0.57) = 0.80.

The reliability coefficients of these scales are satisfactory.

Finally, a measure of *Social Economic Status* (SES) was constructed based on an additive index of educational level and income.

Results

Table 2 shows the bivariate correlations between the dependent and independent variables. The results with regard to the experienced problems clearly indicate that experienced

Table 2. Interest in information and independent variables

	Scales						
	IIS	IIA	IIF	IIL	IIP	IID	IIC
Independent variables:							
Sex	0.00	0.08	–0.03	–0.16^t	0.07	0.07	0.02
Age	0.07	0.25^t	–0.11*	–0.14*	0.04	0.06	0.04
Marital status	0.11	0.02	0.10	0.04	–0.04	–0.04	–0.05
SES	–0.16^t	0.03	–0.22^t	0.00	–0.08	–0.04	–0.13*
Sub. exp. health	–0.10	–0.15^t	–0.12*	0.03	–0.11	–0.12*	0.11*
Fatalism	0.08	–0.09	0.11	–0.07	–0.03	0.00	0.03
Prev. orientation	0.18^t	0.01	0.09	–0.06	0.04	0.15^t	0.02
Internal control	0.02	0.08	–0.04	0.02	–0.03	0.03	0.01
Unconcern	–0.05	0.09	–0.01	–0.06	–0.07	–0.14*	0.03
Problems of ageing	0.16^t	0.22^t	0.14*	–0.06	0.14*	0.18^t	0.19^t
Financial problems	0.16^t	–0.01	0.34^t	0.07	0.16^t	0.07	0.16^t
Leisure time spend. probl.	0.19^t	0.03	0.25^t	–0.02	0.11*	0.12*	0.27^t
Feeling unsafe	0.36^t	0.10	0.21^t	0.02	0.20^t	0.21^t	0.23^t

Notes: Columns contain bivariate correlation coefficients;
n=319. *$P < 0.05$ (two-sided) $^t P < 0.01$ (two-sided).
Scales: IIS: Interest in Information about Safety (IIS); IIA: Interest in Information about psychological and physical problems of Aging (IIA); IIE: Interest in Information about Financial matters (IIF); IIL: Interest in Information about spending Leisure time (IIL); IIP: Interest in Information about Patient's rights and legal provisions (IIP); IID: Interest in Information about Diseases and use of medicine (IID); IIC: Interest in Information about (social) Contacts and solitude (IIC)

problems in certain domains stimulate an interest in information about these domains. The correlations between problems on a certain field and the need for information about that field are the strongest. However, it also appears that correlations exist between experienced problems on a certain field with interest in information about other domains. This may be partly explicable by the fact that there are strong correlations among the different types of experienced problems. This implies that persons who experience problems in a certain domain also experience problems more often in other domains.

At any rate, the assumption in the first hypothesis is strongly supported here: persons who experience problems in the financial domain particularly show interest in information about income and making ends meet. Persons, who feel unsafe like to be informed about safety matters, etc. It may thus be concluded that indicators of experienced problems clearly correlate stronger with interest in information about specific domains than all other independent variables.

When the following scales are taken as indicators for the need for specific health information[1] – need for Safety information (IIS), for information about the psychological and physical problems of Aging (IIA), for information about Patient's rights (IIP) and for information about Diseases (IID) – it is striking that sex shows no significant correlation with the need for specific health information. On the other hand, age appears to be significantly correlated with IIA, which means that with aging the need for information about physical and psychological problems increases.

Apart from this, age shows no significant correlation with the other indicators of the need for health information. But, regarding SES, there is a significant negative correlation with IIS. Consequently, the lower the socio-economical status the higher the need for information about safety. As expected, SES correlates negatively with the need for financial information: the lower strata need more information about income and making ends meet than the higher ones. The lower strata also need more information about social contacts and solitude.

No significant correlation between sex and the need for financial information could be observed. This is in contrast with a correlation between sex and age, on the one hand, and information about the spending of leisure time, on the other: men show more interest in this information (leisure) than women, and this interest is stronger the younger one is. It may thus be concluded that – with the exception of the correlation between SES and the need for financial information – the assumptions in the second hypothesis are not supported very strongly.

Concerning the health orientations, it is striking that they correlate with the indicators of the need for specific health information to a lesser extent, as expected. Both fatalism and internal control do not significantly correlate with any of the indicators.

---

1   The need for specific health information can be seen as a multi-dimensional concept, of which only four aspects (dimensions) were measured here. More aspects may be distinguished, but these were not included in the first study.

Table 3. Regression analysis – interests in types of information

Dependent variable Interest in:	R^2	Independent variables in the comparison	β	T	p (sig. T)
Information Safety	0.14	Feeling of unsafety	0.34	6.42	0.000
		Prev. orientation	0.11	2.14	0.033
Information on Ageing	0.11	Age	0.22	4.08	0.000
		Probl. ageing	0.19	3.49	0.001
		Fatalism	–0.11	2.11	0.035
Information Financial	0.14	Financial problem	0.29	5.21	0.000
		Spending leisure time	0.15	2.77	0.006
Information on Leisure time	0.04	Sex	–0.15	–2.71	0.007
		Age	–0.12	–2.13	0.033
Information Patients' rights	0.04	Feeling unsafe	0.20	3.59	0.000
Information on Diseases	0.06	Feeling unsafe	0.20	3.67	0.000
		Unconcern	–0.12	–2.11	0.035
Information Social contact	0.08	L. time spend. probl.	0.21	3.38	0.001
		Feeling unsafe	0.13	2.10	0.037

Note: Only those independent variables are mentioned which contribute significantly to the explained variance; n=319.

A preventive orientation (PO) is positively correlated with the need for safety information (IIS) and the need for information about diseases (IID). This finding supports the third hypothesis. It also appears that Unconcern (UC) is negatively correlated with the need for information about diseases. The more one is concerned about one's health the more one needs that particular information.

Finally, it appears that the subjectively experienced state of health (the extent one feels healthy) correlates in the expected (negative) direction with the indicators for interest in health information. However, in general, the correlations are weak and are only significant with the variables IIA and IID. Consequently, the fourth hypothesis is, albeit weakly, supported.

Multiple regression

In order to find out which factors significantly contribute to the explained variance in the indicators of information interest and in order to control for other factors, a multiple regression analysis was performed. Each variable of interest in (specific) information was in turn used as a dependent variable against all independent variables. Table 3 shows the results of this analysis.

From the data in Table 3 it appears that, per dependent variable, only a few independent variables remain which explain a significant part of the variance. The explained variance varies from 0.14 up to 0.04 and is consequently very weak. Besides the limited explaining

173

power of the independent variables, it appears that – with the exception of interest in information about spending leisure time – experienced problems plays the most important role. Interest in information about safety appears to be determined especially by feeling unsafe. Also, a preventive health orientation contributes significantly here.

Besides age, interest in information about physical and psychological problems of aging is also determined by the experience of problems in this domain. Finally, it appears that a less fatalistic health orientation is related to this interest.

Interest in information about financial affairs appears to be determined especially by experience with these problems, but also by experience with problems related to spending leisure time. Probably financial matters play an important role here, in the sense that finances create more opportunities to spend one's time as one desires.

In this respect it is striking that apparently interest in information about leisure is not determined by problems in this field, but depends more on sex and age. Men show more interest in information about spending leisure time, and this interest is higher the younger one is. The same results were found in the bivariate analysis. So, experiencing problems in this field (spending leisure time) leads to interest in information about income and making (financial) ends meet, but not to interest in information about spending leisure time.

The only factor which seems to be of importance for interest in information about patient's rights is the experience of feeling unsafe. This factor is also jointly responsible for interest in information about diseases. A higher concern about one's health leads to a higher interest in this field, too. And finally, it appears that interest in information about social contacts and solitude is determined by experience of leisure problems, on the one hand, and by experience of feeling unsafe, on the other. This problem area can be seen as related to problems in the area of solitude, in the sense that solitude and the lack of social contacts probably stimulate negative experiences with spending leisure time, and that the lack of social contacts reinforces feeling unsafe.

Conclusions

It appeared from this study that, in general, the experience of 'problematic' problems in a certain area stimulates interest in information about that area. Of course, this holds only insofar as the assumptions about causality used here are justified. However, this cannot be proved conclusively on the basis of cross-sectional research. It may be concluded that the results clearly support the reference frame as developed by Bosman *et al.* (1989) with regard to the emergence of demand for information.

With one exception, the social structural variables appear to be of little direct relevance. It is striking that the relationships of the indicators of interest in health information with sex are not at all observable in this study. The same goes with regard to the general negative correlations with SES which were found in the bivariate analysis. Very probably, a low

SES leads to larger problems in the field of finances and also in the health area. In turn, these problems lead further to higher interest.

The experienced problems, then, can be seen as intervening variables in the process of the emergence of a demand for information. In turn, they themselves are dependent on the financial circumstances of the particular person. An interesting finding is that experienced problems in a certain field do not automatically bring about exclusive interest in information about that particular domain. So, for instance, it appears that the experience of feeling unsafe leads not only to an interest in information about safety, but also to an interest in information about diseases and the use of medicine, to an interest in information about patient's rights and about social contacts and solitude.

It may also be concluded that experiencing problems in a certain field in some cases leads to interest in information about other domains, like those regarding problems about spending leisure time. Such problems lead to interest in information about financial affairs and about social contacts, but not to an interest in information about spending time. This finding is explicable by the (probable) fact that in order to spend leisure time as one wishes, conditions such as sufficient finances and social contacts must first be met.

A clear discrepancy was found between the results of previous research (Van der Rijt, 1990) and this study. In the first investigation, sex appeared to be an important factor in explaining the interest in health information. Here, however, sex is of no significance. A possible explanation for this might be that in the earlier research, conducted in 1990, interest in health information was measured by asking more general questions, while in this study the measuring has been directed at specific information of relevance for the respondents – the elderly – and directed at their problems.

Interest in information about specific problems is probably highly determined by related experience with these problems. This means that the process of obtaining information as described at the beginning of this chapter (experience of a 'problematic' problem leads to an individual demand for information) may be treated as an appropriate theoretical model. In the case of a general interest in health information, the model of information seeking behaviour in a routine manner seems more appropriate. Hence, both types of processes lead to a demand for (health) information, but probably have different roots and determinants and thus cannot be combined.

A second explanation for the found discrepancy may well be that this study was conducted under a completely different population (elderly in Rotterdam) than the research group used in the 1990 study (clients of family doctors). A handicap in testing the assumptions adequately stems from different research methods: in the first study problem specific interests are not measured, while in the second study measures of more general interests in information about health were not included. An adequate test requires measurement of both types of variables in the same investigation. Only then is it possible to establish whether both types of processes can be distinguished empirically and whether both processes have different determinants.

In both studies – in contrast with the initial assumption – SES does not appear to be an important (direct) determinant of interest in health information, insofar as it plays any role at all. This is probably because SES is an indirectly operating factor. This means that it, in some way, influences the experience of 'problematic' problems, which in turn leads to information seeking behaviour.

The role of health orientations in the process of the emergence of an information demand is not yet clear. Although it was initially found that, in general, a preventive orientation seems to stimulate interest in health information and that the other health orientations did not play a role of importance (Van der Rijt, 1990), it appears from this study that several health orientations are related to various (areas of) specific health interests. While a preventive orientation seems to stimulate interest in information about safety, concern about one's health stimulates an interest in information about diseases and the use of medicine, and fatalism stimulates – somewhat less – interest in information about physical and psychological problems of aging.

These results suggest that health orientations play different roles depending on which condition, a general or specific information interest, is involved. This needs to be clarified in future research. Therefore, in a follow-up study these seemingly conflicting findings must be taken into consideration, and the following research questions should be posed:

- Which factors determine the need for information and information seeking behaviour in the field of health and medical information?

- Are different processes of information seeking behaviour dependent on different conditions (general or specific interests)?

- To what extend is it possible to speak of routine interest and routine information seeking behaviour, and to what extent of problem related interest and problem related information seeking behaviour?

- What differences exist between the two processes and under which conditions do both processes occur?

- How and in what way are these processes related to active and passive exposures to health information?

Thus, the assumption is that it is possible to speak of two types of processes. The first one, the routine process, is a more general orientation, while the second, the problem directed information seeking process, is focused upon a more specific orientation: problem solving information. The first process will be determined more by professional interest in health information, while the second one will be more determined by concrete problematic health problems. In subsequent study both types of variables should be included. Dependent variables should include variables which measure a 'general information interest' or 'general seeking behaviour' (in the field of health information), and variables which measure a 'specific problem oriented interest' or 'specific seeking behaviour' (in the same field). In addition to these four concepts another one, which must be seen as a special dependent variable should be included: the concept 'factual consumption of health information in the media.' Variables, measuring the concepts 'experienced health problems,' 'health orientations,' 'professional interest in health information,' 'life style,' and other conventional demographic variables should also be included.

The results of the present study also suggest that future target group research conducted around information campaigns should investigate whether specific 'problematic' situations occur, and if so which ones. Further, it is important to determine to which specific demands for information they lead, and how people are inclined to gather the appropriate information in that specific field. Such research may contribute to the identification of different target groups and to insight into how they can be best reached and addressed.

Bibliography

Aa, F. van der and Neeve, M. de (1983) *Alleenstaan: Leefsituatie, knelpunten en mogelijkheden,* Amersfoort: De Horstink.

Abrahamson, U.B. (1993) 'When women watch tv,' *Nordicom Review* 2: 37-52.

Adoni, H. and Mane, S. (1984) 'Media and the social construction of reality,' *Communication Research* 11: 323-340.

Adorno, T.W. (1963a/1970) 'Prolog zum Fernsehen,' in T.W. Adorno, *Eingriffe. Neun Kritische Modelle,* Frankfurt am Main: Suhrkamp.

Adorno, T.W. (1963b/1970) 'Fernsehen als Ideologie,' in T.W. Adorno, *Eingriffe. Neun Kritische Modelle,* Frankfurt am Main: Suhrkamp.

Al-Menayes, J.J. and Sun, S. (1993) 'Processing information: What are the cognitive units and how are they related?,' *Gazette* 52: 57-84.

Altheide, D.L. (1985) 'Symbolic interaction and 'uses and gratification': Towards a theoretical integration,' *Communications* 11: 51-60.

Anderson, J. (1987) *Communication research. Issues and methods,* New York: McGraw-Hill.

Anderson, J. and Meyer, T.P. (1988) *Mediated communication: A social action perspective,* Newbury Park, CA: Sage.

Ang, I. (1991) *Desperately seeking the audience. How television viewership is known,* London: Routledge.

Arts, K., Hendriks Vettehen, P., and Pelzer, B. (1990a) 'Het tijdsbestedingsonderzoek van 'MASSAT 1989',' in K. Renckstorf and J. Jansen (red.) *Communicatiewetenschappelijke Bijdragen 1989-1990,* Nijmegen: ITS.

Arts, K., Hollander, E., Renckstorf, K., and Verschuren, P. (1990b) *Grootschalig onderzoek naar media-uitrusting, media-exposure en mediagebruik in Nederland 1989. Verantwoording en Beschrijving van de data,* Nijmegen: ITS.

Atkin, C.K. (1973) 'Instrumental utilities and information seeking,' in P. Clarke (ed.) *New models for mass communication research,* Beverly Hills, CA: Sage.

Atkin, C.K. and Freimuth, V. (1989) 'Formative evaluation research in campaign design,' in R.E. Rice and C.K. Atkin (eds) *Public communication campaigns,* London: Sage.

Barnlund, D.C. (1970) 'A transactional model of communication,' in C.I. Sereno and K.K. Mortensen (eds.) *Foundations of communication theory*, New York, Harper & Row.

Barton, A.H. (1968) 'Bringing society back in survey research and macro-methodology,' *American Behavioural Scientist* 11: 1-9.

Bauer, R.A. (1964) 'The obstinate audience,' *American Psychologist* 19: 319-328.

Bauer, R.A. (1973) 'The audience', in W. Schramm, I. de Sola Pool, N. Maccoby, E.B. Parker and F.W. Frey (eds.) *Handbook of Communication*, Chicago: Rand McNally.

Becker, H.S. (1963/1973) *Outsiders: Studies in the sociology of deviance*, New York: Free Press.

Becker, H.S., Hughes, E.C., Geer, B., and Strauss, A.L. (1961) *Boys in white*, Chicago: University of Chicago Press.

Beliën M. and Kanters, H.W. (1990) 'Gezondheidsbevordering bij ouderen: een vernieuwing voor GVO?,' *Tijdschrift Gezondheidsbevordering* 11, 3: 14-24.

Berger, P.L. and Luckmann, T. (1967) *The social construction of reality. A treatise in the sociology of knowledge*, New York: Doubleday.

Berger, P.L. and Luckmann, T. (1970) *Die Gesellschaftliche Konstruktion der Wirklichkeit. Eine Theorie der Wissenssoziologie*, Frankfurt: S. Fisher.

Berry, C. (1983) 'Learning from television news: a critique of the research,' *Journal of Broadcasting* 27: 359-370.

Blumer, H. (1969) *Symbolic interactionism. Perspective and method*, Englewood Cliffs, NJ: Prentice Hall.

Blumler, J.G. (1979) 'The role of theory in uses and gratifications studies,' *Communication Research* 6: 9-36.

Blumler, J.G. and Katz, E. (eds.) (1974) *The uses of mass communications. Current perspectives in gratifications research*, Beverly Hills, CA: Sage.

Blumler, J.G., Gurevitch, M. and Katz, E. (1985) 'Reaching out: a future for gratifications research', in K.E. Rosengren, L.A. Wenner and P. Palmgreen (eds.) Media gratifications research: current perspectives. Beverley Hills: Sage.

Bogart, L. (1972) *The age of television*, New York: Ungar.

Bonfadelli, H. (1983): 'Der einfluss des Fernsehens auf die Konstruktion der sozialen Realität: Befunde aus der Scheiz zur Kultivierungshypothese,' *Rundfunk und Fernsehen* 31, 3–4: 415–430.

Bosman, J., Hollander, E., Nelissen, P., Renckstorf, K., Wester, F. and Woerkum, C. van (1989) *Het omgaan met kennis – en de vraag naar voorlichting. Een multidisciplinair theoretisch referentiekader voor empirisch onderzoek naar de vraag naar voorlichting*, Nijmegen: ITS.

Bosman, J. and Renckstorf, K. (1992) 'Het concept informatiebehoefte en de samenhang tussen subjectief ervaren problemen, informatie-interesse en informatieconsumptie,' in K. Renckstorf, P. Hendriks Vettehen, and L.B. van Snippenburg (red.) *Communicatiewetenschappelijke Bijdragen 1991-1992*, Nijmegen: ITS.

Bourdieu, P. (1979/1984) *Distinction: A social critique of the judgement of taste*, London: Routledge.

Bouwman, H. (1987) *Televisie als cultuurschepper*, Amsterdam: VU Uitgeverij.

Brants, K. and Zoonen, L. van (1992) *Angst en walging in Europa: De sociale constructie van 'culturele identiteit'*, paper, Sommatie '92, Veldhoven, The Netherlands.

Brehm, B. (1994) *Televisiekijken als handelingspatroon*, Nijmegen: KUN.

Brosius, H.B. and Berry, C. (1990) 'Ein Drei-Faktoren-Model der Wirkung von Fernsehnachrichten,' *Media Perspektiven* 14: 20-30.

Brosius, H.B. (1993) 'The effects of emotional pictures in television news,' *Communication Research* 20: 105-124.

Brown, J.R. and Linné, O. (1976) 'The family as mediator of television's effects,' in R. Brown (ed.) *Children and Television*, London: Collier Macmillan.

Bruyn, S.T. (1966) *The human perpsective in sociology: The methodology of participant observation*, Englewood Cliffs, NJ: Prentice Hall.

Burdach, K. (1981) 'Methodische Probleme der Vielseherforschung aus psychologischer Sicht. Zur Kontroverse Gerbner/Hirsch,' *Fernsehen und Bildung* 15 (1-3): 99-113.

Buß, M. (1985) *Die Vielseher. Fernseh-Zuschauerforschung in Deutschland*, Frankfurt am Main: Metzner.

Chaffee, S.H., McLeod, J.M., and Wackman, D.B. (1973) 'Family communication patterns and adolescent political participation,' in J. Dennis (ed.) *Socialization to Politics: A Reader*, New York: John Wiley.

Chaffee, S.H. and Izcaray, F. (1975) 'Mass communication functions in a media-rich developing society,' *Communication Research* 2: 367-395.

Chaffee, S.H. and Schleuder, J. (1986) 'Measurement and effects of attention to media news,' *Human Communication Research* 13: 76-107.

Chaney, D. (1972) *Processes of mass communication*, London: Macmillan.

Charlton, M. and Neumann, K. (1985) *Medienkonsum und Lebensbewältigung in der Familie*, München: Psychologie Verlags Union.

Charlton, M. and Neumann, K. (1986) *Medienkonsum und Lebensbewältigung in der Familie. Methode und Ergebnisse der strukturanalytische Rezeptionsforschung, mit funf Falldarstellungen*, München: Weinheim.

Claessens, D. (1968) *Instinkt, Psyche, Geltung. Bestimmungsfaktoren menschlichen Verhaltens*, Köln: Opladen.

Cleophas, F. and Vermeulen, P. (1990) *Voorlichting aan ouderen via lokale TV; een onderzoek naar de haalbaarheid en zinvolheid van een ouderen programmema via lokale TV*, GGD, Afdeling GVO, Research Report nr.108, Rotterdam: GGD.

Comstock, G. (1989) *The evolution of american television*, Newbury Park, CA: Sage.

Cuilenburg, J. van (1983) *Overheidsvoorlichting in overvloed: Overvoorlichtingsonderzoek in het informatietijdperk*, Amsterdam: Vrije Universiteit.

181

Dahlgren, P. (1986) 'Beyond information: TV news as a cultural discourse,' *Communications* 12: 125-136.

Dahlgren, P. (1988) 'What's the meaning of this? Viewers' plural sense-making of TV news,' *Media, Culture and Society* 10: 285-301.

Darmon, R.Y. (1976) 'Determinants of TV viewing,' *Journal of Advertising Research* 16: 17-20.

Davis, D.K. and Puckett, T. (1992) 'Mass entertainment and community: Toward a culture-centered paradigm for mass communication research,' in S.A. Deetz (ed.) *Communication Yearbook 15*, Newbury Park, CA: Sage.

Davison, W.P. (1960) 'On the effects of communication', *Public Opinion Quarterly* 10: 344–360.

DeFleur, M.L. (1970) *Theories of mass communication*, New York: McKay.

DeFleur, M.L. and Ball-Rokeach, S. (1982) *Theories of mass communication*, New York: Longman.

Dekker, G. (1981) 'Gereformeerde en gereformeerd is twee', in W. Goddijn and G. van Tillo (eds.) *Hebben de kerken nog toekomst*, Baarn: Ambo.

Dekker, G. and Peters, J. (1989) *Gereformeerden in meervouud. Een onderzoek naar levelsbeschouwing en waarden van de verschillende gereformeerde stromingen*, Kampen: Kok.

Denzin, N.K. and Lincoln, Y.S. (eds.) (1994) *Handbook of qualitative research*, Thousand Oaks: Sage.

Denzin, N. (1978) *The research act. A theoretical introduction to sociological methods*, New York: McGraw-Hill.

Dervin, B. (1981) 'Mass communication: changing concceptions of the audience', in R. Rice and W. Paisley (eds.) *Public communication campaigns*, Beverley Hills: Sage.

Dervin, B. (1983) 'Information as a user construct: The relevance of perceived information needs to synthesis and interpretation,' in S.A. Ward, and L.J. Reed (eds.) *Knowledge structure and use: Implications for synthesis and interpretation*, Philadelphia, PA: Temple University Press.

Dervin, B. (1989): 'Audience as listener and learner, teacher and confidante: The sense-making approach', in R.E. Rice and C.K. Atkin (eds.) *Public communication campaigns*, 2nd edn. Beverley Hills: Sage.

Donohew, L. and Tipton, L.A. (1973) 'A conceptual model for information seeking, avoiding and processing,' in P. Clarke (ed.) *New models for mass communication research*, Beverly Hills, CA: Sage.

Doob, A. and Macdonald, G. (1979) 'Television viewing and fear of victimization: is the relationship causal?' *Journal of Personality and Social Psychology* 37: 170–179.

Driest, P. (red.) (1986) *Voorlichting aan ouderen*, 's Gravenhage: VUGA.

Edgar, P. (1977) 'Families without television,' *Journal of Communication* 27: 73-77.

Eisinga, R. and Peters, J. (1989) 'Community and commitment in the Netherlands. An examination and extension of localism theory,' paper, SSSR-RRA conference, Salt Lake City, Utah.

Elliott, P. (1974) 'Uses and gratifications research: a critique and a sociological alternative', in J.G. Blumler and E. Katz (eds.) *The uses of mass communications. Current perspectives in gratifications research.* Beverley Hills: Sage.

Fauconnier, G. (1986) *Algemene communicatietheorie*, Leiden/Antwerpen: Nijhoff.

Fauconnier, G. (1990) *Mens en media*, Leuven: Garant Uitgevers.

Felling, A., Peters, J., and Schreuder, O. (1983) *Burgerlijk en onburgerlijk Nederland. Een nationaal onderzoek naar waardenoriëntaties op de drempel van de jaren tachtig*, Deventer: Van Loghum Slaterus.

Felling, A., Peters, J., and Schreuder, O. (1987) *Religion in Dutch society. Documentation of a national survey on religious and secular attitudes in 1985*, Amsterdam: Steinmetz Archive.

Festinger, L.A. (1957) *A theory of cognitive dissonance*, Evanston, IL: Row, Peterson.

Filstead, W. J. (ed.) (1970) *Qualitative methodology: Firsthand involvement with the social world*, Chicago: Markham.

Findahl, O. and Höijer, B. (1985) 'Some characteristics of news memory and comprehension,' *Journal of Broadcasting* 29: 379-396.

Fishbein, M. and Ajzen, I. (1975) *Belief, attitude, intention, and behaviour: An introduction to theory and research*, Reading, MA: Addison-Wesley.

Fiske, J. (1987) *Television culture*, London: Methuen.

Forsey, S.D. (1963) 'The influence of family structures upon the patterns and effects of family viewing,' in L. Arons and M. May (eds.) Television and human behaviour: *Tomorrows research in mass communication*, New York: Appleton-Century-Crofts.

Forsyth, D.R. (1990) *Group dynamics*, Pacific Grove, CA: Brooks/Cole.

Frissen, V. (1988) 'Towards a conceptualization of heavy viewing,' in K. Renckstorf and F. Olderaan (red.) *Communicatiewetenschappelijke Bijdragen 1987-1988*, Nijmegen: ITS.

Frissen, V. (1992) *Veelkijken als sociaal handelen. Een empirisch onderzoek naar het verschijnsel veel televisiekijken in Nederland*, Nijmegen: ITS.

Frissen, V., Renckstorf, K. and Verschuren, P. (1989) 'Op weg naar een verklaring van het veelkijken,' in K. Renckstorf and F. Olderaan (eds.) *Communicatiewetenschappelijke Bijdragen 1988/1989*, Nijmegen: ITS.

Frissen, V. and Wester, F. (1990) 'Recente toepassingen van de interpretatieve onderzoeksbenadering in de communicatiewetenschap,' *Massacommunicatie* 2: 153-175.

Fritz, A. (1987) 'Vier Wochen mit Fernsehen: Bericht über ein Beispiel zur Fernsehforschung in Familien,' *Publizistik* 32: 159-165.

Ganzeboom, H., De Graaf, P., and Kalmijn, M. (1987) 'De culturele en economische dimensie van beroepsstatus,' *Mens en Maatschappij* 62: 153-175.

Garfinkel, H. (1967) *Studies in ethnomethodology*, Englewood Cliffs, NJ: Prentice Hall.

Gaziano, C. (1983) 'The knowledge gap: An analytical review of media effects,' *Communication Research* 10: 447-486.

Gerbner, G. (1964) 'On content analysis and critical research in mass communication,' in L.A. Dexter and D.M. White (eds.) *People, society and mass communications*, New York: Free Press.

Gerbner, G. (1969) 'Violence and television drama,' in R.K. Baker and S.J. Ball (eds.) *Violence and the media: A staff report to the national commission on the causes and prevention of violence*, Washington D.C.: US Government Post Office.

Gerbner, G. (1973) 'Cultural indicators: The third voice,' in G. Gerbner, L. Gross, and W. Melody (eds.) *Communication tachnology and social policy*, New York: Wiley.

Gerbner, G. and Gross, L. (1976a) 'Living with television: The violence profile,' *Journal of Communication* 26, 2: 173-199.

Gerbner, G. and Gross, L. (1976b) 'The scary world of TV's heavy viewer,' *Psychology Today* 10, 11: 41-45.

Gerbner, G., Gross, L., and Melody, W. (eds.) (1973) *Communications technology and social policy: Understanding the new 'cultural revolution'*, New York: Wiley.

Gerbner, G., Gross, L., Signorielli, N., Morgan, M., and Jackson Beeck, M. (1979) 'The demonstration of power: Violence profile no.10,' *Journal of Communication* 29, 3: 177-196.

Glaser, B.G. (1978) *Theoretical sensitivity, advances in the methodology of grounded theory*, Mill Valley, CA: Sociology Press.

Glaser, B.G. and Strauss, A.L. (1967) *The discovery of grounded theory. Strategies for qualitative research*, Chicago: Aldine.

Goffman, E. (1959) *The presentation of self in everyday life*, New York: Doubleday.

Goodhardt, G.J., Ehrenberg, A.S., and Collins, M.A. (1975) *The Television audience: patterns of viewing*, Farnborough: Saxon House.

Graber, D. (1984) *Processing the news: How people tame the information tide*, New York: Longmann.

Greenberg, B.S. (1974) 'Gratifications of television viewing and their correlates for British children,' in J.G. Blumler and E. Katz (eds.) *The uses of mass communication*. Beverly Hills, CA: Sage.

Greenwald, A.G. and Leavitt, C. (1984) 'Audience involvement in advertising,' *Journal of Consumer Research* 11: 581-592.

Groebel, J. (1981) 'Vielseher und Angst. Theoretische Überlegungen und einige Langschnittergebnisse,' *Fernsehen und Bildung* 15, 1-3: 114-136.

Groot, A.D. de (1969) *Methodology: Foundations of inference and research in the behavioural sciences*, The Hague: Mouton.

Guba, E.G. (1981) 'Criteria for assessing the thrustworthiness of naturalistic inquiries,' *Education, Communication and Technology Journal* 29: 75-91.

Gunter, B. (1987) *Poor reception: Misunderstanding and forgetting television news*, London: Lawrence Erlbaum.

Gunter, B. and Svennevig, M. (1987) *Behind and in front of the screen: Television involvement with family life*, London: Libbey.

Haferkamp, H. (1972) *Soziologie als Handlungstheorie*, Düsseldorf: Bertelsmann Universitätsverlag.

Hall, S. (1980/1973) 'Encoding and decoding in the television discourse,' in S. Hall, D. Hobson, and P. Lowe (eds.) *Culture, media, language*, London: Hutchinson.

Hall, S. (1982) 'The rediscovery of ideology: Return of the repressed in media studies,' in M. Gurevitch, T. Bennett, J. Curran, and J. Woollacott (eds.) *Culture, Society and the Media*, London: Methuen.

Hammersma, M. (1990) 'Horen, zien & cijfers: Resultaten van 25 jaar Kijk-en Luisteronderzoek,' in K. Renckstorf and J. Janssen (red.) *Communicatiewetenschappelijke Bijdragen 1989-1990*, Nijmegen: ITS.

Hanneman, G.J. and Greenberg, B.S. (1973) 'Relevance and diffusion of news of major and minor events,' *Journalism Quarterly* 50: 433-437.

Hasebrink, U. and Krotz, F. (1992) Individuelle Fernsehnutzung: Zum Stellenwert von Unterhaltungssendungen, *Rundfunk und Fernsehen* 3: 398-411.

Hawkins, R. and Pingree, S. (1980) 'Some processes in the cultivation effect', *Communication Research* 7, 2: 1993–226.

Hawkins, R. and Pingree, S. (1983) 'Television's influence on social reality,' in E. Wartella and C. Whithney (eds.) *Mass Communication Review Yearbook* 4, Beverly Hills, CA: Sage.

Heeter, C. and Greenberg, B.S. (1988) *Cable viewing*, Norwood, NJ: Ablex.

Heinsman, L.J. (1982) *De kulturele betekenis van de instroom van buitenlandse televisieprogrammema's in Nederland*, 's Gravenhage: Staatsuitgeverij (WRR-rapport M3 1982).

Heinsman, L. and Servaes, J. (eds.) (1991) *Televisie na 1992: Perspectieven voor de Vlaamse en Nederlandse omroep*, Leuven: Acco.

Helle, H.J. (1968) 'Symbolbegriff und Handlungstheorie,' *Kölner Zeitschrift für Soziologie und Sozialpsychologie* 20: 17-37.

Hendriks Vettehen, P. (1993) 'Handelingstheoretisch gefundeerd onderzoek naarmediagebruikspatronen: De "beredenerende" benadering', in K. Renckstorf, P. Hendriks Vettehen, W. Mutsaers and L. van Snippenburg (eds) *Communicatiewetenschappelijke bijdragen 1993–1993*, Nijmegen: ITS.

Hendriksen, P.M. (1979) 'Omroepen in de woestijn,' *Massacommunicatie* 7: 55-66.

Hermans, L. and Snippenburg, L.B. van (1993) 'Nieuws-gierigheid van vrouwen: Een interpretatief onderzoek naar de manier waarop vrouwen omgaan met televisienieuws,' *Massacommunicatie* 21: 120-135.

Heuvelman, A. (1989) *Buiten beeld*, Amsterdam: Swetz and Zeitlinger.

Hietbrink, N.R. (1993) 'Issue involvement, gratifications and television news viewing activities,' in K. Renckstorf, P. Hendriks Vettehen, W. Mutsaers, and L.B. van Snippenburg (red.) *Communicatiewetenschappelijke Bijdragen 1992-1993*, Nijmegen: ITS.

Himmelweit, H., Oppenheim, A. and Vince, P. (1958) *Television and the child. An empirical study of the effect of television on the young*, London: Oxford.

Hirsch, P. (1980) 'The 'scary world' of the non-viewer and other anomalies: A reanalysis of Gerner et al.'s findings on cultivation analysis. Part 1,' *Communication Research* 7: 403-456.

Hirsch, P. (1981) 'On not learning from one's own mistakes. A reanalysis of Gerbner et al.'s findings on cultivation analysis. Part 2,' *Communication Research* 8, 1: 3-37.

Höijer, B. (1990) 'Studying viewers reception of television programmes: Theoretical and methodological considerations,' *European Journal of Communication* 5: 29-56.

Horkheimer, M. and Adorno, T.W. (1969) *Dialektik der Aufklärung. Philosophische Fragmente*, Frankfurt: Suhrkamp.

Horton, D. and Wohl, R. (1956) 'Mass communication and para-social interaction: Observations on intimacy of a distance,' *Psychiatry* 19: 215-229.

Hovland, C.I. (1959) 'Reconciling conflicting results derived from experimental and survey studies of attitude change', *The American Psychologist* 14: 8–17.

Hsia, H.J. (1988) *Mass communication research methods*, Hillsdale NJ: Lawrence Erlbaum.

Hughes, E. (1958) *Men and their work*, Glencoe, IL: Free Press. Himmelweit, H., Oppenheim, A., and Vince, P. (1958) *Television and the child. An empirical study of the effect of television on the young*, London: Oxford University Press.

Hughes, M. (1980) 'The truth of cultivation analysis. A reexamination of the effects of television watching on fear of victimization, alienation and the approach of violence,' *Public Opinion Quarterly* 44: 287-302.

Hulett, J.E. (1966) 'A symbolic interactionist model of human communication,' *AV Communication Review* 14, 5-33: 203-220.

Hunziker, P. (1976) 'Fernsehen und interpersonelle Kommunikation in der Familie,' *Publizistik* 21: 180-195.

Hunziker, P. (1988) *Medien, Kommunikation und Gesellschaft*, Darmstadt: Wissenschaftliche Buchgesellschaft.

Huth, S. (1982) 'Zur Wirkung des Vielfernsehens. Ergebnisse aus derempirische Forschung in de USA', *Fernsehen und Bildung* 16: 149–234.

Iyengar, S., Peters, M.D., and Kinder, D.R. (1982) 'Experimental demonstrations of the 'not-so-minimal' consequences of television news programmes,' *The American Political Science Review* 76: 848-858.

Jackson-Beeck, M. (1977) 'The non-viewers: Who are they?,' *Journal of Communication* 27, summer: 62-72.

Jackson-Beeck, M. and Sobal, J. (1980) The social world of heavy television viewers. *Journal of Broadcasting* 24, 1: 5-11.

Jankowski, N.W. and Wester F. (1991) 'The qualitative tradition in social science enquiry: contributions to mass communication research', in K.B. Jensen and N.W. Jankowski (eds) *A handbook of qualitative methodologies for mass communication research*, London: Routledge.

Jensen, K.B. (1986) *Making sense of the news*, Aarhus: Aarhus University Press.

Jensen, K.B. (1987) 'Qualitative audience research: Toward an intergrative approach to reception,' *Critical Studies in Mass Communication* 4: 21-36.

Jensen, K.B. (1990) 'The politics of polysemy; television news, everyday consciousness and political action,' *Media, Culture and Society* 12, 1: 57-77.

Jensen, K.B. (1992) 'Reception analysis: Mass communication as the social production of meaning,' in N.W. Jankowski and K.B. Jensen (eds) *A handbook of qualitative methodologies for mass communication research*, London: Routledge.

Jensen, K.B. and Rosengren, K.E. (1990) 'Five traditions in search of the audience,' *European Journal of Communication* 5: 207-238.

Jensen, K.B. and N.W. Jankowski (eds.) (1991) *A handbook of qualitative methodologies for mass communication research*, London: Routledge.

Jong-Gierveld, J. de (1969) *De ongehuwden: Een sociologisch onderzoek naar de levensomstandigheden en levensinstelling van ongehuwde mannen en vrouwen*, Alphen a/d Rijn: Samson.

Kaase, M. and Schulz, W. (1989): 'Perspektiven der Kommunikations-forschung' in M. Kaase and W. Schulz (eds) *Kölner Zeitschrift für Soziologie und Sozialpsychologie*, Sonderheft 30, 'Massenkommunikation: Theorie, Methoden, Befunde', 9–27.

Kaiser, A. (1989) *De relatie publiek en journalistiek*, Utrecht: Rijksuniversiteit Utrecht.

Katz, E. (1959) 'Mass communications research and the study of popular culture,' *Studies in Public Communication* 2: 1-6.

Katz, E. (1961) 'Communication research and the image of society: convergence of two traditions,' in H. Dexter, and D.M. White (eds.) *People, society and mass communications*, New York: Free Press.

Katz, E. (1980) 'On conceptualizing media effects,' *Studies in Communications* 1: 119-141.

Katz, E. (1987) 'Communications research since Lazarsfeld,' *Public Opinion Quarterly* 51: 25-45.

Katz, E. and Lazarsfeld, P.F. (1955) *Personal influence. The part played by people in the flow of mass communications*, New York: Free Press.

Katz, E. and Foulkes, D. (1962) 'On the use of the mass media as 'escape'. Clarification of a concept,' *Public Opinion Quarterly* 26: 377-388.

Katz, E., Blumler, J.G., and Gurevitch, M. (1974) 'Utilization of mass communication by the individual,' in J.G. Blumler and E. Katz (eds.) *The uses of mass communications. Current perspectives in gratifications research*, Beverly Hills, CA: Sage.

Kazee, T.A. (1981) 'Television exposure and attitude change: The impact of political interest,' *Public Opinion Quarterly* 45: 507-518.

187

Kellerman, K. (1985) 'Memory processes in media effects,' *Communication Research* 12: 83-131.

Kepplinger, H.M. (1979) 'Paradigm change in communications research,' *Communications* 4: 163-182.

Kerstholt, F. (1989): *Tussen rationele keuze en Durkheimiaanse solidariteit: Over voortgang in theorie en onderzoek van sociale ongelijkheid*, Tilburg: Tilburg University Press.

Kiefer, M. (1987) 'Vielseher und Vielhörer. Profile zweier Mediennutzergruppen,' *Media Perspektiven* 11: 677-692.

Kiefer, M.L. (1987a) Massenkommunikation III. In K. Berg and M.L. Kiefer (red.) *Massen-kommunikation III. Eine Langzeit-studie zur Mediennutzung und Medienbewertung 1964-1986*, Frankfurt am Main: Metzner.

Kiefer, M.L. (1987b) 'Massenkommunikation 1964 bis 1985,' *Media Perspektiven* 11: 137-148.

Klapper, J. (1958) 'What we know about the effects of mass communication: The brink of hope,' *Public Opinion Quarterly* 21: 453-474.

Klapper, J.T. (1960) *The effects of mass communication*, New York: The Free Press.

Klaus, G. (1970): *Wörterbuch der Philosophie*, 2 Bde., Berlin.

Kleefmann, F. (1985) *Handelen, handelingscontext en planning. Een theoretisch-sociologische verkenning*, Wageningen: Landbouwhogeschool.

Kleinnijenhuis, J., Peeters, A., Hietbrink, N., and Spaans, D. (1991) 'Het nieuwsaanbod van NOS en RTL en wat kijkers ervan leren,' *Massacommunicatie* 19: 197-226.

Knulst, W. (1982) *Mediabeleid en cultuurbeleid*, 's-Gravenhage: Staatsuitgeverij.

Knulst, W. and Kalmijn, M. (1988) *Van woord naar beeld? Onderzoek naar de verschuivingen in de tijdsbesteding aan de media in de periode 1975-1985*, Cahier Nr. 66/1988, Rijswijk: Sociaal-Cultureel Planbureau.

Krappmann, L. (1969) *Sozologische Dimensionen der Identität: Strukturelle Bedingungen für die Teilnahme an Interaktionsprozessen*, Stuttgart: Klett.

Krappmann, L. (1972) 'Neuere Rollenkonzepte als Erklärungsmöglichkeit für Sozialisa-tionsprozess,' in: b:e-Redaktion (ed.) *Familienerziehung, Sozialschiocht und Schulerfolg*, Weinheim: Beltz.

Kraus, S. and Davis, D. (1976) *The effects of mass communication on political behaviour*, Philadelphia: Pennsylvania State University Press.

Krippendorff, K. (1993): Schritte zu einer konstruktivistischen Erkenntnistheorie, in: G. Bentele and M. Rühl (eds.) *Theorien öffetnlicher Kommunikation*, München: Öhlschäger.

Lanzetta, J.T., Sullivan, D.G., Masters, R.D., and McHugo, G.J. (1985) 'Emotional and cognitive responses to televised images of political leaders,' in R.M. Perloff and S. Kraus (1985) *Mass Media and Political Thought*, Beverly Hills, CA: Sage.

Lasswell, H.D. (1948/1964) 'The structure and function of communication in society,' in L. Bryson (ed.) *The communication of ideas*, New York: Cooper Square Publishers.

Lazarsfeld, P.F., Berelson, B., and Gaudet, H. (1948) *The people's choice*, New York: Columbia University Press.

Lazarsfeld, P.F. and Merton, R.K. (1948/1960) 'Mass communication, popular taste and organized social action,' in W. Schramm (ed.) *Mass communications*, Urbana, IL: University of Illinois Press.

Levy, M.R. (1979) 'Watching TV news as para-social interaction', *Journal of Broadcasting* 23: 69–79.

Levy, M.R. and Windahl, S. (1984) 'Audience activity and gratifications: A conceptual clarification and exploration,' *Communication Research* 11: 51-78.

Levy, M.R. and Windahl, S. (1985) 'The concept of audience activity,' in K.E. Rosengren, P. Palmgreen, and L. Wenner (eds.) *Media gratifications research: Current perspectives*, Beverly Hills, CA: Sage.

Liebes, T. and Katz, E. (1990): *The export of meaning*, New York: Oxford University Press.

Lindlof, T.R. and Copeland, A.C. (1982) 'Television rules of prepartum new families,' in Burgoon, M. (ed.) *Communication Yearbook 6*, Beverly Hills, CA: Sage.

Lindlof, T.R., Shatzer, M.J., and Wilkinson, D. (1988) 'Accomodation of video and television in the American family,' in J. Lull (ed.) *World families watch television*, Beverly Hills, CA: Sage.

Linschoten, C.P. van and Heuvel, W.J.A. van den (1989) 'GVO/Preventie voor ouderen. Aanknopingspunten voor beleid,' *Tijdschrift Gezondheidsbevordering*, 10: 53-62.

Lippmann, W. (1922) *Public opinion*, New York: Harcourt Brace.

Littlejohn, S.W. (1983) *Theories of human communication*, Belmont, CA: Wadsworth Publishing Company.

Livingstone, S. (1990) *Making sense of television*, Oxford: Pergamon.

Lo, V. (1994) 'Media-use, involvement and knowledge of the Gulf War,' *Journalism Quarterly* 71, 1: 43-54.

Lowery, S.A. and DeFleur, M.L. (1988) *Milestones in mass communication research*. Media effects, London: Longman.

Lull, J. (1978) 'Choosing television programmes by family vote,' *Communication Quarterly* 26: 53-57.

Lull, J. (1980a) 'Family patterns and the social uses of television,' *Communication Research* 7: 319-334.

Lull, J. (1980b) 'The social uses of television,' *Human Communication Research*, 6: 197-209.

Lull, J. (ed.) (1988) *World Families watch television*, Newbury Park, CA: Sage.

Lull, J. (1990) *Inside family viewing: Etnographic research on television audiences*, London: Comedia.

Lüscher, K. (1975) 'Jurisprudenz und Soziologie,' in F. Kübler (ed.) *Medienwirkung und Medienverantwortung: Überlegungen und Dokumente zum Lebach-Urteil des Bundesverfassungsgerichts*, Baden-Baden: Nomos Verlagsgesellschaft.

189

Maccoby, E. (1954) 'Why do children watch television?,' *Public Opinion Quarterly* 18: 239-244.

Maccoby, E. (1964) 'Die Wirkung des Fernsehens auf Kinder,' in W. Schramm (ed.) *Grundfragen der Kommunikationsforschung*, München: Juventa Verlag.

Maletzke, G. (1963): *Psychologie der Massenkommunikation*, Hamburg: Hans Bredow Inst.

Maletzke, G. (1967): *Publizistikwissenschaft zwischen Geistes- und Sozialwissenschaften*, Berlin: Spiess.

Maletzke, G. (1963): *Massenkommunikation*, Tübingen: Niemeyer.

Manschot, B. and Brug, H. van der (1986) 'Televisieseries: Kijkgedrag en voorkeur,' *Massacommunicatie* 14, 1: 30-35.

Manis, J.G. and Meltzer, B.N. (eds.) (1972) *Symbolic interaction*, Boston: Allyn and Bacon.

McDonald, D.G. (1986) 'Generational aspects of television coviewing,' *Journal of Broadcasting and Electronic Media* 30, 1: 75-85.

McLuhan, M. (1978) 'The brain and the media: The 'Western' Hemisphere,' *Journal of Communication* 28: 54-60.

McQuail, D. (1969) *Towards a sociology of mass communications*, London: Collier-Macmillan.

McQuail, D. (1985) 'With the benefits of hindsight: reflections on uses and gratifications research', in M. Gurevitch and M.R. Levy (eds.) *Mass communication review yearbook*, vol. 5, Beverley Hills: Sage.

McQuail, D. (1992) *Media performance. Mass communication and the public interest*. Newbury Park: Sage.

McQuail, D. (1994) *Mass communication theory*, London: Sage.

McQuail, D. and Gurevitch, M. (1974) 'Explaining audience behavior: three approaches considered', in J.G. Blumler and E. Katz (eds.) *The uses of mass communications. Current perspective on gratifications research*, Beverly Hills: Sage.

McQuail, D., Blumler, J., and Brown, J. (1972) 'The television audience: a revised perspective,' in D. McQuail (ed.) *Sociology of mass communications*, Harmondsworth: Penguin.

McQuail, D. and Windahl, S. (1993) *Communication models for the study of mass communication*, London: Longman.

Mead, G. (1934/1970) *Mind, self, and society*, Chicago: University of Chicago Press.

Meier, U. and Frissen, V. (1988) 'Zwijmelen tussen de schuifdeuren: Televisie kijken,' in L. van Zoonen (ed.) *Tussen plezier en politiek*, Amsterdam: S.U.A.

Meier, U. and Peeters, A. (1988) 'Kijken naar televisie: Een huiselijk melodrama?,' *Massacommunicatie* 16, 1: 23-34.

Miles, M.B. and Huberman, A.M. (eds.) (1984) *Qualitative data analysis: A sourcebook of new methods*, Beverly Hills, CA: Sage.

Miller, G.A. and Buckhout, R. (1973) *Psychology: The science of mental life*, New York: Harper and Row.

Morley, D. (1980): *The nation-wide audience: Structure and decoding*, London: BFI TV Monographs.

Morley, D. (1986) *Family television: Cultural power and domestic leisure*, London: Comedia.

Morley, D. (1989) 'Changing paradigms in audience studies,' in E. Seiter, H. Borchers, G. Kreutzner, and E.M. Warth (eds.) *Remote control: Television, audiences, and cultural power*, London: Routledge.

Morley, D. (1992): *Television, audiences and cultural studies*, London: Routledge.

Morley, D. and Silverstone, R. (1991) 'Communication and context: Ethnographic perspectives on the media audience,' in K.B. Jensen and N.W. Jankowski (eds.) *A Handbook of qualitative methodologies for mass communication research*, London: Routledge.

Mutsaers, W. (1993) 'Televisiekijken als sociale activiteit: De invloed van kijkers en medekijkers op het kiezen van en kijken naar televisieprogrammema's,' in K. Renckstorf, W. Mutsaers, and L.B. van Snippenburg (eds.) *Mediagebruik in Nederland*, Nijmegen: ITS.

Mutsaers, W. and Vierkant, P. (1991) 'Televisiekijkgedrag en gezinssituatie: beknopte rapportage met conclusies,' *Bulletin Kijk-en Luisteronderzoek* B91-134.

Mutsaers, W., Snippenburg, L.B. van, and Vierkant, P. (1992) 'Samen televisiekijken en conflicterende interesses,' *Massacommunicatie* 3: 235-253.

Naschold, F. (1973) 'Kommunikationstheorien,' in J. Aufermann, H. Bohrmann, and R. Sülzer (eds.) *Gesellschaftliche Kommunikation und Information: Forschungsrichtungen und Problemstellungen: Ein Arbeitsbuch zur Massenkommunikation*, Frankfurt am Main: Athenäum Fischer Taschenbuch Verlag.

Nelissen, P. (1991) *Het omgaan met kennis en de vraag naar voorlichting. Een communicatiewetenschappelijk perspectief voor empirisch onderzoek naar de vraag naart voorlichting*, Nijmegen: ITS.

Nelissen, P. (1992) 'Toegepast versus fundamenteel publieksonderzoek: Integratie van inzichten en werkwijzen,' paper t.b.v. workshop internationaal media-, opinie-en marktonderzoek, Sommatie '92, Veldhoven, The Netherlands.

Nie, N.H., Hull, C.H., Jenkins, J.G., Steinbrenner, K., and Bent, D.H. (1975) *SPSS: Statistical Package for the Social Sciences (2e ed.)* New York: McGraw-Hill.

Niven, H. (1960) 'Who in the family selects the TV programme?,' *Journalism Quarterly*, 37: 110-111.

Noelle-Neumann, E. (1973) 'Return to the concept of powerful mass media,' *Studies in Broadcasting* 9: 67-112.

Noelle-Neumann, E. (1991) 'The theory of public opinion: the concept of the spiral of silence', in J.A. Anderson (ed.) *Communication yearbook*, vol. 14, Newbury Park, CA: Sage.

NOS/KLO (1975) *TV-ontvangstmogelijkheden. Kwantiteit, kwaliteit, behoefte aan uitbreiding*, Hilversum: NOS.

NOS/KLO (1976) *Journaal 1975/1976*, Hilversum: NOS.

NOS (1990b) *Kijk-en Luisteronderzoek*. Hilversum: NOS.

NOS/KLO (1991) *Kijk-en Luisteronderzoek.* Hilversum: NOS.

NOS/KLO (1992a) *Bulletin N.O.S. Kijk-en luisteronderzoek,* B92-193, Hilversum: NOS.

NOS/KLO (1992b) *Beoordeling NOS-journaal en RTL-4 nieuws,* Hilversum: NOS.

NOS/KLO (1992c) *Bulletin N.O.S. Kijk-en luisteronderzoek,* B92-076, Hilversum: NOS.

NOS/KLO (1994) *Bulletin N.O.S. Kijk-en luisteronderzoek,* B94-059, Hilversum: NOS.

NOS (1988) *Horen, zien en cijfers. Vijfentwintig jaar Kijk-en luisteronderzoek,* Hilversum: NOS.

O'Keefe, G.J. and Reid-Nash, S. (1987) 'Crime news and real world blues', *Communication Research* 14: 147-163.

Olderaan, F. and Jankowski, N.W. (1988) 'De uitbreiding van het media-aanbod en de reactie van de Nederlandse gebruikers,' in K. Renckstorf and F. Olderaan (red.) *Communicatiewetenschappelijke Bijdragen 1987-1988,* Nijmegen: ITS.

Palmgreen, P. and Rayburn, J. (1982) 'Gratifications sought and media exposure: an expectancy value model,' *Communication Research* 9: 561-580.

Palmgreen, P., Wenner, L. and Rayburn, J. (1985) 'Uses and gratifications research: the past ten years', in K. Rosengren, L. Wenner and P. Palmgreen (eds.) *Der Positiivismusstreit in der deutschen Soziologie,* Berlin: Luchterhand.

Parsons, T. (1937/1968) *The structure of social action,* vol. 2, New York: Free Press.

Patton, M.G. (1980) *Qualitative evaluation methods,* Beverly Hills, CA: Sage.

Pearlin, L. (1959) 'Social and personal stress and escape television viewing', *Public Opinion Quarterly* 23: 255-259.

Peeters, A.P. (1990) 'De beoordeling van het NOS-journaal en het nieuws van RTL-Veronique,' *NOS Kijk-en Luisteronderzoek,* Bulletin B90-015.

Perse, E.M. (1989) 'Cultivation and involvement with local television news,' in N. Signorelli and M. Morgan (eds.) *Cultivation analysis: New directions in media effects Research,* Newbury Park, CA: Sage.

Perse, E.M. (1990a) 'Involvement with local television news: Cognitive and emotional dimensions,' *Human Communication Research* 16, 4: 556-581.

Perse, E.M. (1990b) 'Media involvement and local news effects,' *Journal of Broadcasting and Electronic Media* 34, 1: 17-36.

Peters, J. (1986) 'Institutional sources of intellectual poverty in communication research'. *Communication Research* 13: 527–559.

Peters, J. (1989) 'Sociaal-culturele achtergrond van kijkfrequentie en omroeplidmaatschap,' in K. Renckstorf and F. Olderaan (red.) *Communicatiewetenschappelijke Bijdragen 1988-1989,* Nijmegen: ITS.

Peters, V. and Wester, F. (1989) *Theory and practice of qualitative analysis,* Nijmegen: University of Nijmegen.

Peters, V. and Wester, F. (1994) *Kwalitan 40.0. A support programme for the analysis of qualitative data,* Nijmegen: University of Nijmegen.

Petty, R.E. and Cacioppo, J.T. (1986) 'The elaboration likelihood model of persuasion,' in L. Berkowitz (ed.) *Advances in Experimental Social Psychology*, New York: Academic Press.

Postman, N. (1985) *Amusing ourselves to death*, New York: Viking/Penguin Inc.

Popper, K.R. (1970) 'Die Logik der Sozialwissenschaften', in T.W. Adorno *et al.* (eds.) *Der Positiivismusstreit in der deutschen Soziologie*, Berlin: Luchterhand.

Radway, J. (1984) *Reading the romance*, Chapel Hill: University of North Carolina Press.

Rayburn, J. and Palmgreen, P. (1984) 'Merging uses and gratifications and expectancy-value theory,' *Communication Research* 11: 537-562.

Renckstorf, K. (1977a) *Neue Perspektiven in der Massenkommunikationsforschung. Beiträge zur Begründung eines alternativen Forschungsansatzes*, Berlin: Spiess.

Renckstorf, K. (1977b) 'Neue Perspektiven in der Massenkommunikationsforschung,' in K. Renckstorf (ed.) *Neue Perspektiven in der Massenkommunikationsforschung*. Berlin: Spiess.

Renckstorf, K. (1980a) 'Erinnerungen von Nachrichtensendungen im Fernsehen: Konturen des 'Aktiven' Publikums,' *Media Perspektiven* 4: 246-255.

Renckstorf, K. (1980b) *Nachrichtensendungen im Fernsehen (1): Zur Wirkung von Darstellungsformen in Fernsehnachrichten*, Berlin: Spiess.

Renckstorf, K. (1984) *Menschen und Medien in der postindustriellen Gesellschaft. Neuere Beiträge zur Begründung eines alternativen Forschungsansatzes*, Berlin: Spiess.

Renckstorf, K. (1989) 'Mediennutzung als soziales Handeln: Zur Entwicklung einer handlungstheoretischen Perspektive der empirischen (Massen-)kommunikationsforschung,' *Kölner Zeitschrift für Soziologie und Sozialpsychologie, Sonderheft* 30, Massenkommunikation: 314-336.

Renckstorf, K. (1994) *Mediagebruik als sociaal handelen. Een handelingstheoretische benadering voor communicatiewetenschappelijk onderzoek*, Nijmegen: ITS.

Renckstorf, K. (1995) *Kommunikationswissenschaft als sozialwissenschaftliche Disziplin*, Nijmegen: Stichting voor Duitsland Studies.

Renckstorf, K. and Rohland, L. (1980) *Nachrichtensendungen im Fernsehen (2): Absichten, Interessen und Muster der Medienzuwendung*. Berlin: Verlag Volker Spiess.

Renckstorf, K. and P. Nelissen (1989) 'Mediennutzung als Soziales Handeln,' in K. Renckstorf and F. Olderaan (red.) *Communicatiewetenschappelijke Bijdragen 1988-1989*, Nijmegen: ITS.

Renckstorf, K., Mutsaers, W. and van Snippenburg, L. (eds.) *Mediagebruik in Nederland* vol. 1, Nijmegen: ITS.

Renckstorf, K. and Hendriks Vettehen, P. (1992) 'Het kijken naar buitenlandse televisienetten,' in K. Renckstorf, P. Hendriks Vettehen, and L.B. van Snippenburg (red.) *Communicatiewetenschappelijke Bijdragen 1991-1992*, Nijmegen: ITS.

Renckstorf, K. and Wester, F. (1992) 'Die handlungstheoretische Perspektive empirischer (Massen-) Kommunikationsforschung,' *Communications* 17: 177-196.

Renckstorf, K. and Wester, F. (1993) 'Het omgaan met televisienieuws: een handelingstheoretisch communicatiewetenschappelijk perspectief,' in K. Renckstorf, P. Hendriks Vettehen, W. Mutsaers, and L.B. van Snippenburg (eds.) *Communicatiewetenschappelijke Bijdragen 1992-1993*, Nijmegen: ITS.

Rijt, G.A.J. van der (1990) 'Sociale ongelijkheid, oriëntaties op gezondheid en behoefte aan gezondheidsinformatie,' *Tijdschrift voor Sociale Gezondheidszorg*, 68: 261-267.

Riley, M.W. and Flowerman, S.H. (1951) 'Group relations as a variable in communications research,' *American Sociological Review* 16: 174-180.

Riley, M. and Riley, J. (1951) 'A sociological approach to mass communications research,' *Public Opinion Quarterly* 15: 445-460.

Riley, M.W. and Riley, J.W. (1959) 'Mass communication and the social system,' in R.K. Merton, L. Broom, and S. Cottrell (eds.) *Sociology Today*, New York: Basic Books.

Robinson, J.P. and M.R. Levy (1986) *The main source: Learning from television news.* Beverly Hills, CA: Sage.

Rosengren, K.E. (1974) 'Uses and gratifications: A paradigm outlined,' in J.G. Blumler and E. Katz (eds.) *The uses of mass communications*, Beverly Hills, CA: Sage.

Rosengren, K.E. (1993) 'From field to frog ponds,' *Journal of Communication* 33: 6-17.

Rosengren, K.E., Wenner, L.A. and Palmgren, P. (eds.) (1985) *Media gratification research. Current perspectives.* Beverley Hills, Sage.

Rubin, A. (1984) 'Ritualized and instrumental television viewing,' *Journal of Communication* 34: 67-77.

Rubin, L. (1979) *Women of a certain age*, New York: Harper and Row.

Ruhrmann, G. (1989) *Rezipient und Nachricht*, Opladen: Westdeutscher Verlag.

Saxer, U. (ed.) (1985) *Gleichheit oder Ungleichheit durch Massenmedien? Homogenisierung-Differenzierung der Gesellschaft durch Massenkommunikation*, München: Verlag Ölschläger.

Schenk, M. (1978) *Publikums- und Wirkungsforschung*, Tübingen, JCB Mohr.

Schenk, M. (1987) *Medienwirkungsforschung*, Tübingen, JCB Mohr.

Schramm, W. (1968) 'The nature of news,' in A. Casty (ed.) *Mass media and mass man*, New York: Holt, Rinehart and Winston.

Schramm, W., Lyle, J., and Parker, E.B. (1961) *Television in the lives of our children*, Stanford, CA: Stanford University Press.

Schulz, W. (1982) 'Ausblick am Ende des Holzwegs,' *Publizistik* 27: 49-73.

Schulz, W. (1986a) 'Fernseh-Paranoia und andere psychische Auffälligkeiten. Langzeitwirkung des Vielsehens?,' in W. Mahle (ed.) *Langfristige Medienwirkungen*, Berlin: Verlag Volker Spiess.

Schulz, W. (1986b) 'Das Vielseher-Syndrom. Determinanten der Fernsehnutzung,' *Media Perspektiven* 10: 762-776.

Schulz, W. (1987) 'Determinanten und Folgen der Fernsehnutzung. Daten zur Vielseher-Problematik,' in M. Grewe-Partsch and J. Groebel (eds.) *Mensch und Medien*, München: KG Saur.

Schulz, W. (1993) 'Mangel an Makrotheorien der Medienwirkungen?' in G. Bentele, and M. Rühl (eds.) Theorien öffentlicher Kommunikation, Mncen: Öhlschläger.

Schütz, A. (1932/1967) *The phenomenology of the social world*, Evanston, IL: Northwestern University.

Schütz, A. (1970) *Reflections on the problem of relevance*, London: Yale University Press.

Schütz, A. (1964) 'The well-informed citizen. A treatise on the social distribution of knowledge,' in A. Schütz *Collected papers II* The Hague: Nijhoff.

Schütz, A. (1972) 'The well-informed citizen. A treatise on the social distribution of knowledge,' in A. Schütz, *Collected papers*, The Hague: Nijhoff.

Schütz, A. (1976) 'The well-informed citizen. An essay on the social distribution of knowledge,' in A. Schütz (1976), *Collected papers II*, The Hague: Nijhoff.

Schütz, A. and Luckmann, T. (1979) *Strukturen der Lebenswelt*, Bd. 1, Frankfurt: Suhrkamp.

Schütz, A. and Luckmann, T. (1984) *Strukturen der Lebenswelt*, Bd. 2, Frankfurt: Suhrkamp.

Schwartz, H. and Jacobs, J. (1979) *Qualitative sociology: A method to the madness*, New York: Free Press.

Seiffert, H. (1972) *Einführung in die Wissenschaftstheorie*, Bd.1, München: C.H.Beck.

Seiffert, H. (1973) *Einführung in die Wissenschaftstheorie*, Bd.2, München: C.H.Beck.

Seiter, E., Borchers, H., Kreutzner, G., Warth. E.M. (eds.) (1989) *Remote control: Television, audiences, and cultural power*, London: Routledge.

Sereno, C.I. and Mortensen, K.K. (eds.) (1970) *Foundations of communication theory*, New York: Harper and Row.

Servaes, J. (1992) ''Europe 1992': The audiovisual challenge,' *Gazette* 49: 75-97.

Servan-Schreiber, J.J. (1967) *Le défi américain*, Paris: Denoël.

Silverstone, R. (1994) *Television and everyday life*, London: Routledge.

Sixma, H. and Ultee, W. (1983) 'Een beroepsprestigeschaal voor Nederland in de jaren tachtig,' *Mens en Maatschappij* 59: 360-382

Smith, R. (1986) 'Television addiction', in J. Bryant and D. Zillman (eds.) *Perspectives on media-effects*, Hillsdale NJ: Lawrence Erlbaum.

Snippenburg, L.B. van (1991) 'Objectieve maatschappelijke positie, subjectieve behoeften en kijken naar informatieve televisieprogrammema's,' *Massacommunicatie* 2: 101-116.

Sociaal-Cultureel Planbureau (1990) *Sociaal en cultureel rapport 1990*, Rijswijk: Sociaal-Cultureel Planbureau.

Spradley, J.P. (1980) *Participant observation*, New York: Holt, Rinehart and Winston.

Stappers, J.G., Reijnders, A.D., and Möller, W.A.J. (1990) *De werking van massamedia*, Amsterdam: Arbeiderspers.

Strauss, A.L. (1969) *Mirrors and masks*, San Francisco: Sociology Press.

Strauss, A.L. (1987) *Qualitative analysis for social sciences*, Cambridge: University Press.

Sturm, H. (1981a) 'Der Vielseher als Schlüsselproblem einer psychologisch-orientierten Medienwirkungsforschung,' *Fernsehen und Bildung* 15, 1-3: 9-15.

Sturm, H. (1981b) 'Der Vielseher im Sozialisationsprozess. Rezipientenorienter Ansatz und der Ansatz der formalen medienspezifischen Angebotsweisen,' *Fernsehen und Bildung* 15, 1-3: 137-148.

Swanson, D.L. (1977) 'The uses and misuses of uses and gratifications,' *Human Communication Research* 3: 214-221.

Tankard, J.W. and Harris, M.C. (1980) 'A discriminant analysis of television viewers and nonviewers', *Journal of Broadcasting* 24: 399–409.

Thomas, W.I. and Thomas, D.S. (1928) *The child in America: behaviour problems and programmes*, New York: Knopf.

Tichenor, Ph.J., Donohue, G.A., and Olien, C.N. (1970) 'Mass media flow and differential growth in knowledge,' *Public Opinion Quarterly* 34: 159-170.

Tillo, G. van (red.) *Hebben de kerken nog toekomst?*, Baarn: Ambo.

Tims, A.R. and Masland, J.L. (1985) 'Measurement of family communication patterns,' *Communication Research* 12: 35-57.

Verwey, M. (1986a) 'Nieuwe methoden voor vaststelling en verklaring van TV-kijkgedrag: verklaring kijkfrequentie TV-actualiteitenrubrieken: een causale analyse,' *Massacommunicatie* 2, 3: 144-155.

Verwey, M. (1986b) 'Verklaring kijkfrequentie TV-actualiteitenrubrieken: Een causale Analyse,' *Massacommunicatie* 14: 144-155.

Vierkant, P. (1987) *Televisiekijkers in Nederland. Een onderzoek naar het televisiekijkgedrag van de Nederlandse bevolking*, Meppel: Krips.

Vorderer, P. (1992) *Fernsehen als Handlung. Fernsehfilmrezeption aus motivationspsychologischer Perspektive*, Berlin: Sigma.

Vroon, P. (1992) *Wolfsklem. De evolutie van het menselijk gedrag*, Baarn: Ambo.

Wand, B. (1968) 'Television viewing and family choice differences,' *Public Opinion Quarterly* 32: 84-94.

Weaver, D.H. (1981) 'Audience need for orientation and media effect', *Communication Research* 7,3: 361–376.

Weber, M. (1905/1985) *The protestant ethic and the spirit of capitalism*, London: Unwin.

Weber, M. (1922/1987) *Over klassen, standen en partijen*, Kampen: Kok Agora.

Weber, M. (1907/1956) *Wirtschaft und Gesellschaft: Grundriss der Verstehenden Soziologie*, Tübingen: Mohr.

Webster, J.G. and J.J. Wakshlag, (1982) 'The impact of group viewing on patterns of television programme choice,' *Journal of Broadcasting* 26: 445-455.

Westendorp, P. H., van. (1981) 'A new dimension in public opinion research: Standard multidimensional measurement of involvement with social problems: technique and applications,' *Journal of the Market Research Society* 23, 3: 161-180.

Wester, F. (1991) *Strategieën voor kwalitatief onderzoek*, Muiderberg: Coutinho.

Wilde, G. (1992) 'Der Markt für Fernsehprogramme in Westeuropa 1990 bis 2000,' *Media Perspektiven*, 16: 108-115.

Wilson, T.P. (1970) 'Conceptions of Interaction and Forms of sociological explanation,' *American Sociological Review* 35: 697-710.

Wittebrood, K. (1992) 'Het politieke kennisniveau van de Nederlandse burger,' *Acta politica* 5: 135-159.

Wober, M. (1978) 'Television violence and paranoid perception: the view from Great Britain', *Public Opinion Quarterly* 42: 315–321.

Woldringh, C.I. and Knapen, M.H. (1980) *Vrij en alleen: Een explorerende studie in enkele grotere steden van Nederland naar de situatie van ongehuwden en hun beleving daarvan*, Nijmegen: ITS.

Woodall, W.G., Davis, D.K., and Sahin, H. (1983) 'From the boob tube to the black box: Television news comprehension from an information processing perspective,' *Journal of Broadcasting* 27: 1-23.

Wright, Ch. R. (1986) *Mass Communication. A sociological perspective*, New York: Random House.

Yin, R.K. (1984) *Case study design and methods*, Beverly Hills, CA: Sage.

Zahn, S.B. and Baran, S.J. (1984) 'It's all in the family: Siblings and programme choice conflict,' *Journalism Quarterly* 21: 847-852.

Zajonc, R.B. (1980) 'Feeling and thinking: Preferences need no inferences,' *American Psychologist* 35, 2: 151-175.

Zijderveld, A. (1974a) *De relativiteit van kennis en werkelijkheid*, Meppel: Boom.

Zijderveld, A. (1974b) *De theorie van het symbolisch interactionisme*, Meppel: Boom.

Zoonen, L. van (1991) 'A tyranny of intimacy? Woman, femeninity and television news,' in P. Dahlgren and C. Sparks (eds.) *Communication and Citizenship*, London: Routledge.

Contributors

Jan Bosman (1951) is Associate Professor at the Department of Communication, University of Nijmegen in the Netherlands. He lectures on marketing communication and consumer behavior. A background in psychology, his main interests are in the psychological aspects of communication. He is currently involved in research on halo effects in marketing communication.

Valerie Frissen (1960) is Associate Professor at the Department of Communication Studies, University of Amsterdam in the Netherlands. She received her PhD from the University of Nijmegen based on a study examining heavy viewing from a social action perspective. Currently, her research interests are in the field of audience behavior and cultural studies. She has published on communication research methodology, audience research, new information and communication technologies and gender issues. She is presently coordinator of an international network on Gender and New Information Technologies (GRANITE).

Paul Hendriks Vettehen (1962) is researcher at the Department of Communication, University of Nijmegen in the Netherlands. He has conducted studies on several topics in audience research and is presently involved in a dissertation project on the interconnections between theory building and measurement in audience research.

Liesbeth Hermans (1960) is a PhD candidate at the Department of Communication, University of Nijmegen in the Netherlands. Her research concerns the work procedures of journalists, and is being conducted from a social action perspective. Other research interests and publications relate to use of television news.

Niek Hietbrink (1962) is a PhD candidate at the Department of Communication, University of Nijmegen in the Netherlands. He studied business economics and marketing at the University of Rotterdam. His forthcoming dissertation involves an investigation into the ways people choose, watch and use television news. He has participated in a comparative study of the Dutch public and commercial newscasts, and in an experimental study of news recall.

Nicholas Jankowski (1943) is Associate Professor at the Department of Communication, University of Nijmegen in the Netherlands. He has conducted qualitative and quantitative research of small-scale media since the mid-1970s and is co-editor of *The People's Voice;*

Local Radio and Television in Europe. He has carried out several studies of interactive media and is currently editing a volume on multimedia. Jankowski further serves on the board of directors of the European Institute of Communication and Culture (EURICOM).

Denis McQuail (1935) is Professor of Mass Communication at the University of Amsterdam in the Netherlands. He is the author of, among other works, *Mass Communication Theory* (third edition, 1994) and *Media Performance; Mass Communication and the Public Interest.* His research has included studies on the effects of political communication, effectiveness of educational television, content analysis and audience research. McQuail is also an editor of *The European Journal of Communication.*

Wilbert Mutsaers (1969) studied communication science at the University of Nijmegen in the Netherlands and subsequently occupied a research post at the Department of Communication at the same university. During 1992-1994 he was involved in a large-scale study of media use in the Netherlands. In addition to publications related to this study, he has written on social aspects of viewing television.

Karsten Renckstorf (1944) is Professor of Communication and Head of the Department of Communication, University of Nijmegen in the Netherlands, where he has been coordinating the MASSAT research programme since 1988. He studied sociology at the University of Hamburg and obtained his PhD at the University of Bremen. Between 1970 and 1992 he was an editor of the quarterly *Rundfunk und Fernsehen*, and is presently co-editor of the series *Communicatiewetenschappelijke Studies*. Renckstorf has published extensively on the impact of television news, the role of local and regional media, and the use people make of mass media and mediated messages.

Gerrit van der Rijt (1941) is Associate Professor at the Department of Communication, University of Nijmegen in the Netherlands. He has conducted numerous studies on health communication, directed particularly at audience behavior. He has also performed several evaluations of information campaigns.

Leo van Snippenburg (1942) is Associate Professor at the Department of Communications, University of Nijmegen in the Netherlands. Research interests concern information-oriented audiences, political communication, media and reality construction, and new media technologies. In addition to Dutch and international publications on these studies, he has written on epistemological and methodological topics. At the moment he is also involved in a comparative survey project involving Sweden and the Netherlands.

Fred Wester (1947) is Associate Professor of Research Methodology in the Faculty of Social Sciences, University of Nijmegen in the Netherlands. He is the author of several books and articles on interpretive sociology and qualitative research methods. A recent work which he co-authored, *Qualitative Analysis in Practice*, examines uses of the computer in qualitative research. He is currently involved in research on television drama and news, and the methodology of qualitative content analysis.